(RE)IMAGINING HUMANE GLOBAL GOVERNANCE

In this important and path-breaking book, esteemed scholar and public intellectual Richard Falk explores how we can re-imagine the system of global governance to make it more ethical and humane.

Divided into three parts, this book first scrutinizes the main aspects of global governance, including geopolitics, the future of international law, climate change and nuclear weapons, 9/11, global democracy, and the UN. In the last part, Falk moves the discussion on to the search for progressive politics, the Israel–Palestine conflict and the World Order Models Project. Drawing on, but also rethinking the normative tradition in international relations, he examines the urgent challenges that we must face to counter imperialism, injustice, global poverty, militarism and environmental disaster. In so doing, he outlines the radical reforms that are needed on an institutional level and within global civil society if we are to realize the dream of a world that is more just, equitable and peaceful.

This important work will be of interest to all students and scholars of global politics and international relations.

Richard Falk is Albert G. Milbank Professor of International Law and Practice Emeritus at Princeton University, USA where he was a member of the faculty for 40 years. Since 2002 he has been a Research Professor at the Orfalea Center for Global and International Studies at the University of California–Santa Barbara, USA. He has been Special Rapporteur on Occupied Palestine for the UN Human Rights Council since 2008, and served on a panel of experts appointed by the President of the UN General Assembly, 2008–9.

GLOBAL HORIZONS

Series Editors: Richard Falk, Princeton University, USA; and R. B. J. Walker, University of Victoria, Canada

We live in a moment that urgently calls for a reframing, reconceptualizing, and reconstituting of the political, cultural and social practices that underpin the enterprises of international relations.

While contemporary developments in international relations are focused upon highly detailed and technical matters, they also demand an engagement with the broader questions of history, ethics, culture and human subjectivity.

GLOBAL HORIZONS is dedicated to examining these broader questions.

(RE)IMAGINING HUMANE GLOBAL GOVERNANCE

Richard Falk

LONDON AND NEW YORK

First published 2014
by Routledge
2 Park Square, Milton Park, Abingdon, Oxon OX14 4RN

Simultaneously published in the USA and Canada
by Routledge
711 Third Avenue, New York, NY 10017

Routledge is an imprint of the Taylor & Francis Group, an informa business

British Library Cataloguing in Publication Data
A catalogue record for this book is available from the British Library

Library of Congress Cataloging in Publication Data
(Re)imagining humane global governance / Richard Falk.
1. International relations--Moral and ethical aspects. 2. International
organization--Moral and ethical aspects. 3. International cooperation--Moral and
ethical aspects. 4. Human rights. I. Title.
JZ1306F35 2013
341.01--dc23
2013011071

ISBN: 978-0-415-81556-7 (hbk)
ISBN: 978-0-415-81557-4 (pbk)
ISBN: 978-1-315-88708-1 (ebk)

Typeset in Bembo
by Integra Software Services Pvt. Ltd, Pondicherry, India

Printed and bound by CPI Group (UK) Ltd, Croydon, CR0 4YY

For Hilal,
my love always

CONTENTS

NOTE OF ACKNOWLEDGEMENT

As with any book written over a period of years, I owe thanks for help and stimulation, including even disagreement and provocation, to many persons, but I will name only a few here.

My thinking and work in various respects bears the influence of Stephen Gill, Isa Baake, Burns Weston, Saul Mendlovitz, Fred Dallmayr, Phyllis Bennis, Robert Jay Lifton, Asli Bali, Tom Farer, Fred Branfman, Robin Broad, Paul Wapner, David Krieger, Gerry Spence, Elisabeth Weber, and Hilal Elver.

Interaction with students over the last several years in my UCSB graduate course devoted to global governance has been a most enjoyable part of preparing this book for publication, and influential in the shaping of my reasoning.

I also want to thank Mark Juergensmeyer and Victor Faessel for providing me with a warm and congenial working atmosphere in the Orfaela Center of the University of California at Santa Barbara. Among many colleagues who I learn from are the following: Rich Appelbaum, Avery Gordon, Mark Juergensmeyer, Chris Newfield, Esther Lezra, Lisa Hajjar, Paul Amar, Winddance Francis Twine, and John Foran.

I thank Emilie Olson for providing me with such intelligent and enjoyable assistance in taking care of the final stages of this manuscript.

I want to thank Craig Fowlie, Peter Harris, Andy Souter, Lisa Salonen, and the Routledge staff for a satisfying long-term working relationship that has made more enjoyable and efficient my role as author and series editor.

The dedication to Hilal Elver only begins to express the love, gratitude, and admiration that I feel and how blessed I am to be her life partner; these feelings grow with each passing year, allowing me to experience more fully her talents, integrity, warmth, life-sustaining courage, and most of all, her love.

I want finally to thank the following publishers for permission to draw upon previously published work: Fordham University Press, Cambridge University Press, *Millennium – Journal of International Studies*, *Globalizations*, and *Transnational Law and Contemporary Problems*.

INTRODUCTION

Understanding the evolving nature of global governance seems ever more critical to the overall management of planetary life. In some respects, the realities of multiple forms of interrelatedness make this undertaking more complex and fragile than it has ever been. The apocalyptic dimensions of nuclear weaponry and climate change are the most disturbing items on a long global agenda of policy challenges. Resistance to meeting these challenges, which have moral, legal, and political aspects, is both structural and ideological.

The essential *structural* reality of global governance is a state-centric arrangement of political authority that combines notions of territorial sovereignty with ideas relating to the global commons. What is less formally appreciated is that this state-centric structure has an important mixture of *horizontal* and *vertical* features. The horizontal orientation is based on notions of juridical equality among sovereign states, a principle that shapes diplomatic and commercial transnational relations, membership and participation in most international institutions, including the United Nations, and the governance of all routine transactions across borders in relation to flows of people and capital. The vertical orientation is based on the actualities of geopolitical inequality and dominates such concerns as the use of international force, including humanitarian intervention, the shaping of global economic policy, the role of global and regional leadership, the decision process in the UN Security Council, the division between nuclear-have and have-not states, and the implementation of international human rights and criminal law standards. The balance between horizontal and vertical aspects of global governance varies over time, reflecting the rise and fall of so-called 'Great Powers', changing technology, the emergence of international norms, patterns of conflict, the presence of environmental and economic challenges, and the style and goals of global leadership.

While acknowledging the structural persistence of this complicated state-centric world order it is also necessary to point to the roles of a variety of non-state actors associated with media, religion, business and finance, and civil society activism. These actors influence the climate of public opinion, and affect the range of choices available to governments in forming their policies and strategies. Assessments of the roles and impacts of these actors in various policy domains vary greatly over time and space, and often also reflect the diversity of outlook arising from a wide range of national, ethnic, cultural, economic, and geographic perspectives.

The United States has tended to be responsible for much of the verticality of world order in the period since 1945. Its execution of this hegemonic role has changed priorities and approach on several occasions. During the Cold War the United States focused its energies on the containment of the Soviet Union, and subordinated other goals to this overarching preoccupation. After the fall of the Berlin Wall and the collapse of the Soviet Union, American projections of influence were shifted to the central task of accelerating the expansion of neoliberal globalization, especially during the 1990s. After the 9/11 attacks, the orientation of American grand strategy reverted to a more traditional foreign policy agenda that emphasized global security issues, as was expressed by the 'Long War' launched against al Qaeda and its affiliates, and shifted its regional interests away from Europe and toward, first, the Middle East and then in the direction of Asia. The degree of vertical influence is often summarized by distinguishing between the bipolarity of the Cold War era as compared to the unipolarity of the late twentieth century and the potential multipolarity of the global future. One sign of this emergent, yet unsettled and uneven multipolarity, is associated with a changing geopolitical landscape that features the spectacular rise of China, India, Brazil, and Russia to positions of world prominence, mainly due to economic achievements and endowments. Another sign is the uncertain move toward regionalism that had seemed until the recent world recession to be a wave of the future led by the European Union, but now is regrouping to avoid implosion due to serious problems of sovereign debt and related issues in several member countries that have diminished confidence in the overall post-statist undertaking.

The essential *ideological* reality of global governance rests on the universal commitment to maximizing economic growth as measured by aggregate yardsticks, especially gross national product. This iron law of policy can take a variety of forms, but almost all accept the centrality of private sector entrepreneurship in the domains of business and finance. There are critical differences, of course, between the neoliberal assumptions of Western capitalism and the more state-directed economic approaches of the Asian countries, but both forms of market-driven development seek to promote growth as inherently beneficial while acknowledging to varying degrees the importance of curtailing such harmful side effects as global warming, pollution, poverty, and various forms of human insecurity. In effect, the ideological mood is still reflective of a TINA ('there is no alternative') political outlook that precludes all adjustments that impinge upon economic growth prospects or restrict consumptive excesses, including per capita energy and water use.

In effect, state-centricism is ideologically homogeneous, or nearly so. With the collapse of the Soviet Union, there occurred a severe weakening of adherence to socialism as an alternative approach to production and distribution that gave far greater emphasis to social justice, including the avoidance of gross inequality of circumstance and reward. Capitalist ideas about production and distribution are flexible and alter over time in response to a variety of pressures. One consequence of the collapse of socialism as an alternative to capitalism was to remove the ethical pressure on the private sector to avoid the cruel excesses of market manipulations. This development was further accentuated by the weakening of the labor movement, partly as a consequence of post-industrial patterns of manufacturing and business administration that made the organization of workers both more difficult and less meaningful. This absence of countervailing ideological forces also has the tendency to reduce the political leverage of advocates of environmental protection, which are dismissed as anti-business.

It seems evident that this structural/ideological approach to global governance bears the imprint of its West-centric origins. The early systematizing of world order was almost exclusively a European undertaking of regional scope that took its general modern shape at the Peace of Westphalia in 1648, but was preceded and followed by many variations. This West-centric pattern reached its acme in the period between the eighteenth and twentieth centuries during which several European countries established overseas colonial empires. With the collapse of colonialism in the decades after World War II, state-centricism was universalized, the vertical control of world order was partly weakened and partly reconstituted by the United States and the Soviet Union, and later by the United States on its own. At the same time, the post-colonial form of state-centricism has been uneven, with some regions able to establish national governance of an effective kind and others periodically subject to various forms of Western intervention. Asia has been generally able to handle the transition to political independence in accord with the expectations of territorial sovereignty, while sub-Saharan Africa has been the scene of frequent Western interventions. Asian problems in the transition from colonial rule were most severe in the two divided countries of Korea and Vietnam, both giving rise to bloody wars, and in the Korean case to a simmering conflict without an end in sight.

Global governance is usually approached from an explicitly descriptive perspective without explicit reference to its relationship to *human security*, which implies minimizing violence, enhancing human rights, protecting the environment, and promoting social justice. By incorporating such normative perspectives into appraisals of world order it seems more appropriate to draw a distinction between 'global governance' as currently constituted and 'humane global governance' as including goals associated with achieving higher standards of human security. The current system of global governance is shaped by the primacy accorded to the security of states, and especially of dominant states, and to ensuring conditions for the borderless efficiency of capital with regard to trade and investment. Humane global governance is, in contrast, dedicated to the security of people and to development paradigms that are people-oriented, giving priority to food, water, health, and employment security rather than fulfilling the expectations of billionaire venture capitalists and hedge fund managers.

A recurrent theme of the essays that comprise this volume is the increasing frustration of global problem-solving mechanisms that are dependent directly or indirectly on the aggregation of distinct national interests. This was not a serious issue in the period up to the end of World War II, but with the advent of nuclear weapons and long range delivery systems, the growth of world population coupled with rising living standards, and the exponential increases in the burning of fossil fuels, it was less and less sensible to view a state-centric system of world order as capable of providing policy outcomes that accorded with *global* and *human* interests and wellbeing as distinct from *national* interests of big and small states. In relation to nuclear weaponry, the approach has been overtly a matter of what the hegemonic United States believed to be in service of its national security, with secondary reinforcement based on the views of other nuclear weapons states. In effect, the vertical dimension of statist world order predominates. With respect to climate change, at least formally and up to the present time, the mechanism for negotiating global policy has been based on the horizontal dimensions of world order presided over nominally by the United Nations as providing the auspices. In practice this mechanism that is inclusive with regard to the participation of all governments has been seeking to find bargains that accord with diverse perceptions of national interests, and so far with disappointing results that fall far below the threshold of prudence with respect to greenhouse gas emission being recommended by the great majority of climate science specialists. Although the global character of climate change is widely admitted, the response is completely beholden to what the governments of states are prepared to do, with scant deference to the scientific consensus and to global/human interests.

There are several tectonic shifts taking place that are shaking the foundations of world order based on territorial sovereign states and the shared management of the global commons. In contemplating the prospects for global governance it is becoming evident that these developments must be better understood. On the one side, territorial sovereignty is becoming more permeable due to the deepening transnational character of all aspects of human existence, from the impact of social networking and the Internet to patterns of conflict that accentuate the interplay of non-state extremist political movements and drone warfare and covert special forces units roaming the planet. Such a phenomenon can be grasped under the rubric of 'the deterritorializing of the state', and is being resisted by such seemingly archaic and futile instruments of territorial reassertion of authority as separation walls built along international borders and Internet censorship.

At the same time, less noticed, is an extraordinary development of the territorialization of the global commons via surveillance, militarization, and expanded coastal claims to offshore living and non-living resources. Such a trend was manifest in the evolving law of the seas, with an expanding pattern of territorial claims, moving from the classic 3-mile limit to 12 miles, and then in the Law of the Seas Treaty of 1982, adding a 200-mile exclusive economic zone and vesting a further right to seabed resources as far beyond 200 miles as the continental shelf below the ocean extends. This territorialization of the oceans is also apparent from the increasing tensions about international maritime disputes pertaining to islands of minimal habitation in the eastern Mediterranean, East China Sea, South China Sea, and South Atlantic. The salience of these disputes reflects the presence of large natural gas and oil deposits at a time when the search for energy security and supplies is given the highest priority in the formation of national policy objectives. That is, sovereignty claims that in the past were symbolic have now been elevated due to their resource and energy implications.

The future of global governance is being linked increasingly to this changing rhythm of territorializing and deterritorializing developments, and how best to interpret them from the perspective of human and global interests as well as from the perspective of national interests. Such a clarification will have great significance for how it might be most useful to conceptualize the future of state-centric world order, and particularly whether the time has come to give greater attention to the need for *global* law as a complement to *international* law, and if so, what should be the venues most appropriate for its development in those global issue-areas that cannot be satisfactorily addressed by relying on international or regional legal regimes.

There exists a further fundamental shift in emphasis with profound conceptual and policy implications. It is the shift in emphasis from *boundaries* to *limits*. Such a formulation may be misleading to the extent that it suggests a disregard of boundaries, which is not intended. The turn toward limits in relation to people, carrying capacity of the earth, greenhouse gas emission levels, war making tactics, and economic growth contradicts the Westphalian ethos of unconstrained material progress within the boundaries of sovereign states and underscores the weakness of mechanisms for acknowledging and adjusting to these limits. Such thinking also bears directly on the adequacy of the structural and ideological dispositions of twenty-first-century state-centricism, which remains beholden to the dualistic thinking of 'self' and 'other', in relation to the management of overlapping claims to resources contained in the global commons. It is not possible to conceive of a global imaginary responsive to the relevance of these global limits on all levels of human behavior emerging within state-centric forms of world order. The best that might occur, is for a benevolent global leader to emerge that was willing to constrain its own short-term gains for the sake of safeguarding the global public good. Such a dynamic is almost beyond the realm of plausibility, as the impinging of limits is most likely to prompt a leading state to use its leverage to secure national advantages in the face of such pressures rather than to act from the viewpoint of the future and on behalf of the *species* rather than the *state*.

The chapters that follow try to wrestle with this overall situation from different angles of concern. In a sense, the subject matter of global governance is the unifying theme, with a special emphasis on the growing pressures to find improved ways to protect global and human interests, which presupposes a longer time horizon than is common even for governments that define their national interests as encompassing the responsibilities of acting as a global leader. It is important to realize that even from a national interest perspective, all political leaders representing governments are caught up in time cycles that assess performance by what takes place in the next few years. For a constitutional democracy such as the United States this consideration exerts great pressure to satisfy the immediate concerns and expectations of the citizenry, which has been conditioned to improving the economic situation and safeguarding the security of the country against real and imagined foreign threats. Even in authoritarian societies, political stability depends on creating an impression that material conditions are being addressed with efficiency and conviction, subject only to meeting serious security threats.

PART I
General contours

1

(RE)IMAGINING HUMANE GLOBAL GOVERNANCE

Preliminary complexities

There are three sets of concerns that bear upon a discussion of global governance, and related discourses on the adequacy of world order to meet the challenges of the early twenty-first century. They are: regulating the world economy from the perspective of human security; eliminating nuclear weapons by way of a negotiated disarmament process; and limiting greenhouse gas emissions in a manner that is responsive to the dangers of adverse climate change.

As used here, global governance is concerned with the establishment of order in the absence of world government or strong enough international institutions to implement global norms in relation to political actors. These governance concerns raise a series of difficulties that if resisted strongly or left unattended will have serious negative policy consequences for the peoples of the world. Closely related to global governance is the idea of world order, which is primarily focused on the structure of relations and interplay among those political actors that are the makers of world history at any given time.

I Regulatory authority in the domain of transnational economic activity

The era of neoliberal ideological hegemony following the Soviet collapse favored a minimization of regulatory authority in the world economy, relying on market forces and crisis management to ensure optimal development and economic growth based on the efficient deployment of capital. This approach more or less dominated the policy scene in the 1990s, although coming under increasing scrutiny due to the mobilization of social forces dissatisfied with the neoliberal distribution of benefits and the hegemonic shaping of global economic policy. The backlash achieved notoriety initially due to the so-called 'Battle of Seattle' in 1999 that exhibited a growing challenge being mounted by both populist forces ('globalization-from-below') and by many governments of the South no longer willing to defer to Euro-American control over domains of trade and investment (exclusionary regimes established in accord with the priorities of 'globalization-from-above').

The worldwide deep recession that started in late 2008 was caused mainly by irresponsibly risky and abusive practices in the banking, financial, and real estate sectors of the American economy. The painful impact of these market failures has pointed to the urgent need for greater governmental supervision and for socially sensitive forms of economic regulation at national, regional, and global levels. The unsatisfactory character of American leadership on matters of trade, finance, and fiscal policy also underlay the push for global economic reform, including international financial institutions. This push for regulatory authority is strong, but so is corporate and banking resistance to interferences with either market self-management or national sovereignty. At present, governmental actors are seeking to shape a more benevolent world economic order by way of diplomacy, especially to address issues of alleged currency imbalances, as with China, and excess indebtedness, as with Greece. International economic institutions, especially the International Monetary Fund, are an important part of the governance pattern, but less than previously, having been somewhat discredited by their handling of the Asian Financial Crisis that occurred a decade earlier, but these institutions do offer governments a somewhat flexible instrument for international cooperation and crisis management.

As of now, concerns about inadequate regulation of the world economy persist on two levels: the continuing unwillingness to address claims of an unfair distribution of benefits, including insufficient attention to the plight of the poor throughout the world, and the absence of effective oversight over devious and imprudent banking and accounting practices associated with financing and indebtedness.

II Climate change and nuclear weaponry

In both settings, there is a rhetorical commitment by governmental leaders acknowledging concerns, and expressions of a willingness to take appropriate adaptive steps. For both climate change and nuclear weaponry, the relationship between problem and solution seems concentrated in a very few governmental representatives of sovereign states. For nuclear weapons, the nine states that possess the weaponry, led by the United States, appear to lack the political will to achieve their elimination, or even to embrace a declaratory policy that renounces all options of first use.[1] Those states that possess nuclear weapons have devoted most of their political energy to preventing the further spread of the weaponry to additional countries, especially those countries believed to be challenging Western security interests. The overall preoccupation with the nonproliferation regime misleadingly implies that the principal danger arises from the countries that do *not* possess nuclear weapons rather from those that do. This diversion of concern serves to remove pressure from the nuclear-weapons states to engage in serious disarmament negotiations instead of participating in an unending series of arms control negotiations whose modest outcomes are designed to achieve no more than the efficient and safe management of existing nuclear weapons arsenals.

When it comes to climate change, the issues raised relate mainly to policy priorities and intergovernmental disagreements as to the appropriate allocations of adaptive obligations. To what extent should the level of pre-1990 contributions to the overall buildup of carbon emissions be taken into account in assessing and allocating relative responsibilities? The insistence of China that these earlier patterns of industrial development must be factored into any overall scheme for global policy, coupled with the refusal of the United States to accept such an approach, was a major reason why the Copenhagen UN climate change conference of 2009 was generally viewed as a failure. It is also evident that a state-centered approach to climate change will neglect the human security impacts that would be emphasized by a people-centered approach that accorded emergency priority to the peoples and persons most disadvantaged by and vulnerable to global warming. As fundamental as these disagreements about apportioning responsibility for reducing carbon emissions is a parallel obstacle arising from the determined reluctance on the part of most governments and societies to incur large *present* economic costs for the sake of *future* benefits. Short cycles of political accountability greatly hamper the capacity and willingness of governments to meet longer term challenges until they produce crisis conditions, perceived as such, and then it may be too late.

Against this background, both in relation to nuclear weaponry and climate change, skeptics believe that only in response to a catastrophe will it become politically feasible to meet these challenges of global scope. It also appears to be the case that waiting for a catastrophe may well be a matter of waiting too long to deal with either nuclear weapons or global warming. In the first instance, the damage done by a nuclear war may be so great as to preclude recovery, while in the second instance, the time lag associated with a carbon buildup would mean that the adverse effects would intensify even after a crisis response.[2]

III Twenty-first-century security challenges

Since the 9/11 attacks on the United States, there has arisen a preoccupation with the vulnerability of even the most powerful states to severe harm inflicted by non-state actors with scant resources but a dedicated will and a cadre of warriors ready to die for the cause, including even a readiness to sacrifice their own life in pursuit of political goals. The ideas about security that developed in the modern era of inter-state warfare and rivalry do not seem to fit the new circumstances of extremist resentments and tactics that cannot be territorially confined, making traditional military doctrine and capabilities of questionable relevance. The recourse to war by the United States in response to 9/11 illustrates the enormous costs and uncertain results of treating threats posed by transnational terrorism as if they created a suitable occasion for waging war. From a governance perspective it would have made more sense to rely on enhanced global policing, intelligence gathering, and law enforcement. Such a law and intelligence approach seems more sensitive to the specificities of the terrorist threat and incurs far lower economic and political costs. Yet such a soft power approach remains politically suspect in governmental settings, as existing political bureaucracies are accustomed to relying on their military capabilities when addressing a security threat. What does seem correct is that the old delimitations associated with a world of sovereign states now provide almost no guidance, either because the preparation of an attack and even the overt acts involved in carrying it out may take place anywhere on the planet, with or without the support of a territorial sovereign.

Global governance: shifting patterns

It was the English School of international relations that most effectively conceptualized the dual assertions of the anarchical structure of the world political system as complemented by a normative order based on international law, diplomatic prudence, and informal linkages of comity.[3] These ideas were particularly appropriate in the setting of various Westphalian discourses articulating the logic of the state system as a moderating modification of the Machiavellian worldview associated with various forms of unalloyed realism.[4] Especially Martin Wight and Hedley Bull were keen, as well, on distancing themselves from those who advocated more ambitious renderings of the normative dimensions of international relations that they associated with the Grotian tradition in international law. Some of these notable international relations specialists and leading statesmen stressed the promise of international institutions and favored the extension of the coverage of international law even to the point of overriding the sovereignty of states and the impunity of governmental leaders.[5] This view of international relations rested the prospects for good global governance on hegemonic self-restraint by leading states in their enactment of benevolent managerial roles, taking full advantage of the ordering potentialities of a pluralist framework composed of territorial states whose sovereign status entitled their governments to a wide margin of respect and autonomy.

With the rise of transnational economic relations and human rights, both with respect to actors and arenas, and with the multidimensional salience of transnational networks sustained by a variety of information technologies, the Westphalian discourse seems increasingly outmoded, or at the very least, in need of being enlarged to take into account some post-Westphalian perspectives.[6] This essay seeks to do this in the context of an evolving critical understanding of 'globalization', not with the goal of negating the primacy of the state system, but in complicating the explication of how politics and authority operate at a global level. The pluralist tilt of the English School must now be adapted to encompass the role of actors in the global marketplace (trade, investment, currency), in the domain of human rights, and among civil society actors (transnational voluntary associations, militant global citizens and their networks). Strict Westphalian understandings of power and security were also deeply challenged by the 9/11 attacks and the American response, producing an essentially non-territorial war between two actors, neither of which is a state in the generally accepted sense of a territorially delimited entity. Of course, the United States seems a traditional state if we cast our gaze only upon a world map, but if we take proper account of its global presence in space, oceans, and foreign bases, as well as the global scope of its security zone and popular culture, then it seems more useful to abandon the notion of 'state' and signal the conceptual rupture by considering it to be the first instance of a 'global state'.[7]

With suitable qualifications, an international society perspective still remains illuminating, principally because it calls our attention to the continuing absence of either effective centralized authority structures or a globally constituted security and problem-solving system operating efficiently under the aegis of the United Nations. Some readings of American grand strategy attribute to the global stature of the United States a condition of primacy that confers an opportunity, if not a responsibility, to administer global security from Washington, which since 2001 has focused on what the Pentagon calls 'the long war', and what others describe simply as 'the war on terror' or counter-terrorism.[8] To the extent that an American global state achieves coherent control over world politics, it would diminish the historical relevance of a pluralist account of world politics. Such American preeminence would offer the first instance of a solidarist world order of global scope, although not necessarily a benevolent or effective version. It would likely be widely regarded by opponents and skeptics as a species of dystopia rather than being viewed in positive terms as an idealistic or even utopian alternative to alleged chaos or anarchy, giving rise to a disposition toward violent geopolitics associated with pluralist experience. The actual trends with respect to the interplay of sovereign states suggest the re-emergence of a more multipolar, but less Western, geopolitical pattern featuring the rise of China, but also the emergence of India and Brazil, and the renewed relevance of Russia, as major global players, as well as dominant regional presences.[9]

This chapter will consider several solidarist tendencies and alternatives evident in present world society within the framework of a reconstituted discourse on globalization. A final brief section will revisit the question of 'whither international society?' but under the preferred rhetorical banner of 'the future of world society'. This latter language is preferred because it frees the political and moral imagination from the bonds of a purely statist or materialist framing of political reality that linguistically presupposes that relations among 'nations' or 'states' remains the only fruitful focus for an explanation of cooperative and norm-governed behavior as constraining influences. But at the same time, such a terminology does not ignore the continuing role of states and the state system, which for many dimensions of international life continues to be decisive, including setting membership rules for access to almost all important international institutions, arenas, and procedures (including treaty-making). What is currently needed given this growing complexity, but is not yet clearly enough discernible to articulate, is a global imaginary responsive to twenty-first-century beliefs, behavioral patterns, and aspirations.[10]

'Globalization' under stress

In the 1990s it was evident that 'globalization,' despite objections about the unsatisfactory nature of the term as misleading or vague, was widely accepted as usefully descriptive and explanatory: namely, that the world order sequel to the Cold War needed to be interpreted largely from an economic perspective, and that the rise of global market forces was displacing the rivalry among sovereign states as the main preoccupation of world order. This perception was reinforced by the ascendancy of Western-style capitalism, ideologized as 'neoliberalism' or geopolitically labeled as 'the Washington consensus', a circumstance reinforced by the collapse of the Soviet Union and the discrediting of a socialist alternative. It seemed more illuminating to think of the 1990s in this economistic light signified by reference to globalization than it was to hold in abeyance a re-inscription of world politics by the evasive 'the Post-Cold War era'. There were other ways of signaling that something new and important was taking place in the global setting. Some spoke convincingly of 'networking' as the signature of the information age highlighting the restructuring of international life that was being brought about by the computer and Internet. In my judgment, such a label, while far from ridiculous, still seemed less resonant with the more pervasive emphasis on economic growth via neoliberalism than does an acceptance of the terminology of globalization.[11]

But the 9/11 attacks came along to complicate matters further. These attacks strangely both revived and revolutionized the modern discourse of world politics, at once highlighting anew the severity of security concerns, war/peace issues, facing leading states, yet also giving rise to doctrines and practices that could not be understood by reference to the prior centuries of interaction among territorial political communities. The concealed transnational terrorist network that displayed the capability to inflict severe substantive and symbolic harm to the heartland of the dominant global state could not be comprehended, much less targeted and defeated, by resorting to a traditional war of territorial self-defense. There was no suitable statist adversary that could be blamed, and then attacked and defeated once and for all, although this fundamental and disquieting reality was provisionally disguised by the once-plausible designation of Afghanistan as responsible for the attacks due to its role in providing a safe haven for al Qaeda.[12] Although this initial phase of the Afghanistan War produced a 'victory' in the form of the replacement of the Taliban regime and the destruction of the al Qaeda infrastructure situated within the country, it became clear that such a campaign was only marginally related to a 'victory' in this new type of 'war', if by victory is meant the elimination of the threat, as it turns out, even in relation to Afghanistan. For one thing, most of the al Qaeda leadership and many of its cadres escaped, slipping across the border and quickly relocating in the remote tribal regions of Pakistan. This development underscored the novelty of the situation, especially the absence of any fixed territorial base for the enemy or any way to secure a meaningful victory on a territorial battlefield. Unable or unwilling to confront the threat according to its distinctive features, the US government shaped its response as if the security threat emanated from the 'axis of evil' countries rather than from a mega-terrorist multinational network with a long agenda of grievances, some legitimate, some not.

These moves in world politics dramatized the originality of the global setting as well as the confusing interplay of an expansionist grand strategy being executed by the neoconservative operatives in the Bush White House with a supposed security preoccupation after 9/11 with al Qaeda and terrorism. Bewildering questions of discourse and terminology arose as the Westphalian style of response to the al Qaeda threat seemed increasingly misleading and unsuccessful, as well as conceptually misdirected.[13] At the same time, the central contention of this essay is that 'globalization' retains its relevance as a descriptive label for the current phase of international relations, but that it needs to be interpreted far less economistically, and more comprehensively, since the events of 2001. The final section will consider approaches to global governance and world society given this altered understanding of 'globalization.'

The changing geopolitical context of globalization and global governance

To set the stage for this extended view of globalization as incorporating the new geopolitics of post-statist political conflict, it is necessary to review briefly the evolution of world politics after the Cold War.

The breakdown of the geopolitical discipline of bipolarity that had managed conflict during the Cold War era generated a security vacuum that could be and was filled in various ways. The Iraqi conquest and attempted annexation of Kuwait in 1991 was an initial expression of this breakdown. It would have seemed virtually certain that during the Cold War epoch, without the approval of Moscow and Washington, Iraq would not have embarked on a path of aggressive warfare against its small neighbor. The American-led coalition that restored Kuwaiti sovereignty was the mark of a new era being shaped by essentially uncontested American global leadership, seemingly a geopolitical debut for unipolarity in the global security sphere. The fact that the United Nations Security Council endorsed the defensive effort, accorded America full operational control of the Gulf War, and supported the subsequent ceasefire burdens that Washington insisted on being imposed upon Iraq, was far more expressive of the actuality of unipolarity than it was a sign that Woodrow Wilson's dream of an institutionalized international community upholding the peace collectively was finally coming true. What emerged from the Gulf War more than anything else was the extent to which the United Nations Security Council seemed willing to allow itself to be used as a legitimating mechanism for controversial US foreign policy initiatives that seemed to stretch the limits on the use of international force contained in both international law and the United Nations Charter.

Another course of action could have been followed, and seemingly was even encouraged by the first President Bush's initial rhetorical invocation of 'a new world order' in 1990 as a means of generating public and governmental support at the UN for authorizing a collective security response to Iraqi aggression. Such reliance on the procedures of the Security Council to fashion and supervise a response could have represented a genuine realization of the Wilsonian project to shift the locus of authority and responsibility in war/peace matters from the level of the state to that of the world community. But there was no such disposition in the White House of the Bush I presidency. Instead, the United States moved to fill the security vacuum by acting on its own to the extent that it deemed necessary, while seeking Security Council approval so as to possess a legitimating rationale that would mobilize support for the use of force and deflect criticism.

The initiation of the Kosovo War under NATO auspices in 1999 made this new American orientation toward law and power clear, and the fact that it was under-taken during the Clinton presidency suggested the bipartisanship of this geopolitical unilateralism in the aftermath of the disappearance of the Soviet Union as a state capable of deterring the United States. With the prospect of a Russian and Chinese veto in the offing, the US government avoided the United Nations Security Council, while organizing 'a coalition of the willing' to attack the Serbian presence in and control of Kosovo under the formal and operational umbrella of NATO. This created a geopolitical precedent for use of non-defensive force without a mandate from the Security Council. Such action represented a serious depart-ure from the discipline of international law and the UN Charter, although there were extenuating circumstances associated with averting a humanitarian catastrophe that exerted interventionary pressures. The action taken was controversial, although endorsed by public opinion and governmental policy throughout Europe and in the United States.[14] It was justified as an exceptional claim necessitated by the perceived imminence of an ethnic cleansing crisis in Kosovo and against the background of the earlier UN failure to protect the Bosnian peoples, as epitomized by the 1995 Srebrenica massacre of an estimated 7,000–8,000 Bosnian males while UN peacekeepers scandalously stood by as disempowered spectators.

The Iraq War of 2003 was a more revealing and consequential departure from the UN framework of restraint with respect to the use of international force in circumstances other than self-defense. Instead of circumventing the Security Council as in Kosovo, the US tried hard to enlist the UN in its war plans, and initially succeed in persuading the entire membership of fifteen countries to back SC resolution 1441, which implicitly accepted the American position that if Iraqi weapons of mass destruction were not found and destroyed by Baghdad's voluntary action or as a result of the United Nations inspection process, then an American-led war with UN blessings would obtain political backing and international legitimacy. Tensions within the Security Council surrounded mainly the timing and the alleged requirement that acting on 1441 required a further explicit authorization for recourse to war. Evidently concerned that inspection might obviate the case for war, and that an additional Security Council mandate might never be obtained, the US went ahead on its own in March 2003, inducing a rather unimpressive coali-tion of more or less willing partners to join in the military effort, which produced a quick, although deceptive, battlefield victory, followed by a bloody, expensive, and inconclusive occupation.[15]

In an important sense President George W. Bush was implementing a vision of a new world order, but not the one that his father appeared to favor in 1990–91 or that Wilson pushed so hard for after World War I. Unlike the Gulf War of 1991 when the response, which was endorsed by the United Nations Security Council, was an instance of collective defense against prior aggression and conquest, or the Kosovo War where the military action appeared necessary and justified as humanitarian intervention in circumstances where there were reasonable grounds to anticipate a potential humanitarian catastrophe for Albanian Kosovars, the 2003 war against Iraq rested on neither a legal nor moral grounding that was persuasive to most governments in the world, was opposed by an incensed global public opinion, and seemed politically imprudent, even perverse, from the perspective of meeting the al Qaeda challenge of transnational terrorism. The Bush Doctrine of preemptive war as applied to Iraq, lacking a persuasive factual showing of imminent threat, seemed at the time to be a flagrant repudiation of the core international law prohibition of non-defensive force. It also established a precedent that, if followed by other states, could produce a series of wars and undermine the authority of the UN Charter and modern international law.[16] The US approach seemed to be filling the security vacuum that existed after the Cold War with the unilateralism and lawlessness of hegemonic prerogatives and geopolitical ambitions. This seemed to widen even the already contested claim of preemptive self-defense by resorting to war in the absence of an imminent threat, and possibly in the absence of any threat whatsoever, thereby embracing unilateralism and discretionary recourse to war in a manner that went beyond the already dangerous expansiveness of so-called 'preventive war'. For the United States to attack Iraq, a relatively weak state except within the Middle East, a state that had been weakened further by its lengthy war with Iran during the 1980s, by a devastating defeat in the Gulf War, and by more than a decade of harsh sanctions, involved launching a war without international or regional backing in a context where there was absent a credible past, present, or future threat.

This display of audacity by the US government, repeatedly, although unconvincingly, rationalized by continuous references to the distinctive challenges posed by global mega-terrorism made manifest in the 9/11 attacks, was exhibited in efforts to reconstitute world order in three crucial respects: seriously eroding the sovereignty of foreign countries by potentially converting the entire world into a battlefield for the conduct of the American war against al Qaeda; greatly weakening the restraints associated with the international law of war and accompanying collective procedures of the organized world community while carrying on its campaign of counter-terrorism; re-establishing the centrality of the role of war and force in world politics, while dimming the lights that had been illuminating the rise of markets, the primacy of *corporate* globalization, and the displacement of statist geopolitics. In effect, the focus on the terminology of globalization and the operations of the world economy was being partially eclipsed by a novel twenty-first-century pattern of geopolitics in which the main adversaries were a concealed transnational network of political extremists and a global state engaging in multiple military interventions and operating without consistent regard for the sovereign rights of territorial states, especially those situated in the global South.[17]

For both of these political actors the framework of diplomacy and conflict that has evolved since the dramatic events of 9/11 has radical, rather than moderate, world order implications. But there are important continuities, as well, that give persisting relevance to the role of the United Nations and international law. In view of this, it seems far better to deal with the current global situation by reference to its distinctive features as modifying our understanding of world order, rather than claiming that a unique set of circumstances justify the depiction of a new system and the adoption of a new political vocabulary. On balance, I believe that despite there being some merit in favoring an entirely new set of descriptive labels for this early twenty-first-century period as compared to the 1990s, it remains on balance advantageous to retain and revise the globalization discourse, especially in light of the increasing relevance of global governance as a pre-occupation with respect to the complexities of global policy. A different conclusion on these conceptual issues might well be preferable if the discussion was focused exclusively on an appraisal of the 'political economy' or 'global security' aspects of world order rather than on the overall quality of governance as it affects the wellbeing of the peoples throughout the planet.

The Peace of Westphalia in 1648 that led over time to an agreed framing of political behavior in a world of sovereign states was now being treated as more often anachronistic with respect to the resolution of acute transnational conflict.[18] Seen in this light, reliance on the discourse of globalization seems useful to emphasize the extent to which crucial dimensions of contemporary world history are being addressed in such a way as to underscore the much diminished role for the agency and boundaries of sovereign states in many, but not all, settings. For instance, in extending control over the oceans and space, as well as insulating borders against unwanted and illegal migrants, the state in the early years of the twenty-first century is more assertive than it had been in the prior century. Above all states provide the boundaries that still shape the political geography of the world, and dominate our imaginative projections of how the world is organized. We are not likely to abandon this statist map of the world in the foreseeable future, despite its exaggerated reliance on territorial demarcations of human and natural activities.

Seven globalizations for the twenty-first century

Against this background framing, the future of global governance is inherently problematic. The contours and ideological orientation of globalization and governance will remain highly contested and fluid for decades, far more so than was the case during the placid 1990s, and the future of world order will hang precariously in the balance. The old political language of statism will continue to be relied upon in many formal settings, including leading international conferences devoted to global policy concerns, but it will not illuminate the multi-layered and transnational complexities of world order nearly as comprehensively as a revamped reliance on the language of globalization.

Seven overlapping approaches to global governance can be identified as the structural alternatives for the future of world order. These will be briefly depicted, and a few conclusions drawn: corporate and financial globalization; civic globalization; imperial globalization; apocalyptic globalization; regional globalization; ecological globalization; and normative globalization. The emerging structure of world order is a complex composite of these interacting and overlapping elements, varying with conditions of time and space, and therefore incapable of positing a unified 'construction' as a generalized account of the new reality of the global lifeworld. In other words, many partial constructions of world order compete for plausibility and adherence, but none has so far gained the sort of consensus that would qualify it as the defining reality. The contours and meanings of globalization are embedded in a dialogic process, further complicated by sharply divergent perceptual perspectives, uneven material circumstances and historical memories, and by a bewildering array of shifting policy challenges. Commentators upon the global setting must be content with partial, imprecise, tentative formulations of this evolving world order articulated by reference to multiple globalizations. These should be put forward with an accompanying realization that changing conditions and unanticipated developments may require frequent reformulations.[19]

Corporate and financial globalization

In the 1990s, with the resolution of the East/West conflict, the center of global attention shifted to the ideas, arenas, and practices associated with the functioning of financial markets, currency arrangements, and world trade and investment, as guided by a privileging of capital formation and efficiency, and a celebration of capitalist ascendancy. The role of governments was increasingly seen as subordinate to this cultic commitment to the efficiency of capital, and governments were expected to play facilitative roles that trusted the mechanisms of self-regulation. Political elites and elected leaders, to achieve and sustain 'legitimacy', struggled to win the support, and prominent participation in government, of private sector elites. Ideological adjustments were made to upgrade markets, privatize a wide range of undertakings previously situated within the public sector, and to minimize the role of government in promoting social goals associated with health, employment, and human security. Keynesianism was out, neoliberalism was in. New informal non-governmental arenas of policy formation emerged to reflect this shift in emphasis away from electoral politics and welfare state expectations. The nanny state of welfare was out, the neoliberal state of self-reliance was in. In this atmosphere great weight was given to the pronouncements and outlook of such organizations as the World Economic Forum, an annual gathering of invited global business leaders in Davos, Switzerland, reinforced by the participation of top political figures. Political leaders seemed eager to receive invitations to speak at Davos, and whenever given the opportunity tended to express their enthusiasm for promoting the goals of a neoliberal world economy even if it meant subordinating such national priorities as jobs and domestic investment. Governments and international financial institutions (IMF, World Bank) accepted and promoted this economistic agenda with enthusiasm, creating intergovernmental frameworks dedicated to the goals of the transnational private sector, such as the yearly economic summit (Group of Seven, then Eight, and still later, Twenty) that first brought together the political heads of state of the principal advanced industrial countries in the North, and then later incorporated rising states in the South.

In the 1990s there seemed to be a rather neat displacement of the territorial and security features of the state system by the capital-driven concerns of the world economy conceived along these neoliberal lines. It appeared that a new non-territorial diplomacy associated with trade, investment, and monetary flows was taking precedence over older concerns with strategic alliances, as well as dividing sovereign states between friends and enemies, giving priority to the security and wellbeing of each specific territorial community of citizens. As long as corporate and monetary globalization was sustained by impressive growth statistics – even if accompanied by evidence of persistent massive poverty, widening disparities among and within states and regions with respect to income and wealth, and a disturbing neglect of economic stagnancy in sub-Saharan Africa – there was little mainstream dissent from the pro-globalization consensus. This economistic consensus was also believed to have political side benefits. There was a widespread belief that global economic growth would encourage shifts away from authoritarian forms of governance and toward the more decentralized patterns of governance associated with various types of constitutional democracy and the protection of essential human rights.[20] Such attitudes reflected, in part, the belief that the victory of the West in the Cold War could be ideologically explained by pointing to the superior economic performance of the liberal economies of the West, that was itself sustained by constitutional democracy that allowed private sector creativity to flourish.

It was only in the wake of the Asian Financial Crisis that began in 1998, and its reverberations in such disparate countries as Argentina, Japan, and Russia, that serious criticism began to produce a controversy as to whether the future of corporate and financial globalization should be entrusted to the untender mercies of neoliberal guidance. In such an altered atmosphere, the reformist voices of such insiders as George Soros and Joseph Stiglitz began to be heard more widely, lending credibility to previously ignored leftist critics. And then in late 1999, the Seattle demonstrations directed at an IMF ministerial meeting signaled to the world the birth of a wide and multi-faceted anti-globalization movement deeply opposed to the basic policies associated with neoliberalism even when it succeeded in producing global economic growth. The reaction to Seattle finally generated a serious debate, still far from resolved, on the effects of globalization-from-above, assessing its benefits and burdens, and focusing especially on whether the poor of the world were being massively victimized or impressively helped.[21]

In the Bush II presidency, despite its obsessions with global security and the war against mega-terrorism, the US government dogmatically and unconditionally reinforced its commitment to corporate globalization as the *sole* foundation of legitimate governance at the level of the sovereign state.[22] These policies were promoted without much fanfare because of the neoconservative espousal of an expansive grand strategy labeled by critics as 'the global domination project'. Corporate and monetary globalization at the present time is subject to a variety of challenges resulting from a deep and lingering global recession and by a robust worldwide grassroots movement that is more than a negative response to globalization-from-above, providing some vision of more equitable and sustainable forms of globalization.

In the early twenty-first century confidence in capitalism has further retreated, especially in the aftermath of a global recession that started in 2008, and is not yet clearly over, and generates worries that a worse unraveling of the world economy might well occur in the years ahead. The seemingly superior capacity of centralized and authoritarian political orders, such as China and Malaysia, to withstand economic turbulence and declines in world trade and investment, also has weakened the ideological hold of capitalism on the political imagination, especially in its neoliberal 1990s form. The high-risk banking and financial practices that led to the economic collapse and a jobless recovery have not disappeared, which has had disillusioning effects on claims that market-driven economic policies are to be viewed as socially beneficial. At the same time, the business and banking leadership, abetted by rising economic nationalism that emphasizes competitive advantages in the global marketplace, has made it almost impossible to establish appropriate forms of national and international regulation to restore confidence in corporate and monetary globalization.[23]

Civic globalization

As suggested, the effects of corporate and financial globalization have generated a counter-movement on the level of ideas and practices, a movement that seeks a more equitable and sustainable world economy, although not necessarily opposed to 'globalization' as such despite some elements supportive of local sustainability. That is, if globalization is understood as the compression of time and space as a result of technological innovation and social/economic integration, and if its policy emphasis becomes people-oriented rather than capital-driven, then it is more accurate to consider civic globalization as favoring 'another globalization' rather than being identified as anti-globalization populism. Over the years, civic globalization has clarified its dominant tendencies, despite diverse constituencies from North and South, including activist groups with distinct and sometimes clashing priorities, including human rights, economic wellbeing, and environmental protection, as well as a range of commitments to participatory and substantive democracy. Not surprisingly civic globalization has yet to convey a coherent image of what is meant by a people-oriented approach.[24]

As already suggested, especially through the annual gatherings of the World Social Forum in Porto Allegre, Brazil and elsewhere, it has been exhibiting both its vibrant and its divergent tendencies, creating the impression of anarchic energy but not yet a coherent political project. There is a certain negative unity among militant adherents of civic globalization – a systematic repudiation of the main tenets of corporate and monetary globalization, and the further belief that capitalism cannot be reformed, but must be transformed into a type of political economy that has not previously existed. In the search for coherence and a positive program, there is an increasing disposition to view civic globalization as essentially a movement dedicated to the achievement of *global* democracy, which emphasizes the call for a more participatory, transparent, and accountable process of shaping and implementing global economic and political policy, especially within regional and global economic institutions, in relation to regulated marketplaces, and within the UN system generally.

As might be expected, those concerned with the impact of corporate and financial globalization are also deeply disturbed by and generally opposed to the American response to the 9/11 attacks, and view resistance to imperial globalization, and its accompanying militarism, as ranking with, or even regarded as more serious and urgent, than opposition to the predatory effects of corporate and monetary globalization. The mobilization of millions to oppose the Iraq War in early 2003 was mainly a phenomenon in the countries of the North, but it attracted many of the same individuals who had earlier been part of grassroots campaigns associated with opposition to corporate globalization. There is an uncertainty, at present, as to whether anti-war and anti-imperial activism will merge successfully with the struggle for a transformed world economy and for substantive democracy, and whether the experience of prolonged global recession will move this struggle forward, or shift attention to incremental reform and temporary recovery.

Imperial globalization

Even at the high point of corporate and financial globalization in the mid-1990s, there were a variety of critical assessments that pierced the economistic veil to depict and lament the American project of global domination.[25] It was notable that during the 1990s the United States failed to use its global preeminence constructively. It failed to promote nuclear and general disarmament or to create a more robust UN peacekeeping capability, or to address the major unresolved conflicts throughout the world. Instead, the United States government put its energies into the identification of new enemies whose existence would justify high defense spending, the strengthening of its worldwide network of military bases and regional naval commands, the retention of its nuclear arsenal, and the continuation of an expensive program dedicated to the militarization of space. In retrospect, it seems difficult to deny the charges that US policy, whether or not with full comprehension by its leaders and many of its citizens, was seeking a structure for world order that rested on American imperial authority.[26] True, the apparent priority goal in the 1990s for American global leadership was to keep the world profitable for corporate and financial globalization, deflecting criticism and threatening potential opponents.

The 'election' of George W. Bush in 2000 as a representative of the radical right in America, a result greatly abetted by the national emergency atmosphere following the 9/11 attacks, gave an unanticipated wide opening to the most ardent advocates of imperial globalization situated within the American policymaking community. It converted the undertaking from one of indirection and closet advocacy in conservative think tanks to that of the most vital security imperative in the history of the country with intense and widespread popular backing. There was, of course, no official American acknowledgement that the government was pursuing imperialist ideas and goals. The need for American military dominance everywhere and the associated projection of military force to various corners of the globe were justified as essential security adjustments to the post-9/11 global setting. In the immediate aftermath of the attacks a globally aggressive conception of security provided the most powerfully persuasive rationale for the global projection of US military power since the Cold War era, and it did so in a setting where the absence of strategic and ideological statist rivalry allowed the US government to promise a future world order without wars and geopolitical rivalry among states, and thus assure foreign governments that they would be able to enjoy the benefits of a reinvigorated corporate and financial globalization.[27]

As suggested earlier, the counter-terrorist consensus loomed large at first, giving rise to strong support at home and abroad for the US decision to wage war against Afghanistan, and to dislodge the Taliban regime from control. The move toward war with Iraq disclosed the limits of this global consensus as well as the *diplomatic* limits of the American capacity to generate active political support for its project of global dominance. As with Afghanistan, the Iraqi regime was widely deplored by other governments as oppressive and militarist, but unlike Afghanistan, Washington's claims of preemption as directed toward Iraq seemed unconvincing and were generally regarded as much more connected with plans for unrelated geopolitical expansion, especially in the Middle East, than qualifying as a genuine response to 9/11 related to credible claims of defensive necessity with respect to the continuing threats posed by the al Qaeda network. Indeed, as critics of the Iraq War pointed out during the pre-war debate, the probable effect of the war would be to heighten the al Qaeda threat rather than diminish it. This critical view was accompanied by the surfacing of many suspicions about what was the *real* motivation for military intervention in Iraq, prompting explanations relating to ensuring future control over Gulf oil reserves, Israel's security, containment of political Islam, nonproliferation and regional hegemony.

The perception of imperial globalization is a matter of interpretation, as are its probable effects on the governance of political behavior in the world. The advocates of the new imperialism emphasize its benevolent potentialities, with reference to the spread of constitutional democracy and human rights, and the geopolitical availability of peacekeeping capabilities that could act far more effectively than what could be achieved by reliance on the United Nations.[28] The critics make several main arguments. Some are concerned with prospects for a geopolitical backlash in the form of a new strategic rivalry, conceivably involving a Sino–European alliance. Others stress that this commitment to global militarism will lead to the further weakening of American republicanism at home and abroad. Given these developments, it seems prudent to worry about the emergence of some new oppressive political order that might be most accurately described as 'global fascism', a political fix without historical precedent.[29] Of course, the proponents of imperial globalization resent the friction produced by civic globalization, and despite the claims of support for 'democracy' prefer compliant governmental elites and passive citizenries. Bush 'rewarded' and lavishly praised governments that ignored and overrode the clearly evidenced anti-war sentiments of their citizens, especially Britain, but also Italy and Spain, while 'punishing' those countries that refused to fully support recourse to an aggressive and unlawful war against Iraq, including France, Turkey, and Germany. To a small degree, these concerns have abated since Barack Obama became president of the United States in 2009, although the structure of American militarism persists, as does the resolve to deal with persistence of threats associated with the 9/11 experience by foreign military intervention. The Obama presidency, at first, escalated American and NATO military operations in Afghanistan and has kept tensions high in relation to Iran by relying on threat diplomacy reinforced by escalating sanctions.

Apocalyptic globalization

There is no entirely satisfactory designation for the sort of political stance associated with Osama Bin Laden's vision of global governance. It does appear reliant upon extreme forms of political violence that challenge the West, especially the US, by a 'war' without limits. Without possessing any military capabilities, the strongest consolidation of state power in all of human history was seriously challenged. The al Qaeda capability to pose such a challenge was vividly demonstrated on 9/11, attacking the United States symbolically and substantively more severely than at any time throughout the course of its entire history with the possible exception of the War of 1812. The Bin Laden vision also embodies very far reaching goals that if achieved would restructure world order as it is now known: driving the United States out of the Islamic world, replacing the state system with an Islamic *umma*, and converting the residual infidel world to Islam, thereby globalizing the *umma*. It is here characterized as 'apocalyptic' because of its religious and absolutist embrace of violent finality that radically restructures world order on the basis of a specific religious vision, as well as its seeming willingness to resolve the historical tensions of the present world by engaging in a war of extermination against the 'crusader' mentality of those designated as enemies, including Jews, Christians, and atheists, an avowedly genocidal agenda. Since the United States as the target and opponent of al Qaeda also expresses its response in a political language of good and evil, but with the moral identities inverted, the term 'apocalyptic globalization' is descriptive of the outlook.[30] This designation also conforms to the concern about nuclear weaponry, both as a safeguard for the established order and as a potential danger to the established order should such weapons of mass destruction fall into the hands of al Qaeda or affiliates of similar disposition.

Perhaps, it confers on al Qaeda an exaggerated prominence by treating its vision as sufficiently relevant to warrant a distinct status as a new species of globalization that approaches the future with its own formula for global governance. At present, the scale of the attacks, as well as the scope of the response, seems to validate this prominence, even though it may seem highly dubious that such an extremist network has any enduring prospect of toppling statism or permanently weakening either corporate and financial globalization or imperial globalization. As far as civic globalization is concerned, there exists a quiet antagonism, and an even quieter basis for limited collaboration. The antagonism arises because the main support for civic globalization comes primarily from those that regard themselves as secularists, or at least as opponents of extremist readings of any particular world religion that gives rise to a rationale for unrestricted holy war waged against civilian society. The collaboration possibility, if it exists at all, is implicit and a result of convergent goals rather than active cooperation. This convergence is present because of certain shared goals, including justice for the Palestinians and opposition to imperial and corporate and financial globalization.

Regional globalization

As with apocalyptic globalization, the terminology presents an immediate problem. Does not the postulate of a regionalist world order contradict trends toward globalization of a planetary scope? The language may seem to suggest such a tension, but the intention is coherent, to imply the possibility that global governance may in the future be partially, or even best, conceived by reference to a world of regions. The basic perspective, of longer range than the others, is to view European regionalism as an ambitious exploratory venture, which if it evolves and becomes vindicated in the eyes of the world, will lead to imitative behavior in other principal regions of the world. What would constitute success for the European Union is not entirely clear, and is impossible to specify at this time. It would undoubtedly include economic progress, social democracy, conflict resolution in relation to ethnic and territorial disputes, and resistance to – or at least the moderating of – imperial, apocalyptic, and corporate and financial manifestations of globalization. Such regionalizing prospects are highly speculative at this stage, but still worth entertaining, given the dramatic transformations experienced by Europe during the past 50 years, and the difficulties associated with establishing beneficial world order alternatives.[31] It needs to be admitted that prospects for regionalism in Europe and even the world were far brighter before the onset of the Eurozone crisis of confidence and related severe sovereign debt difficulties in several European countries.

Regionalism is conceptually and ideologically appealing as a feasible synthesis of functional pressures to form enlarged political communities and the rise of identity politics associated with civilizational and religious orientations. Regionalism is geopolitically appealing as augmenting the capabilities of the sovereign state without abandoning its centrality in political life at a national level, especially to allow non-American centers of action to compete economically and to build bulwarks of political resistance to the threats posed by imperial and apocalyptic globalization.

It is also well to acknowledge grounds for skepticism with respect to regional globalization. The United States, as well possibly as China, Russia, Japan, Brazil, and India, seem likely either to oppose or to try their best to dominate any strong regionalizing moves outside of Europe. The disparities and rivalries among countries in the non-Western regions are so great as to make ambitious experiments in regionalism seem implausible for the foreseeable future. Also, regional frameworks are not entirely congruent with the supposed recognition of civilizational and religious identities. Even in Europe there are large non-Western, non-Judeo-Christian minorities, and in Asia and Africa, the civilizational and religious identities cannot be homogeneously categorized without neglecting the realities of their basic condition of heterogeneity.

Ecological globalization

The advent of growing concerns about the adverse effects of climate change presents a statist world order with a series of difficult problems that can only be addressed through intergovernmental cooperation on an unprecedented scale and scope. The Copenhagen UN climate conference at the end of 2009 exhibited the realization that some portions of the world are exceedingly worried about the harmful effects of global warming in the coming decade. This seems especially true for low-lying island communities facing the prospects of rising ocean levels due to the melting of polar and glacial ice, and parts of sub-Saharan Africa that are threatened with particularly high temperatures and catastrophic drought in conditions where the human struggle for survival is already exceedingly difficult. There are related issues concerning deforestation, the danger that marine life will be devastated by acidification of the oceans, reduced biodiversity, a rising incidence of extreme weather, and a variety of harms associated with growing scarcities of fresh water.

Normative globalization

By normative globalization is meant the impact of international law, the United Nations, human rights, and religious and secular forms of humanism upon transnational behavior and policy agendas. It represents a recognition of the role of values and rights both in public consciousness and in political behavior. By considering these influences within a framework of globalization, there is also a recognition that national identity frameworks are being superseded to varying degrees by universalistic and civilizational identities. Civic globalization is also often the bearer of undertakings that reflect commitments to the *human* interest and to *human* security rather than to more exclusive perspectives centering on nation, religion, ethnicity. The rise of human rights and humanitarian intervention are expressive of this tendency, but also operate in a contradictory manner as disguised carriers of imperial or apocalyptic globalization, and even of corporate and financial globalization.[32] The development of a global rule of law is a central goal of normative globalization.

A concluding observation

The basic argument made here is that it remains useful to retain the descriptive terminology of globalization in addressing the challenge of global governance, but that its provenance should be enlarged to take account of globalizing tendencies other than those associated with the world economy and the anti-globalization movement that formed in reaction. The discourse on globalization, to remain useful, needs to extend its coverage to the antagonism produced by the encounter between the United States and al Qaeda, acknowledging its borderless character and the degree to which both antagonists sponsor a visionary solution to the problem of global governance, which seems radically inconsistent with the values associated with human rights and global democracy. As well, the European experiment in organizing many aspects of political community on a regional basis suggests what many find to be an attractive alternative to reliance on statism (which had been accepted without raising questions at the time the United Nations was established), as well as a potential source of resistance to both imperial and apocalyptic menaces.[33] Ecological stresses, especially those associated with climate change and global warming, also seem to require such high levels of cooperation among sovereign states that perceive their interests very unevenly as to generate a variety of disturbing effects on the collective life of the planet.

Such an appreciation of various globalizations is not intended to serve as a funeral rite for the state system that has shaped world order thinking since the mid-seventeenth century, nor to deride the achievements of territorial sovereignty in promoting tolerance, reason, plural space for self-determination and national security, and a liberal conception of state–society relations. The state may yet stage a comeback, including a normative comeback, providing most of the peoples of the world with their best hope for blunting the sharp and often cruel edges of corporate, financial, imperial, apocalyptic, ecological, and even regional dimensions of globalization.[34] The recovery of a positive world order role for the state may be further facilitated by collaborative endeavors joining moderate states with the transnational social energies of civic globalization, and possibly environmental activism. Such a possibility has already been manifested in impressive populist moves to support the 1997 Kyoto Protocol on climate change, the outlawing of anti-personnel landmines, and especially by the successful movement that led to the establishment of the International Criminal Court in 2002.

The whole project of global governance has been eclipsed by the events of recent years, especially by the advent of unilateralist American foreign policy as of the 2000 presidential elections, followed in 2001 by the unleashing of the border-less war and the deliberate Washington effort to sideline the United Nations and disregard international law to the extent that such sources of authority clash with the policies of imperial globalization by withholding a legitimating seal of certifi-cation. Part of the rationale for reimagining globalization is to encourage a more relevant debate on the needs and possibilities for global governance, that is, sug-gesting that the world situation is not altogether subject to this vivid clash of dark forces, that constructive possibilities exist to move ahead, and deserve the engagement of citizens and their leaders throughout the world. Of course, it will be maintained by some commentators that such an undertaking is merely rescuing globalization from circumstances that have rendered the discussions of the 1990s irrelevant to present concerns, including how to re-stabilize the world economy and provide a regulatory framework protective of human security.

Returning to the observations made at the outset, the postulate of a decen-tralized political order composed of many dispersed actors continues to support a pluralist view of world society, but not one that is elegantly simplified by limiting the class of relevant political actors to sovereign states. Beyond this, the integrative characteristics of the world economy, environmental protection, and global civil society, as well as the American drive for global empire, give unprecedented weight to more unitary or monist constructions of the global reality. Indeed, the most responsive rendering of world order prospects would seem to rest upon the emergence of a creative tension between the two poles of assessment, pluralist and unitary, as conceptualized in an earlier global setting by the English School. We do not yet have a convincing political language with which to express this new dynamic reality, and so during what might be a long waiting period, it seems best to describe the world situation as one of 'complex globalization', a multidimensional viewpoint that is sensitive to the currently anguished, messy, and controversial interplay of the main contending agents of history. Whether a new coherence in the form of a global imaginary will emerge from complex globalization is radically uncertain, although it is plausible to highlight two solidarist candidates for the shaping of the future of world society: the first, associated with the American dominance project, the second associated with the vision of a global democracy that informs the activities of global civil society.[35] An imperial solution for world order would create a negative form of solidarism while a democratic solution, as abetted by environmental activism and civic globalization, would embody a posi-tive form. In either case the pluralist hypothesis is likely to be refuted by the middle of this century. As mentioned in the discussion of a world of regions, that is, regional globalization, it is at least conceivable that a triumphal regionalism will produce a new pluralism rather than lead to political unification in some form, that is, the realization of a partial variant of solidarism as a sequel to the Westphalian era.

The future of world society, it has been argued, is being forged on this anvil of complex globalization. It is most likely to produce a world order that exhibits a high degree of structural hybridity, combining aspects of pluralist and unitary organizational ideas. Whether it will make beneficial contributions to human security will depend, above all, on neutralizing apocalyptic and imperial forms of globalization, as well as democratizing corporate and financial, civic, regional, and even normative and ecological globalization. The peoples of the world will be participants in an ongoing historical cosmodrama that is likely to swerve to and fro before it arrives at some outcome that is sufficiently stable to give rise to a new generalized account of world society.

Notes

1 President Barack Obama delivered a speech in Prague that committed the United States to a vision of a world without nuclear weaponry, but there is no evidence of an intention to follow up on such an initiative, except in managerial arms control/non-proliferation modes as in the New START Treaty or the 2010 Nuclear Posture Review. 'Remarks of President Barack Obama', Hradcany Square, Prague, April 6, 2009; for more general assessment see R. A. Falk, 'A Radical World Challenge: Addressing Global Climate Change and the Threat of Nuclear Weapons', *Globalizations* 3, no. 1, 2010: 131–49. In general, see R. A. Falk and D. Krieger, *The Path to Zero: Dialogues on Nuclear Dangers*, Boulder, CO: Paradigm, 2012.

2 This issue is well depicted by Anthony Giddens, immodestly labeled the 'Giddens Paradox', in: A. Giddens, *The Politics of Climate Change*, Cambridge: Polity, 2009, 2.

3 The contours of the English School have been set forth most definitively by Martin Wight and Hedley Bull. See especially: H. Bull, *The Anarchical Society: A Study of Order in World Politics*, New York: Columbia University Press, 1977; and H. Butterfield and M. Wight, eds, *Diplomatic Investigations: Essays in the Theory of International Politics*, Cambridge, MA: Harvard University Press, 1966. For a sympathetic presentation of the English School, see T. Dunne, *Inventing International Society: A History of the English School*, Basingstoke: Macmillan, 1998; and more recently: A. Linklater and H. Suganami, *The English School of International Relations: A Contemporary Reassessment*, Cambridge: Cambridge University Press, 2008.

4 The effort was to show that both prudent power management respectful of international law and the benefits of inter-state cooperation across a wide spectrum of issues were characteristic of the workings of the state system. For a far more skeptical reading of the Westphalian image of world order, historically and empirically, see various essays in A. Orford, ed., *International Law and Its Others*, Cambridge: Cambridge University Press, 2006.

5 A viewpoint most cogently expressed by H. Bull in his influential essay, 'The Grotian Conception of International Society', in Butterfield and Wight, op. cit., *Diplomatic Investigations*, 51–73.

6 My attempt to treat such concerns is to be found in: R. A. Falk, *The Declining World Order: America's Imperial Geopolitics*, New York: Routledge, 2004.

7 See a graphic depiction of this global reach in: C. Johnson, *The Sorrows of Empire: Militarism, Secrecy, and the End of the Republic*, New York: Metropolitan Books, 2004. The designation of 'empire' needs elaboration, as the American embodiment of the global state makes no formal claim to override the sovereignty of subordinated states, but its disregard of the sovereignty of others is blatant and constitutive of a new, if contingent, twenty-first-century framing of world order.

8 An intelligent expression of this perspective can be found in: S. Brooks and W. Wohlforth, 'Spearheading Reform of the World Order', *Foreign Affairs* 88, no. 2, 2009, 49–63; especially in the period after 9/11, this primacy was articulated as an ideological mission that is indistinguishable from a global domination project.

9 For differing approaches to the changing geopolitical landscape, see R. Kagan, *The Return of History and the End of Dreams*, New York: Knopf, 2008; A. Moravcsik, 'Europe, the Second Superpower', *Current History* 109, March 2010, 91–98.

10 See C. Taylor, *Modern Social Imaginaries*, Durham, NC: Duke University Press, 2004. Others approach this question of world order adaptation in the language of 'paradigm change'.

11 Most influentially by M. Castells in his magisterial three-volume work bearing the overall title *The Information Age: Economy, Society and Culture*, Cambridge, MA: Blackwell, 1996, 1997, 1998.

12 My own misguided early endorsement of the Afghanistan War represented a misplaced view that the threat that produced the attacks was both attributable in part to a government in power and could be significantly reduced, if not eliminated, by recourse to war and regime change. See R. A. Falk, *The Great Terror War*, Northampton, MA: Olive Branch Press, 2003.

13 Ignored here, but not to be dismissed, are continuing calls for a redescription and reappraisal of what actually took place on 9/11, giving rise to a growing ethos of suspicion with respect to truth and governance in American society. See D. R. Griffin, *The New Pearl Harbor Revisited: 9/11, the Cover-up, and the Exposé*, Northampton, MA: Olive Branch Press, 2008; for an inquiry into deeper roots of this malaise, see P. D. Scott, *The Road to 9/11: Wealth, Empire, and the Future of America*, Berkeley, CA: University of California Press, 2007.

14 Perhaps most comprehensively and intelligently defended in: M. J. Glennon, *Limits of Law, Prerogatives of Power: Interventionism After Kosovo*, New York: Palgrave, 2001; for a more nuanced endorsement of the Kosovo intervention that seeks to revise international law to take wider account of humanitarian pressures to erode sovereign rights, see Independent International Commission on Kosovo, *The Kosovo Report: Conflict, International Response, Lessons Learned*, Oxford: Oxford University Press, 2000.

15 For analysis of these issues, including an assessment of the future viability of the Charter's constraints on the use of international force, see R. A. Falk, *The Costs of War: International Law, the UN, and World Order after Iraq*, New York: Routledge, 2008, 69–82.

16 For mainstream assessment, and accompanying official texts appearing as appendices, see L. Korb, ed., *A New National Security Strategy in an Age of Terrorists, Tyrants, and Weapons of Mass Destruction*, New York: Council on Foreign Relations, 2003; for early criticism, see R. A. Falk, 'The New Bush Doctrine', *The Nation* 275, no. 3, July 15, 2002. For a meta-political consideration of deeper and more complex issues involved, see M. W. Doyle, *Striking First: Preemption and Prevention in International Conflict*, Princeton, NJ: Princeton University Press, 2008.

17 For one interpretation of this new framework of global conflict, see R. A. Falk, Note 12 above.

18 For extended discussion, see R. A. Falk, 'Revisiting Westphalia, Discovering Post-Westphalia', *Journal of Ethics* 6, 2002, 11–352.

19 A seminal general inquiry into the relevance of unanticipated intrusions upon expectations is to be found in N. N. Talib, *The Black Swan: The Impact of the Highly Improbable*, New York: Random House, 2007.

20 For a widely read glorification of the benefits of globalization, see T. Friedman, *The Lexus and the Olive Tree: Understanding Globalization*, New York: Farrar, Straus and Giroux, 1999.

21 *The Economist,* in its treatment of the anti-globalization movement that was initiated in Seattle in late 1999 demonstrations against the World Trade Organization, argued that the poor were being much more helped by market-oriented constitutionalism than by social democratic and welfare oriented approaches to economic development.

22 For text of the most authoritative statement, see the opening sentences of the covering letter signed by George W. Bush as president: White House, 'The National Security Strategy of the United States of America', Washington, DC: 2002.

23 An insightful critical response to the failures of economic globalization and possible transformative responses is found in: S. Gill, *Power and Resistance in the New World Order* 2, New York: Palgrave Macmillan, 2008.

24 The dominant tendencies within civic globalization favor democracy as the basis for political life, but are skeptical about procedural forms of democracy that are centered upon periodic and free elections. Instead, what is proposed by those associated with various forms of globalization-from-below is substantive democracy in which the governing process is dedicated to equitable economic, social, and political development, with a bias toward ensuring the wellbeing of the impoverished.

25 For two very different approaches to the emergence of imperial globalization, see M. Hardt and A. Negri, *Empire*, Cambridge, MA: Harvard University Press, 2000; and A. J. Bacevich, *American Empire: The Realities and Consequences of U.S. Diplomacy*, Cambridge, MA: Harvard University Press, 2002.

26 The ending of the Bacevich book, Note 25 above, on p. 244, asserts this challenge: 'The question that urgently demands attention – the question that Americans can no longer afford to dodge – is not whether the United States has become an empire. The question is what sort of empire they intend theirs to be' – whether this question retains its same saliency if the world economic recession recedes and in light of the frustrations faced by American military interventions in Iraq and Afghanistan. In any event, both the American public and its leaders have difficulty discussing this imperial identity or project because the guiding national political myth remains anti-imperial, a legacy of the country's revolutionary origins.

27 Bush writes as follows in the very first sentence of his cover letter attached to the 2002 National Security Strategy document cited in Note 22: 'The great struggles of the twentieth century between liberty and totalitarianism ended with a decisive victory for the forces of freedom – and a single sustainable model of national success: freedom, democracy, and free enterprise'.

28 For influential statements of this pro-imperial outlook, see R. Kagan, 'The Benevolent Empire', *Foreign Policy*, Summer 1998, 24–35; M. Ignatieff, 'The Burden: With a Military of Unrivaled Might, the United States Rule a New Kind of Empire. Will this Cost America its Soul – or Save it?' *New York Times Magazine*, January 1, 2003, 22–27, 50–53.

29 For two rather different lines of argument along these lines, see 'Will the Empire Be Fascist?' in note 5 of R. A. Falk, *The Declining World Order*, New York: Routledge, 2004, 241–52; S. Wolin, *Democracy Inc.: Managed Democracy and the Specter of Inverted Totalitarianism*, Princeton, NJ: Princeton University Press, 2008.

30 My use of the word 'apocalyptic' here is based on conversations with R. J. Lifton.

31 See useful conceptualization and advocacy in: T. E. Paupp, *The Future of Global Relations: Crumbling Walls, Rising Regions*, New York: Palgrave Macmillan, 2009; also: note 6 in R. A. Falk, *The Declining World Order*, New York: Routledge, 2004, 45–65.

32 For several explorations, see A. Orford and D. Kennedy in Orford ed., *International Law and its Others*, op. cit., 131–96.

33 Although this Westphalian consensus that existed at the birth of the United Nations was distinctly West-centric and had no trouble reconciling this conceptual statism with an acceptance of European colonial empires in the non-West as valid political arrangements.

34 This possibility is explored in R. A. Falk, 'State of Siege: Will Globalization Win Out?' *International Affairs* 75, no. 1, January 1997, 123–36.

35 It is important to distinguish between the spread of democracy within states and the democratization of the world order system. The latter includes the procedures of entities such as the IMF and World Bank, and the operations of the UN's principal organs, the General Assembly and the Security Council. For an incisive overview of the interdependent nature and significance of national and global democracy, see D. Archibugi, *The Global Commonwealth of Citizens: Toward Cosmopolitan Democracy*, Princeton, NJ: Princeton University Press, 2008.

2

NONVIOLENT GEOPOLITICS

My attempt here is to articulate a conception of a world order premised on non-violent geopolitics, as well as to consider some obstacles to its realization. By focusing on 'geopolitics' the intention is to consider the role played by dominant political actors on the global stage. It challenges the main premise of realism that security, leadership and influence in the twenty-first century continue to rest primarily on military power, or what is sometimes described as 'hard power' cap-abilities.[1] The contrasting argument that I support is that political outcomes since the end of World War II to a much greater extent than is generally appreciated have been shaped by soft power ingenuity that has rather consistently overcome conditions of military inferiority to achieve a desired political outcome. The United States completely controlled land, air, and sea throughout the Vietnam war, winning every battle, and yet eventually losing the war, killing as many as 4 million Vietnamese on the road to the failure of its military intervention. Ironically, the US government went on to engage constructively with the victorious Vietnam forces, and currently enjoys a friendly and productive diplomatic and economic relation-ship. In this instance, the strategic difference between defeat and victory is almost unnoticeable, making the wartime casualties and devastation even more tragic, and worse than pointless from every relevant perspective.

Nevertheless, US militarists refused to learn from this costly experience, treating the impact of defeat as a kind of geopolitical malady, dubbed the 'Vietnam Syndrome', rather than as a reflection of a historical trend supportive of the legitimate claims of self-determination despite the relative military weakness of such nation-alist movements of resistance. The mainstream realists drew the wrong lesson, insisting that the outcome was the exception rather than the rule, a case mainly of undermining the domestic support for the war back in the United States, not a matter of losing to a stronger adversary.[2] In effect, overcoming the Vietnam Syndrome meant restoring confidence in hard power geopolitics and thereby neutralizing domestic opposition to war making. This revived militarist approach to and control over the shaping of American foreign policy was proclaimed as an achievement of the Gulf War in 1991, which revealingly prompted the American president at the time, George H. W. Bush, to utter memorable words in the immediate aftermath of this military victory on the desert battlefield of Kuwait: 'We finally kicked the Vietnam Syndrome.' His meaning was that the United States had a renewed confidence that it could wage and win wars at acceptable costs, not pausing to notice that such victories were obtained only where the terrain was suited for a purely military encounter, or the capability and will of the enemy to resist was minimal or non-existent. Hard power is not obsolete, but lacks the capacity to shape the outcomes in the most characteristic conflicts of the period since 1945, namely, the political struggles to unseat oppressive rule on behalf of a foreign imperial power or reliance on military intervention. To restructure the politics of a sovereign state, hard power is still decisive in encounters with hard power, or in situations where the weaker side is defenseless, and the stronger side is prepared to carry its military dominance to genocidal extremes and exterminate the other.

It is hardly surprising that the excessive and anachronistic reliance on hard power solutions in situations of conflict have led to a series of failures by the militarily superior side, acknowledged (Iraq War) and unacknowledged (Afghanistan War; Libyan War). As long as the United States invests so much more heavily in military capabilities than any other state it is bound to respond to threats or pursue its interests along a hard power path, thereby refusing to take proper account of clear historical trends favoring soft power dominance in conflict situations involving struggle for control of the state in non-Western foreign societies. Israel also has adopted a similar approach, relying on its military superiority to destroy and kill, but not being able to control the political results of the wars it embarks upon (e.g. the Lebanon War of 2006, the Gaza attacks of 2008–9). An additional cost of hard power or violent geopolitics is to undermine respect for the rule of law in global politics, for the authority of the United Nations, and for efforts to minimize war, thereby diverting resources and losing lives.

A second demonstration of the anachronistic reliance on a violence-based system of security was associated with the response to the 9/11 attacks on the Twin Towers and the Pentagon, the dual symbols of the US imperium. A feature of this event was the exposure of the extreme vulnerability of the most militarily dominant state in the whole of human history to attack by a non-state actor without significant weaponry and lacking in major resources. In the aftermath it became clear that the enormous US military investment in achieving 'full spectrum dominance' had not brought enhanced security, but the most acute sense of insecurity in the history of the country. Once again the wrong lesson was drawn, namely, that the way to restore security was to wage war regardless of the distinctive nature of this new kind of threat, to make mindless use of the military machine abroad and to couple this with the curtailment of liberties at home despite the absence of a territorial adversary or any plausible means–ends relationship between recourse to war and reduction of the threat.[3] The appropriate lesson, borne out by experience, is that such a security threat can best be addressed by a combination of transnational law enforcement and through addressing the *legitimate* grievances of the political extremists who launched the attacks. As Johan Galtung has argued, the Spanish response to the Madrid attacks of March 11, 2004 seemed sensitive to the new realities: withdraw from involvement in the Iraq War, enhance police efforts to identify and arrest violent extremists, and join in the dialogic attempts to lessen tension between Islam and the West.[4] In an informal talk, the former British prime minister, John Major, observed that he only began to make progress in ending the violence in Northern Ireland when he stopped thinking of the IRA as a terrorist organization and began treating it as a political actor with real grievances and its own motivations in reaching accommodation and peace.

The right lesson is to recognize the extremely limited utility of military power in conflict situations within the post-colonial world, grasping the extent to which popular struggle has achieved historical agency during the last 60 years. Such struggle has shaped numerous outcomes of conflicts that could not be understood if assessed only through a hard power lens that interprets history as almost always determined by wars being won by the stronger military side that after victory on the battlefield gets to shape the peace.[5] Every anticolonial war in the latter half of the twentieth century was eventually won by the militarily weaker side, which prevailed in the end despite suffering disproportionate losses along its way to victory. It won because the people were mobilized on behalf of national independence against foreign colonial forces, and their resistance included gaining complete international control of the high moral ground. It won because of the political truth embodied in the Afghan saying: 'You have the watches, we have the time.' Gaining the high moral ground both delegitimized colonial rule and legitimized anti-colonial struggle; in the end even the state-centric and initially empire-friendly UN was induced to endorse anticolonial struggles by reference to the right of self-determination, which was proclaimed by international law as an inalienable right of all peoples.

This ascendancy of soft power capabilities in political struggles was not always descriptive of political reality. Throughout the colonial era, and until the mid-twentieth century, hard power was generally effective and efficient, as expressed by the colonial conquests of the Western hemisphere with small numbers of well-armed troops, British control of India with a few thousand soldiers, or the success of 'gunboat diplomacy' in supporting US economic imperialism in Central America and the Caribbean. What turned the historical tide against militarism was the rise of national and cultural self-consciousness in the countries of the South, most dramatically in India under the inspired leadership of Gandhi, where coercive nonviolent forms of soft power first revealed their potency to the world.

More recently, abetted by the communications revolution, resistance to oppressive regimes based on human rights has demonstrated the limits of hard power governance in a globalized world. The anti-apartheid campaign extended the struggle against the racist regime that governed South Africa to a symbolic global battlefield where the weapons were coercive nonviolent reliance on boycotts, divestment, and sanctions. The collapse of apartheid in South Africa was significantly achieved by developments outside of its sovereign territory, a pattern that is now being repeated in the Palestinian 'legitimacy war' being waged against Israel. The outcome is not assured, and it is possible for the legitimacy war to be won and yet the oppressive conditions sustained, as seems to be currently the case with respect to China's control of Tibet.

Against this background, it is notable, and even bewildering, that geopolitics continues to be driven by a realist consensus that ahistorically believes that history continues to be determined by the grand strategy of hard power exercised by dominant state actors.[6] In effect, realists have lost touch with reality. It seems correct to acknowledge that there remains a rational role for hard power, as a defensive hedge against residual statist militarism, but even here the economic and political gains of demilitarization would seem to far outweigh the benefits of an anachronistic dependence on hard power forms of self-defense, especially those that risk wars fought with weaponry of mass destruction. With respect to non-state political violence, hard power capabilities are of little or no relevance, and security can be best achieved by accommodation, intelligence and transnational law enforcement. The US recourse to war in addressing the al Qaeda threat, as in Iraq and Afghanistan, has proved to be costly, and misdirected.[7] Just as the US defeat in Vietnam reproduced, at great expense and with horrific costs for Vietnamese society, the French defeats in their colonial wars waged in Indochina and Algeria, the cycle of failure has been renewed in the post-9/11 global setting. Why do such lessons bearing on the changing balance between hard and soft power remain so long unlearned in the imperial center of geopolitical maneuver?

It is of great importance to pose this question even if no definitive answer can be forthcoming. There are some suggestive leads that relate to both material and ideological explanations. On the materialist side, there are deeply embedded governmental and societal structures whose identity and narrow self-interests are bound up with a maximal reliance upon and projection of hard power. These structures have been identified in various ways in the US setting: 'national security state', 'military–industrial complex', 'military Keynesianism', and 'the war system'. It was Dwight Eisenhower who more than 50 years ago warned of the military–industrial complex in his farewell speech, notably making the observation only as he was at the end of his presidency.[8] At this time, there seems to be a more deeply rooted structure of support for militarism that extends to the mainstream media, conservative think tanks, a huge intelligence apparatus, an army of highly paid lobbyists, and a deeply compromised Congress, the majority of whose members have substituted patronage and money for conscience and prudence. This politically entrenched paradigm linking realism and militarism makes it virtually impossible to challenge a military budget even at a time of fiscal deficits that are acknowledged by some conservative observers to endanger the viability of the US empire. The scale of the military budget, combined with navies in every ocean, more than 700 foreign military bases, and a huge investment in the militarization of space, exhibit the self-fulfilling inability to acknowledge the dysfunctionality of such a global posture.[9] The US spends almost as much as the entire world put together on its military machine, and more than double what the next ten leading states spend. And for what benefit to either the national or global security?

The most that can be expected by way of adjustment of the realist consensus under these conditions is a certain softening of the hard power emphasis. In this respect, one notes that several influential adherents of the realist consensus have recently called attention to the rising importance of non-military elements of power in the rational pursuit of a grand strategy that continues to frame geopolitics by reference to presumed hard power 'realities', but are at the same time critical of arch militarism attributed to neoconservatives.[10] This same tone pervades the speech of Barack Obama at the 2009 Nobel Peace Prize ceremony. This realist refusal to comprehend a *largely* post-militarist global setting is exceedingly danger-ous given the continuing hold of realism on the shaping of policy by governmental and market/finance forces.[11] Such an outmoded realism not only engages in imprudent military undertakings; it tends also to overlook a range of deeper issues bearing on security, survival and human wellbeing, including climate change, safe energy, water scarcities, fiscal fragility, market freefall, and the many forms of human insecurity, especially as relating to jobs and impoverishment. As such, this kind of policy orientation is incapable of formulating the priorities associated with sustainable and benevolent forms of global governance, and is neglectful of the imperatives of human security.

In addition to the structural rigidity that results from the entrenched militarist paradigm, there arises a systemic learning disability that is incapable of analyzing the main causes of past failures. As a practical matter, this leads policy options to be too often shaped by unimaginative thinking trapped within a militarist box. In recent international policy experience, thinking mainly confined to the military box has led the Obama administration to escalate US involvement in an internal struggle for the future of Afghanistan and to leave the so-called military option on the table for dealing with the prospect of Iran's acquisition of nuclear weapons. An alter-native policy approach in Afghanistan, which has finally been adopted, is based on the recognition that the Taliban is a conservative religious movement seeking nationalist objectives amid raging ethnic conflict. As a result, it comprehends that the US security interests would benefit from an early end of combat operations, followed by the phased withdrawal of NATO forces, a major increase in devel-opmental assistance that avoids channeling funds through a corrupt Kabul govern-ment, and a genuine shift in US foreign policy toward respect for the politics of self-determination. Similarly, in relation to Iran, instead of a program of coercive sanctions, threats of a military strike and destabilizing efforts, a different approach is preferable based on a call for regional denuclearization, including that of Israel. This kind of diplomacy would be expressive of both thinking outside the militarist box, and a recogition of the existence of more hopeful non-military responses to genuine Middle East security concerns.

In conclusion, some form of geopolitics is almost bound to be practiced, given the gross inequality of states and the weakness of the United Nations as the institutional expression of unified governance for the planet. Especially since the collapse of the Soviet Union, the primacy of the United States has inevitably resulted in its unprecedented geopolitical ascendancy. Unfortunately, this position has been accompanied by America's unreconstructed confidence in the hard power paradigm, which combines militarism and realism, producing violent geopolitics in relation to critical unresolved conflicts. The experience of the past 60 years shows clearly that this paradigm is untenable from both pragmatic and principled perspectives. It fails to achieve its goals at acceptable costs, and often not at all. It relies on immoral practices that involve the massive killing of innocent persons and the colossal waste of resources.

A leading test of this thesis is the ongoing struggle for self-determination of the Palestinian people, whether in the form of a secular state encompassing the whole of historic Palestine or an independent and viable state of their own existing alongside Israel, with the borders of 1967. As matters now stand, after decades of occupation, the Palestinian struggle is mainly now a legitimacy war that relies on an array of soft power instruments, including diplomacy and lawfare, a non-violent coercive boycott and divestment campaign, and a variety of transnational civil society initiatives challenging Israeli policies. Uncertainty exists as to the eventual outcome of this long struggle for peace and justice. The whole soft power orientation has taken a giant leap forward as a result of the 'Arab spring' in which unarmed popular movements challenged dictatorial and oppressive regimes with some notable successes, especially in Egypt and Tunisia, and elsewhere at least achieving promises of extensive reforms. Increasingly, I think the potentialities of constructing a world order on the basis of soft power principles is gaining support, shifting nonviolent geopolitics from the domain of utopianism to an emerging status of plausible political project. Of course, there is resistance, most especially from the hard power holdouts throughout government bureaucracies and in militarized sectors of society.

Those political forces relying on the alternative of nonviolent practices and principles, in contrast, have shown the capacity to achieve political goals and a willingness to pursue their goals by ethical means. The Gandhi movement resulting in Indian independence, the Mandela-led transformation of apartheid South Africa, people power in the Philippines and the soft revolutions of Eastern Europe in the late 1980s are exemplary instances of domestic transformations based on nonviolent struggle. None of these soft power victories produced entirely just societies or addressed the entire agenda of social and political concerns, often leaving untouched exploitative and corrupted class relations, massive poverty, and bitter societal tensions, but they did overcome the immediate situation of oppressive state–society relations without significant reliance on violence.

Turning to the global setting, there exist analogous opportunities for the application of nonviolent geopolitics. There is a widespread recognition that war between large states is not a rational option as it is almost certain to involve huge costs in blood and treasure, and reach mutually destructive results rather than as in former times producing a clear winner and loser. The opportunities for a nonviolent geopolitics are grounded in an acceptance of the self-constraining discipline of international law as reinforced by widely endorsed moral principles embodied in the great religions and world civilizations. A further step in this direction would be the repudiation of weaponry of mass destruction, starting with a solemn public pledge not to use nuclear weapons first, and moving on to engage in an immediate and urgent negotiation of a nuclear disarmament treaty that posits as a *non-utopian* goal 'a world without nuclear weapons'. The essential second step is liberating the moral and political imagination from the confines of militarism, and consequent thinking within that dysfunctional box that still remains a staple component of the realist mindset among the leading countries in the West, especially the United States. This psycho-political challenge to move away from reliance on war making as the cornerstone of national and global security is made more difficult by bureaucratic and private sector entrenched interests in a militarist framing of security policy, including an archipelago of military-oriented think tanks.

Notes

1 A mainstream exception is R. Rosecrance, *The Rise of the Virtual State: Wealth and Power in the Coming Century*, New York: Basic Books, 2002.
2 Significantly, every US leader after Nixon did his best to eliminate the Vietnam Syndrome, which was perceived by the Pentagon as an unwanted inhibitor of the use of aggressive force in world politics.
3 Well depicted in D. Cole and J. Lobel, eds, *Less Safe, Less Free: Why America Is Losing the War on Terror*, New York: New Press, 2007; see also my own attempt, R. A. Falk, *The Great Terror War*, Northampton, MA: Olive Branch Press, 2003.
4 This comparison is analyzed in a similar manner in J. Galtung, 'Searching for Peace in a World of Terrorism and State Terrorism', in S. Chiba and T. J. Schoenbaum, eds, *Peace Movements and Pacifism after September 11*, Cheltenham: Edward Elgar, 2008, 32–48.
5 Significantly documented in J. Schell, *The Unconquerable World: Power, Nonviolence, and the Will of the People*, New York: Henry Holt, 2003.
6 It is relevant here to observe that the changes in the global geopolitical landscape associated with the rise of China, India, Brazil and Russia are largely to do with their economic rise, and have little to do with their military capabilities, which remain trivial compared to those of the United States.
7 As interventionary struggles go on year after year with inconclusive results, but mounting costs in lives and resources, the intervening sides contradict their own war rationale, searching for compromises, and even inviting the participation of the enemy in the governing process. This has been attempted in both Iraq and Afghanistan, but only after inflicting huge damage, and enduring major loss of life among their own troops and incurring great expense.
8 Among the valuable studies are R. J. Barnet, *The Roots of War*, New York: Atheneum, 1972; and L. C. Lewin, *Report from Iron Mountain on the Possibility and Desirability of Peace* (for Special Study Group), London: Macdonald, 1968.
9 Most convincingly demonstrated in a series of books by Chalmers Johnson. See especially the first of his three books on the theme, C. Johnson, *The Sorrows of Empire: Militarism, Secrecy, and the End of the Republic*, New York: Metropolitan Books, 2004.
10 See J. S. Nye, *Bound to Lead: The Changing Nature of American Power*, New York: Basic Books, 1990; L. H. Gelb, *Power Rules: How Common Sense can Rescue American Foreign Policy*, New York: HarperCollins, 2009; S. M. Walt, *Taming American Power: The Global Response to American Power*, New York: Norton, 2005. For a progressive critique of

American imperial militarism, see G. Kolko, *The Age of War: The United States Confronts the World*, Boulder, CO: Lynne Rienner, 2006.

11 Several leading scholars have long been sensitive to the disconnect that separates even relatively prudent realists from reality. For a still relevant major work, see J. Galtung, *The True Worlds: A Transnational Perspective*, New York: Free Press, 1980. For other recent perceptive studies along these lines, see K. Booth, *Theory of World Security*, Cambridge: Cambridge University Press, 2007, especially the section on 'emancipatory realism', 87–91; J. Camilleri and J. Falk, *Worlds in Transition: Evolving Governance Across a Stressed Planet*, Cheltenham: Edward Elgar, 2009; J. H. Mittelman, *Hyperconflict: Globalization and Insecurity*, Stanford, CA: Stanford University Press, 2010.

3

TOWARD HUMANE GLOBAL GOVERNANCE

Rhetoric, desire and imaginaries

Toward a global governance imaginary for the twenty-first century[1]

Since the dawning of the nuclear age, there has been a growing anxiety about whether human civilization is sustainable within a state-centric framework of world order, with or without hegemonic geopolitics. Such a restrictive outlook embodies biopolitics on a global scale, and human anxieties as a species living under the threat of bare survival. My preoccupation has been to explore and depict a survival-plus imaginary of the human quest, supplementing this survivalist orientation by coequal concerns coupling the attainment of human dignity for all persons with a spiritual grounding for the meaning of life.[2] For the sake of focus, I label this imaginary as 'humane global governance', choosing words that call our attention to both normative (law, morality, justice, spirituality) and practical (administration, implementation of norms, institutionalized collaboration) dimensions of desirable types of world order.

The conception of what is desirable is historicized in relation to the circumstances of the early twenty-first century. A distinction is also drawn between the normative and practical deficiencies of world order as an operative framing for global activities and of world order *as a system*. This latter category of deficiency casts the darkest shadow across the human future as it presupposes that unless the *structure* of the world is rapidly transformed, the biopolitical future of the human species is severely at risk. These systemic threats include nuclear weaponry, climate change, and economic collapse.

This chapter examines some aspects of this overall effort to diagnose the character of world order challenges, as well as to assess the various responses that seem likely and promising. It includes some reflections on the trajectory of my research and writing over the course of more than five decades.

Establishing global governance: getting beyond illusion

There is little doubt that as the twenty-first century begins to unfold there is a widespread sense that human wellbeing is multiply jeopardized, and that a positive human future will depend upon unprecedented political coordination and cooperation on behalf of global common interests. What follows from this consensus with respect to the institutional arrangements of world politics remains uncertain and highly contested. At one extreme is the historical insistence that the emergence of a world state or government has become the indispensable foundation to achieve the necessary level of coordination, in effect, a sequel to the long experience with various stages of state-centric Westphalian political order. Further along this line of reasoning is the claim that trends toward global governance over the course of the last several decades make the emergence of a world state, or at least a world government, all but inevitable within a relatively short period, say 20 years or less.

Even if it is conceded that such an emergence is likely at some future time, there is a wide disparity of views as to the time frame, and actuating conditions. There are some advocates of world government who think it will come into being as a result of education and the impact of public reason, an overall rational adjustment to impinging realities without any accompanying trauma, and in view of trends toward institutionalizing the integrative pressures of globalization. Many informed observers are skeptical of such a soft landing, and believe that such a world polity will only become a reality, if ever, in a post-catastrophe setting where the old order has been reduced to shambles.[3]

Beyond speculation about emergence, a further issue raised concerns whether this prospect of a world state should be greeted with enthusiasm or not. Some advocates believe that only some form of world government could overcome the most serious biopolitical challenges confronting humanity, mobilizing resources and energies for a coordinated, compassionate, and equitable response to global warming, and reducing dramatically the likelihood of apocalyptic warfare. Others believe that any foreseeable transition to world government would almost certainly freeze or deepen the inequities of present world order, and would necessarily rely on repressive means of governance to sustain stability and maintain control. Such a world government would be widely regarded as a form of global empire of unprecedented scope, and undoubtedly administered by the leadership of a currently hegemonic state actor. Arguably, the American response to the 9/11 attacks during the early years of the Bush presidency was implicitly seeking a world order solution along such lines.[4]

Not everyone believes that the only meaningful focus for systemic global reform entails centralization of political authority in constitutional arrangements that are capable of effective regulation on a global scale. There are also supporters of various models of radical decentralization of power and authority. Such viewpoints emphasize beneficial effects of the anarchic energy that is being currently released by way of the fragmentation of existing states, that is, carrying the logic of self-determination to levels of social order present *within* states, thereby giving approval to forms of order that are reflective of the existence of a historically conditioned sense of community, however it is spatially specified. This anti-centralization bias also expresses itself by effective localized and populist resistance to the geopolitics of empire as the defining structural force of this contemporary period. This vision of an increasingly anarchic future also generates debate about the benefits and drawbacks of political decentralization at this stage of history, including fragmentation of large states.[5]

An intermediate posture between a unified world polity and accelerating political fragmentation involves the rise of regional forms of order as a partial and ambiguous sequel to both the Westphalian framework of sovereign states and the various efforts to achieve empire and hegemony.[6] This kind of political regionalism should be distinguished from renewed interest in a multipolar world order in which China, India, Russia, and Brazil join with the United States and the European Union in reinventing the balance of power for the twenty-first century.[7] Amid such contradictory images of the future of world order, it is more difficult than at earlier stages of the modern period to set policy priorities or even to debate alternative approaches to world order.[8]

Against such a background it seems useful to offer some interpretation of the global setting as a dynamic, evolving reality that is generating challenges not easily met within a still predominantly politically fragmented world of sovereign territorial states. To impart some clarity to the political imagination I have differentiated horizons of feasibility, horizons of necessity, and horizons of desire or aspiration.[9] The realist sensibility arising from a Westphalian world of sovereign states emphasizes the feasible, giving its main attention to the management of hard power as the foundation of security, conceiving of force as a still viable policy option that remains available to militarily strong states for the pursuit of their vital national interests, and treating normative concerns associated with constructing a more just and sustainable world order as falling outside the realm of politics conceived as the art of the possible. In my view, ever since the advent of nuclear weaponry 'realism' as a practical ideology guiding diplomacy has been an anachronistic ideology that imposes intolerable risks on the peoples of the world, exaggerates the contributions of military capabilities to security, and deflects attention from grasping the newer agendas of challenge, opportunity, and limits.[10]

Realism, while being anachronistic, is nevertheless robust and resilient with respect to governmental discourse and outlook, easily absorbing critiques without changing its views as to the structure of world order, or modifying its reliance on military approaches to problem-solving. To some extent, Europe since 1945 has moved impressively, if inconsistently, toward a somewhat demilitarized conception of its security, successfully establishing a culture of peace to govern *internal* European relations. The ambiguity arises because Europe's response to *external* security threats has been based on a close and comprehensive alliance with the United States, which has pursued a militarized, neo-imperial, and interventionary approach to global security. In my judgment, what is 'feasible' is insufficient to meet the world order challenges of the present period, even if realism takes some account of the new and changing global setting. Arguably, also, if feasibility was to be fully realistic in a fragile and complex world setting, it would be more disposed to advocate as generally beneficial an acceptance of the constraints of international law in the context of foreign policy, even by a hegemon, and to acknowledge the limits on military power as demonstrated by the collapse of colonialism and the repeated failure of military intervention in the post-colonial world.

At present, even the least militarist of realists are unwilling to recommend adherence to the norms of international law in relation to war/peace issues.[11] When even the most liberal statespersons discuss foreign policy options, international law is rarely mentioned unless it can be invoked in a partisan spirit as supportive of a controversial geopolitical undertaking or to castigate an adversary. President Barack Obama's appraisal of the wars in Iraq and Afghanistan rested on the distinction between 'wars of choice' and 'wars of necessity' without ever bothering to justify the controversial engagement in Afghanistan by reference to international law or the United Nations.

What reformist pressure exists at intergovernmental levels is largely of a populist character that tends to surface in the aftermath of catastrophic breakdowns of global stability.[12] It exerts only temporary pressure and is inconsequential or trivial so far as overcoming the main anachronistic features of the Westphalian structure and operational behavior.[13] The litmus test of failure is associated with absence of a relevant political will to implement the prohibition of aggressive use of force that has been decreed by international law for the past 80 years.[14] Without the pressure of a catastrophic breakdown that is harmful to dominant political actors, the ideology of realism is likely to continue to shape prevailing ideas and policies about what it is feasible to do. Given the risks associated with war, climate change, and an impending energy/water/food squeeze, such a horizon of feasibility has become dangerously dysfunctional from the perspective of intermediate-term human wellbeing and even species survival.[15]

This conditioning circumstance invites pessimism, or a widespread conspiracy of psychological denial, the stubborn refusal of realism to see reality in relation to problems and a changing historical context, that is, according to the necessities posed, rather than through the familiar and reassuring optic of feasibility.[16] Since the problematic character of the contemporary global circumstance cannot be completely ignored, especially by the liberal wing of the realist consensus, secondary concerns emphasize the goal of stabilizing an increasingly anachronistic world order. These would include enhanced cooperation among states via the disaggregation of the territorial state,[17] the containment of the proliferation of nuclear weaponry, the promotion of human rights, and attention to the curtailment of greenhouse gas emissions by relying on such market correctives as carbon trading. These are plausible initiatives, compatible with horizons of feasibility, and do not demand structural modifications in world order.

A critique of this enclosure of the political imagination can be offered from the perspective of horizons of necessity, which is conceiving of global policy from the perspective of what must be done at the earliest possible time to increase the prospects of human and humane survival and civilizational sustainability. It is from this standpoint that some argue that the political fragmentation of authority embedded in Westphalian, or even neo-Westphalian, systems needs to be overcome by establishing a form of world government with the capacity to regulate effectively the war system, and to impose a global rule of law that constrains and sanctions the strong as well as the weak. Such a world government also presupposes the establishment of a global democracy with a mandate and capacity to lengthen cycles of political accountability now operative at the level of the sovereign state.

As matters now stand, political leaders in the dominant countries depend for their legitimacy and support upon fulfilling short-term expectations that are not compatible with responding to the longer periods of adjustment required to address the twenty-first-century agenda of global challenges. In essence, the horizon of necessity calls for a shift in the balance of influence between the *parts* and the *whole*, as well as between *short-term* political accountability and *intermediate-term* (10–50 years) timelines. A defining feature of Westphalian world order is the sub-systemic dominance of the parts and of the present, complemented by the weakness of the whole or center and the failure to plan for the future. The lengthening of the time dimension for policymaking is less familiar but beginning to be understood within governmental and NGO circles, as suggested by the growing recognition of the needs and even the rights of future generations and by proposals for diminishing the likelihood of harmful climate change. But the prospects of this recent rhetoric of concern being translated into effective government or corporate planning remains highly unlikely.

Additional to feasibility and necessity, there exist various horizons of desire, which incorporate concerns about sustainability and survival, but also add a crucial emphasis on *justice, human dignity, compassion*, and even *individual and collective happiness*. A concern with justice is a matter of fairness that is particularly sensitive to severe deprivation of rights: poverty, oppression, gross inequalities. It is also offers a means of liberating the political and moral imagination to envisage a future for humanity that is dedicated to the fulfillment of the potentials of all persons for a life of dignity.[18] Positing happiness as a collective goal of humanity is an acknowledgement that there is more to a good life than being treated fairly; conditions of beauty and cultural vitality are also public goods that seem eminently worthy of safeguarding and ensuring widespread availability in affordable forms. There is no doubt that many persons who are responsive to horizons of desire favor the establishment as quickly as possible of world government, usually in a federal or confederal form that relies on strict constitutionalism (checks and balances; subsidiarity; separation of powers; substantive constraints) to limit the power of the leaders, and hopefully to contain risks of tyrannical abuses.

My own approach to the horizon of desire is much more conditioned by a bottom-up approach that stresses building normative democracy *within* states and other political communities on a municipal scale, while seeking to find nonviolent pathways to global democracy and global security.[19] In essence, the advocacy of world government is almost certain to produce negative results unless these pre-conditions of democratization and nonviolence are satisfied. The European Union, to the extent that it has established a culture of peace within Europe, built a rights-based social contract for welfare and participation, and created a popularly elected European Parliament that may be regarded to have partially satisfied the preconditions for the establishment of regional government. Such a development in Europe remains a project in the domain of desire, because popular support for such a dra-matic centralization of authority within Europe does not exist at either grassroots or elite levels at this time, and has actually relapsed as the European recession has lingered and imperiled the solvency of several of the weaker national economies among EU members.

It may be helpful to understand activities associated with the horizon of desire as thought experiments that reject the understanding of politics as the art of the pos-sible, that is, as conditioned by horizons of feasibility. Given the way international relations is mainly understood by government officials and academic establishments, this deference to feasibility is expressed by an unconditional reliance on the realist paradigm of understanding and policymaking. This means that if guided by a practical *problem-solving* perspective, only a politics of *impossibility* has any hope at all of meeting the challenges embedded in the current global setting. As such, what is posited is a glaring disconnect between the domain of feasibility, realism, possibility and the domain of actual global problems, humane values, and the quest for global justice. Of course, the idea of 'impossibility' is to some extent polemical, confined to what it is possible to expect from governments and the existing political structures. What makes the impossible possible under certain conditions is the agency of civil society and populist politics, which is unacknowledged or ignored by governmental establishments and their more trusted academic interpreters.

It should be pointed out that the impossible happens rather frequently. Recent instances include decolonization, the American Civil Rights Movement, the lib-eration of Eastern Europe, the collapse of apartheid in South Africa, the election of an African-American as president of the United States, and the Arab Spring. All of these outcomes were impossible in the sense that few, if any, 'responsible' persons envisioned such unfolding narratives as feasible, and scoffed at their proponents. Of course, after the fact, this same corps of responsible observers offered many explanations to account for the outcomes previously neglected or dismissed as impossible.

The long normative march

My own intellectual/political journey was originally nurtured by an Enlightenment confidence that material and moral progress would inevitably follow from the modernist reliance on science, technology, and the guiding role of instrumental reason. To a degree this confidence was shattered by the cumulative impact of the destructiveness of World War II, and particularly the ominous implications for the future of warfare associated with reliance on indiscriminate bombing of cities, long-range missiles, and, above all, by the development of the atomic bomb. This concern was heightened by the growing awareness that the possessors of this technology were more committed to ensuring their geopolitical primacy than in making the world safer by renouncing this weaponry and working to achieve reliably verified disarmament.

The Cold War atmosphere made it appear almost self-evident that the then-current world order was based on the sanity of those competing sovereign states that possessed nuclear weaponry, and as such, was not likely to prove durable. This seemed especially true given the intense ideological rivalries and antagonistic nationalist perceptions of security which emerged after World War II. Such a perspective was admittedly apocalyptic in tone, exhibiting anxieties about survival, both in the elemental physical sense pertaining to the species but also with respect to the civilizational sense of modern urban life styles. So far, despite several close calls, these fears have not been realized, although the underlying set of dangerous circumstances persists even in the absence of serious strategic conflict among states, and has been magnified by the emergence of extremist political non-state actors that embrace tactics of mass destruction.

Coupled with this earlier mood of anxiety was the conviction that even if the worst catastrophes were averted, the continuous preparation for a war fought with weapons of mass destruction would have a negative effect on the quality of collective life, would burden the efforts of poorer countries to develop, and would short-circuit any fundamental effort to live well together on the planet.[20] In essence, so long as the wellbeing, and even the survival of the part, that is, *the state*, continue to be put ahead of the wellbeing of the whole, *the world* or *life on the planet*, it seems obvious that what global bonds of solidarity do exist are far too weak and fragile to cope with the challenges. Not surprisingly these bonds have already demonstrated their inability to overcome world poverty or gross disparities of wealth and resources. We continue to live in a world of statist, classist and individual narcissism, where in the extreme case, leaders of the nuclear-weapons states retain the capabilities and have declared their willingness to use the massive destructive power at their disposal for the sake of national security.[21]

It is against this background that my own journey has led from a stress on intellectual advocacy to a greater reliance on activist engagement, although these two kinds of nonviolent persuasive effort are not mutually exclusive. The advocacy was directed at persuading those who would pay attention that a transformative approach to global politics was needed to achieve safety, security, development, and justice for political actors and the peoples of the world in the nuclear and post-colonial age, and to make that approach compatible with a minimum set of widely shared values held in common by representatives of different civilizations and ideologies.[22] The intention is to foster global-scale collaboration where necessary, while encouraging regional, national, and local diversities and autonomous self-administration to the extent possible. These explorations in thought, premised on transnational interaction with likeminded scholars joined by their opposition to imperial, exploitative, and violent features of existing world order, had no impact on general public opinion and only a marginal influence on the outlook of academic specialists working within the domains of international relations and international law. In these fundamental respects, such scholarly efforts, while making a certain contribution to visionary thinking, lacked any *agency* with respect to promoting the desired transformations of world politics.

On this basis, the engagement as a citizen was more satisfying and seemed more productive of results. For at least a decade I was involved in the anti-war movement formed in reaction to the American intervention in Vietnam. Not only did this involvement have a nurturing effect by establishing communities of dedicated activists spread around the United States, and in Western Europe, but it also provided me with the occasion to experience first-handed injustice and one-sided violence from the perspective of the victim, which was especially a result of two visits to North Vietnam during the Vietnam War.[23] The issue of one-sided violence remains largely unexamined in the literature on either contemporary warfare or even international law, yet should be treated as a crucial component of any effort to (re)frame international *humanitarian* law. American and Israeli operational tactics are illustrative of such one-sided warfare, in which the technologically dominant side chooses the degree and type of destruction to be inflicted with only scant concern about provoking retaliation. For this reason, such military violence resembles torture more than it does warfare between sovereign states of equivalent or near equivalent technological capacity.

Of course, the colonial conquests in Asia, Africa, and Americas were antecedents to modern forms of one-sided warfare, climaxing to date with the atomic attacks on the undefended cities of Hiroshima and Nagasaki. Aside from these learning aspects of activism, the outcome of the Vietnam peace movement seemed to be a vindication of the popular struggle against the American war machine, suggesting at the time that popular democracy was not futile in a modern state. Of course, subsequent militarizing developments, especially in the aftermath of 9/11, cancelled many of these hopeful understandings of the prospect for a more peaceful and just world order that followed from the Vietnam experience.

What did remain, however, was the sense that only a movement of peoples, informed by an anti-realist intellectual analysis, could have any prospect at all of challenging the established structures of statist and market power. As the Cold War came to an end, the realities of these structural impediments to global reform became more evident as the dynamics of neoliberal globalization captured the public imagination in the 1990s. It was only the anti-globalization movement that seemed to grasp the true magnitude of the ethical and ecological challenges being posed by the championship of global economic growth based on making capital as efficient and profitable as possible.[24] In many ways the formation of global policy was shaped increasingly by a dialectical connection between the globalization-from-above operatives who gathered each year at Davos under the auspices of the World Economic Forum, and their populist counterparts who came together annually at the World Social Forum in a South country venue, most often in Porto Alegre, Brazil. It would be naive to suggest that the populist and NGO 'spirit of Seattle' is now or in the foreseeable future in a position to challenge the agenda priorities and policy responses of geopolitical, statist, and corporate/financial forces.[25] Their current role is to provide an awakening presence in crucial global policy-forming venues, such as climate change and world trade meetings, which alerts an apathetic media and global public to the growing dangers and widespread injustices being perpetrated by statist/market collaboration.

In view of this analysis, it is difficult to suppose that the Westphalian approaches to global problem-solving can rectify the existing deficiencies associated with the operations of the world economy or in relation to the menace of nuclear weaponry and climate change. This skepticism is reinforced by the ideological hegemony of neoliberal perspectives, which insist on relying on market solutions to difficulties generated by an insufficiently regulated market. Furthermore, it would be premature to base our hopes on civil society activism given its lack of strength and questionable resolve. Against this background it seems sensible to rethink the role of citizenship in the context of participatory democracy under these twenty-first-century circumstances. An obvious temptation is to recommend the adoption of the outlook of 'a world citizen', thereby acknowledging the global scope of the policy problematique.

It is, of course, beneficial to weaken the nationalist bonds that view political reality through such a self-serving optic, but unless the affirmation of world citizenship is organically linked to a transformative political project it falls into the apolitical Enlightenment trap of disembodied instrumental reason. For this reason I have favored an orientation toward citizenship that is animated by time as well as space, regarding the primary role of citizen to be working toward and embodying a sustainable and just future, a work in progress specified as 'humane global governance'. I call this kind of citizen 'a citizen pilgrim', conceiving of pilgrimage as a journey to a desired re-creation of global governance that may or may not be attainable within the course of a lifetime. Of course, there is no defining *telos* for the citizen pilgrim, as each horizon of aspiration reached will generate a new horizon and start from a different point of departure. This commitment to re-creation of governance implies an understanding of 'the political' in the sense deployed by Sheldon Wolin as 'the commitment to finding the common good'.[26] As with the citizen pilgrim, this conception of citizenship is normative and future-oriented.

To give a sense of direction, it is appropriate to identify tangible steps that could be taken by a citizen pilgrim living in the West to ensure that the recommended identity does not become a new-age refuge for apolitical striving. Among the steps that seem valuable symbolically and substantively, the following can be mentioned for purposes of illustration: (1) the enactment of 'a Tobin tax' to fund at least partially the UN system and a global environmental fund to help economically disadvantaged and vulnerable countries meet the threats posed by global warming;[27] (2) the establishment of a global parliament that is either attached to the UN or operates as an independent institution in the manner of the World Trade Organization;[28] and (3) the conversion of 'advisory opinions' of the International Court of Justice into binding decisions that impose legal obligations on all sovereign states.[29]

A concluding observation

The argument of this chapter has been that an appropriate horizon for global governance cannot be achieved by relying on Westphalian strategies of adaptation, whether horizontally agreed upon by sovereign states or vertically conceived and imposed by hegemonic actors, possibly a new geopolitical co-dominion administered by the United States and China. Such means are beholden to nationalist and market priorities that seem incompatible with eliminating world poverty and nuclear weaponry, as well as adapting sufficiently rapidly to climate change and other environmental threats to avoid severe and possibly irreversible harm of massive proportions. Even if the rhetoric of *necessary* reform were to be invoked, the likely *constraints* on behavior will be insufficient, and even these will probably not be followed in practice or enforced. In effect, relying on the intergovernmental framework to fashion a global governance imaginary responsive to the needs of the twenty-first century is a dead-end invitation to cynicism and nihilism.

The activities and demands of transnational civil society networks are diverse and sometimes contradictory, and variously contextualized, but many share a sense of the political as preoccupied with achieving the common good or promoting *human* interests. It is this normative orientation that is an essential component of a global governance imaginary that deserves the support of the peoples of the world. Such activist striving at present is not formidable enough to claim agency except to the extent of pushing the Westphalian actors to move slightly less slowly down self-destructive paths, but still not nearly slow enough, or attuned sufficiently to the normative demands of global justice. This understanding leads to the encouragement of a more engaged citizenry in democratic societies that has historical confidence built on the record of past achievements of social change in struggles against slavery, racism, gender discrimination, and colonialisms. These transformative developments in each instance involved challenges from below that combined moral passion and a willingness to make personal sacrifices by entering actively into different struggles against the established order. This orientation toward feelings, thought, and action can be given political shape by positing the ideal and encouraging the practices of 'citizen pilgrims'.

We cannot know whether this visionary perspective will ever achieve the status of a viable political project. What we do know with reasonable assurance is that without such a political upheaval from below there will be insufficient movement in the direction of either planetary sustainability or global justice. We also know that what seems implausible from the outlook of now often happens in history, for better and worse. Anticipating the fall of the Berlin Wall, the rise of China, the transformation of apartheid South Africa, and the 9/11 attacks attained plausibility only *in retrospect*. We also know that the unanticipated favorable outcomes did take place because of sacrifice and struggle, making it worthwhile to invest hopes and energies in a desired future, even if we cannot be assured in advance that goals being pursued will ever be achieved. What can be affirmed, without equivocation, is the importance of a humane global imaginary responsive to ethical and ecological imperatives as understood in the year 2013.

Notes

1 The importance of conceiving of political horizons as an imaginary is based on C. Taylor, *Modern Social Imaginaries*, Durham, NC: Duke University Press, 2004.

2 See R. A. Falk, *A Study of Future Worlds*, New York: Free Press, 1975; R. A. Falk, *On Humane Governance: Toward A New Global Politics*. Cambridge: Polity, 1995; R. A. Falk, *The Declining World Order: America's Imperial Geopolitics*, New York: Routledge, 2004, esp. chs 1–7.

3 See D. Deudney, *Bounding Power: Republican Security Theory from the Polis to the Global Village*, Princeton, NJ: Princeton University Press, 2007, 264.

4 Best depicted in the canonical 'National Security Strategy of the United States of America', The White House, 'The National Security Strategy of the United States of America', Washington, DC: 2002.

5 L. Kohr, *The Breakdown of Nations*, New York: E. P. Dutton, 1978.

6 T. E. Paupp, *The Future of Global Relations: Crumbling Walls, Rising Regions*, New York: Palgrave Macmillan, 2009; see also: R. A. Falk, *Declining World Order: America's Imperial Geopolitics*, New York: Routledge, 2004, 45–65.

7 R. Kagan, *The Return of History and the End of Dreams*, New York: Knopf, 2008.

8 H. Bull (*The Anarchical Society: A Study of Order in World Politics*, New York: Columbia University Press, 2nd edn, 1995), co-founder (along with Martin Wight) of the English School of International Relations, is clearest in his view that world order is benefited by a pluralist view of order, and harmed by applications of a more solidarist conception, which he attributes to Grotius and his latter-day heirs (see also: H. Bull, 'The Grotian Conception of International Society', in *Diplomatic Investigations*, ed. H. Butterfield and M. Wight, Cambridge, MA: Harvard University Press, 1968; N. J. Wheeler, *Saving Strangers: Humanitarian Intervention in International Society*, Oxford: Oxford University Press, 2000, 21–52; R. Aron, *Peace and War: A Theory of International Relations*, London: Wiedenfeld and Nicolson, 1966.

9 R. A. Falk, *Achieving Human Rights*, New York: Routledge, 2009, 14–18.

10 For an excellent theoretical approach to security in its contemporary global setting, see K. Booth, *Theory of World Security*, Cambridge: Cambridge University Press, 2007. For realist stress on the relevance of insecurity as foundational for security and instability, see J. J. Mearsheimer, *The Tragedy of Great Power Politics*, New York: Norton, 2001; see also: J. J. Mearsheimer, 'Conversations in International Relations: Interview with J. J. Mearsheimer', *International Relations* 20, 2006: 105–23, 231–43; R. Jervis, *Perception and Misperception in International Politics*, Princeton, NJ: Princeton University Press, 1976. On realist attempts to constrain the militarist sides of American foreign policy, see S. M. Walt, *Taming American Power: The Global Response to U.S. Primacy*, New York: Norton, 2005; L. H. Gelb, *Power Rules: How Common Sense Can Rescue American Foreign Policy*, New York: Harper, 2009.

11 Walt, *Taming American Power: The Global Response to U.S. Primacy*; Gelb, *Power Rules: How Common Sense Can Rescue American Foreign Policy*.

12 J. G. Ikenberry, *After Victory: Institutions, Strategic Restraint, and the Rebuilding of Order after Major Wars*, Princeton, NJ: Princeton University Press, 2001.

13 The most dramatic power-war challenges to a pure Westphalian structure were undoubtedly the two experiments with global political institutions: the League of Nations and the United Nations. Careful examination shows the degree of deference to both sovereign prerogatives and geopolitical status evident in the practice of these organizations, but even in their constitutional arrangements (voting rules; veto power, backroom influence).

14 The 'Pact of Paris' (General Treaty Providing for the Renunciation of War as an Instrument of National Policy) in 1928 made it unlawful to initiate any non-defensive war. This legal commitment was embodied in the UN Charter, Article 2(4), allowing for self-defense as narrowly defined in Article 51 to be the only exception. The prohibition of aggressive war was criminalized by the Nuremberg and Tokyo War Crimes Trials against surviving German and Japanese political and military leaders, but has been

effectively constrained by geopolitical canons of impunity ever since by limits set by geopolitics, despite the surprising establishment of the International Criminal Court in 2002. Yet the non-discriminatory application of international criminal law to the leaders of dominant states seems as unlikely as ever by intergovernmental action. Only elements in global civil society seek to override geopolitics in relation to this norm prohibiting recourse to aggressive war. For serious illustration of a global civil society initiative to implement this prohibition at best symbolically, see M. G. Sökman, ed., *World Tribunal on Iraq: Making the Case Against War*, Northampton, MA: Olive Branch Press, 2008.

15 I have tried to argue this case from a world order perspective in R. A. Falk, 'A Radical World Order Challenge: Climate Change and the Threat of Nuclear Weapons', *Globalizations* 7, nos. 1–2, 2010, 137–55.

16 The 'responsible' domain of political discourse in liberal democracies is so delineated; elected leaders are expected to refrain from acknowledging imperial structures or considerations. Their mere mention is likely to brand the messenger as a radical voice to be excluded from policymaking venues. Elite gatekeeping ensures silence about structural impediments within governmental circles. There is a need not to know, and if known, certainly for government officials to refrain from expressing structural criticisms in public space.

17 A notable attempt along these lines is that of A-M. Slaughter, *The New World Order*, Princeton, NJ: Princeton University Press, 2004.

18 See A. Sen, *The Idea of Justice*, Cambridge, MA: Harvard University Press, 2009; see also: J. Rawls, *The Law of Peoples and the Idea of Public Reason Revisited*, Cambridge, MA: Harvard University Press, 1999; T. Pogge, *World Poverty and Human Rights: Cosmopolitan Responsibilities and Reforms*, 2nd edn, Cambridge: Polity, 2008); M. J. Sandel, *Justice: What's the Right Thing To Do*, New York: Farrar, Straus and Giroux, 2009.

19 I have stressed the importance of substantive democracy, and a bottom-up approach to globalization animated by the wellbeing of peoples rather than the prevailing top-down approach shaped by the efficiency of capital and the interests of governmental elites (see R. A. Falk, *Predatory Globalization: A Critique*, Cambridge: Polity, 1999; see also: D. Archibugi, *The Global Commonwealth of Citizens: Toward Cosmopolitan Democracy*, Princeton, NJ: Princeton University Press, 2008.

20 Trenchantly described by E. P. Thompson in his essay on the detrimental effects on any society that rests its security on preparing to exterminate another society. See Thompson, 'Notes on Exterminism, the Last Stage of Civilisation', *Beyond the Cold War: A New Approach to the Arms Race and Nuclear Annihilation*, New York: Pantheon, 1982, 41–79. On living well together, a phrase explored in illuminating ways by Jacques Derrida, see the collection of essays edited by E. Weber, *Living Together: Jacques Derrida's Communities of Violence and Peace*, New York: Fordham University Press, 2013.

21 For a somewhat feeble attempt to make the role of nuclear weaponry less omnicidal, see K. Lieber and D. Press, 'The Nukes We Need: Preserving the American Deterrent', *Foreign Affairs* 88, no. 6, 2009, 39–51.

22 The World Order Models Project, with which I was associated for many years, worked collaboratively within an agreed framework of five values: peace, economic wellbeing, social justice, ecological stability, and positive identity. No effort was made to establish measurable guidelines for these values, as their vagueness was a further deliberate attempt to safeguard space for civilizational and ideological diversity. For the range of views reflected in the WOMP literature, see S. H. Mendlovitz, ed., *On the Creation of a Just World Order: Preferred Worlds for the 1990s*, New York: Free Press, 1975. For other attempts at depicting a minimum universalism as the basis for a just world order, see J. Rawls, *The Law of Peoples and the Idea of Public Reason Revisited*, and A. Sen, *The Idea of Justice*, as well as the writings associated with the World Parliament of Religions, especially of H. Küng, *A Global Ethic for Global Politics and Economics*, New York: Oxford University Press, 1998.

23 Neither visit was authorized or approved by the US government. They took place in 1968 and 1972, the first at the invitation of the Hanoi government to view the damage

being done by the American air campaign, and the second to assist in escorting three American pilots who had been captured in North Vietnam back to the United States. Revealingly, I was invited prior to the 1968 visit to meet with two then-prominent Department of Defense officials, Leslie Gelb and Morton Halperin, to discuss the trip, and my willingness to deliver a letter sent jointly by the secretaries of defense and state at the time. I would have been entrusted with this mission on one condition, that I pledged not to engage in any further public criticism of the American war effort in Vietnam. Naturally, without hesitation, I refused, and still remain in the dark as to the contents of such a letter, but not as to the unacknowledged sensitivity of government officials to public criticism of war policies.

24 See R. Broad, ed., *Global Backlash: Citizen Initiatives for a Just World Economy*, Lanham, MD: Rowman and Littlefield, 2002; M. Hardt and A. Negri, *Multitude: War and Democracy in the Age of Empire*, New York: Penguin, 2005.

25 This skepticism does not even attempt to take account of the unconscious drivers of state policy or of the often sinister effects of what Peter Dale Scott (P. D. Scott, *The Road to 9/11: Wealth, Empire, and the Future of America*, Berkeley: University of California Press, 2007) has usefully depicted as 'deep politics'. I leave aside, despite their undoubted yet complex relevance, also the special problematics associated with the American global domination project that has ebbed and flowed ever since the end of World War II, followed by the collapse of the European overseas empires.

26 Wolin's book is relevant also because of its powerful argument that even citizenship in its traditional sense has been emptied of influence *within* supposedly democratic states. In other words, there is a crisis of democracy as assessed from the perspective of an engaged citizen, whose efforts are nullified by the way money and private sector influence controls the formation of public policy. See S. Wolin, *Democracy Inc.: Managed Democracy and the Specter of Inverted Totalitarianism*, Princeton, NJ: Princeton University Press, 2008, 66.

27 For the original proposal, see J. Tobin, 'A proposal for international monetary reform', *Eastern Economic Journal* 4, nos 3–4, 1978, 153–59; see sophisticated support for proposal throughout the volume of essays edited by Deepak Nayyar, especially, Amit Bhaduri's chapter, 'Nationalism and Economic Policy in an Era of Globalization', 19–48 (in particular 45–46) in: D. Nayyar, ed., *Governing Globalization: Issues and Institutions*, Oxford: Oxford University Press, 2002.

28 See R. A. Falk, *Achieving Human Rights*, New York: Routledge, 2009, 22–25; for more detailed depiction, see R. A. Falk and A. Strauss, 'Toward Global Parliament', *Foreign Affairs* 80, no. 1, 2001, 212–20; R. A. Falk and A. Strauss, 'On the Creation of a Global People's Assembly: Legitimacy and the Power of Popular Sovereignty', *Stanford Journal of International Law* 36, 2000, 191–220.

29 For instance, it would enhance the status of the rule of law applicable to states. As matters now stand, states regard themselves as free to disregard authoritative views as to legal duties. In one recent case, Israel felt no pressure to comply with a 14–1 advisory opinion of the World Court (2004) with respect to the unlawfulness of its construction of a separation wall on occupied Palestinian territory. Similar remarks apply to the World Court decision on the legality of nuclear weapons (1996).

4

APPROPRIATING NORMATIVE GEOPOLITICS

The theme of this chapter is the extent to which international law and the United Nations serve as both obstacle and instrument in the pursuit of a vision of a just world order that is sensitive to the realization of human rights comprehensively conceived to include economic, social, and cultural rights as well as civil and political rights.[1] It may seem obvious to the more ethically minded commentators on world politics that the most worthwhile undertaking of international law and the UN is to restrain the wrongful exercise of power by states, and that this task is deserving of the utmost and invariable respect of governments and citizens. But the realities of international life and experience are sufficiently complicated, contradictory, and confusing as to resist such formulaic clarity.[2] Both international law and the UN, besides being intertwined, can be twisted by powerful political actors so as to advance regressive, as well as progressive, policy agenda items.

The rules and frameworks that constitute international law, as conventionally understood, continue to owe their authority largely to the consent of the elites that control the governments of the most powerful sovereign states.[3] Such an acknowledgement of legal positivism, as description and prescription, needs to come to terms with the extent to which states, especially dominant or hegemonic states, tend to subordinate or manipulate legal obligations whenever these impinge upon their geopolitical priorities. So conceived, international law from above is less useful as a source of behavioral restraint, especially in relation to the use of force, and more significant as either an instrument of mutually beneficial cooperation (as in relation to trade, investment, maritime safety, and a host of practical transnational concerns) or as a universal language for the communication of claims and grievances.[4] There has, in addition, emerged over the course of the last century a counter-tradition that might be characterized as 'international from below', in which weaker states have effectively used international law as a protective shield to resist various forms of exploitative interference with sovereign rights.[5]

Martti Koskenniemi has provocatively argued that international law has habitually functioned either as a source of apology for the depredations of power (Kant in a similar spirit dismissed the celebrated international jurists of his time as 'miserable consolers') or as a utopian bromide for sentimental dreamers.[6] In essence, such a doubting posture contends that international law either rationalizes the machinations of power and confuses the public or steadfastly ignores the shaping role of power and also confuses the public. Either way the preeminent role of the international lawyer from such a skeptical perspective is one of deliberate or innocent obfuscation, that is, serving the state out of ambition and deference or being too naive to understand the extent to which geopolitics trumps law whenever the grand strategies of major states become engaged. In this respect it is always important to be enough of a realist to see through this apologetic role that international law unquestionably and frequently plays in great power diplomacy, while also having an understanding that is simultaneously wary and even dismissive of fuzzy thinking legalists who believe that merely by positing legal rules it becomes possible to formulate a new behavioral hierarchy of self-actualizing norms that are by their very existence assured of restraining oppressive or exploitative exercises of state-centric violence. The Kelsenite tradition, with its formal rigor and deliberate detachment of law from an interplay with religious and political authority, represented the most influential expression of this depoliticized legalism, especially in Europe between the two world wars.[7] Totalitarian forms of legalism, both Nazi and Soviet, discredited legal positivism nationally, but not internationally.

Nevertheless, the apology/utopia dualism is too simplistic in a number of respects, including overlooking the significance of law as relevant for gaining control over the often crucial high moral ground in a conflict situation, in all manner of 'new wars', especially in those conflicts highlighting the role of social movements and non-state actors.[8] It is notable that ever since the end of World War II that the militarily dominant side in conflicts addressing self-determination concerns have rarely been able to control the political outcome. This was true throughout the period of anti-colonial struggles where the weaker side, as measured by hard power disparities, invariably prevailed, although sometimes after a long interval and at great human cost. Historically this had not always been the case. In the modern era, prior to 1945, the militarily stronger side almost always achieved its goals without great difficulty or sacrifice, with hard power consistently providing efficient and effective historical agency. The establishment of the globe-girdling colonial empires gave territorial and economic expression to this generalization about the geopolitical potency of hard power, especially as deployed by the major states in Western Europe, up through World War II.

No single factor reversed this pattern, but an essential feature of the reshaping of conflict and dominion, especially in the countries of the South, was that the militarily weaker side increasingly understood and took advantage of achieving the normative backing of law and morality (instruments of soft power) in carrying on its struggle. Other factors that contributed to this trend were the greater availability of small arms throughout the world after World War I and the weakening of political will in the colonial North due to the debilitating effects of a costly war that was increasingly experienced in metropole society as being on the wrong side of history, and thereby producing a meaningless loss of life and resources. This new sense of normative advantage was especially relevant to creating a potential mass willingness by a people in bondage to endure heavy burdens over long periods of time due to this new belief in the entitlement and capacity of oppressed or colonized peoples to win their freedom and independence.[9] The United Nations played an important role in creating and reinforcing this anti-colonial consciousness through its endorsement of norms of self-determination and of non-intervention in internal affairs, as well as through its repudiation of colonialism and condemnation of apartheid as an international crime.

The UN, at its start, was conceived and established as a purely Westphalian framework of world order, with governments constituted as the political actors representing sovereign states, alone entitled to membership. States retained full authority in relation to overseas territories subject to their sovereign authority. Yet from its inception the UN was also an arena where issues of normative aspiration were also considered to be matters of law and morality. That is, the shaping of the norms of international law within the UN was an expression of its soft power importance in a global setting that failed to possess supranational governmental authority to settle international disputes. Thus, despite the statist background and the hegemonic modus operandi of the UN, it came gradually to encourage the decolonization process, thereby reflecting a changing global climate of ideas and assessment of contending social forces, including the approval of norms that both empowered struggles against established colonial and racist political arrangements, and disempowered and demoralized entrenched elites seeking to perpetuate existing forms of political order.[10] Of course, this dynamic of constructing such a people-friendly and emancipatory orientation for international law was itself the outcome of an ongoing political process complemented by the activism of non-governmental organizations, particularly those concerned about human rights.[11] It is here that the politics of civil society are shaped and tested through a variety of efforts to construct, validate, and then actualize a normative architecture embodying fundamental ideas of morality, fairness, and justice.[12] Although the historical trend validates the significance of gaining the high moral ground and reliance on soft power instruments, especially during the decades of anti-colonial struggle and during the last stages of the Cold War, there is no assurance about the outcome of any particular conflict. Where the historical trend seems strongest is in relation to the failures of foreign military intervention since 1945, despite hard power dominance, a pattern exemplified by the American defeat in Vietnam. The trend is less pronounced in state–society struggles in which the hard power state may prevail – as in relation to Tibet, Chechnya, or with regard to Sri Lanka – or fail, as in the Shah's Iran or apartheid South Africa. Further, the outcome of these struggles may produce a victory for a supposed liberation movement that itself turns oppressive almost as soon as it gains power, as in Iran after the victory of the Khomeini-led revolution of 1978–79, or of the Taliban in the aftermath of the Afghanistan resistance to Soviet intervention.

But while this portrayal of the continuity between the worldview of progressive activists, the United Nations, and the international legal process contains important insights, it is far from the whole truth about the role and character of the United Nations, international law, and civil society. It is crucial to grasp the significance of the constitutional provision that allows the five permanent members of the Security Council to veto decisions of the Organization in the area of peace and security. This reflects a deliberate and fundamental intention in theory and practice to acknowledge the geopolitical dimension of world order by conferring on the then most powerful states permanent membership in the Security Council and an extraordinary exemption from any obligation or expectation that these five countries, considered the victors in World War II, would be bound by the norms or procedures of the UN Charter. The exemption in the form of the veto is unrestricted in its use for all important decisions of the Security Council, and can be extended to protect friends of the permanent five as well. What may be more troublesome in some respects is the other part of the bargain underlying the formation of the United Nations to the effect that every other member state is legally obligated to act within the bounds set by the UN Charter as interpreted by the Security Council, including being subject to UN-sponsored enforcement actions and punitive measures.

There are at least two ways to view this dualistic legal structure built into the constitutional foundations of the United Nations. It can be seen as a sort of Faustian bargain that was needed to bring the Organization into existence in the first place and to help ensure that it would not fall apart under the strain of political crises as did its predecessor, the League of Nations.[13] This UN deference to the distribution and role of hard power capabilities is at the heart of the realist worldview, and the fact that the UN has achieved and sustained universality of membership would tend to vindicate this approach in many circles; but it also has had several negative consequences. Most obviously, throughout the Cold War it meant gridlock in the Security Council, which translated into a discrediting ineffectuality whenever the superpower antagonists were in disagreement, which was virtually always. The veto also explains a UN legitimacy deficit, embedding double standards in the constitutional sinews of the Organization. This has constrained UN effectiveness, as well as sending the disheartening message that considerations of law and justice must generally give way to the vagaries of hard power. Double standards, so contaminating to the rule of law, can also be observed in other domains of world politics. Most notably is the treaty regime established by the Nonproliferation Treaty in 1968 to manage the control of nuclear weapons and in relation to humanitarian intervention, both in cases where action is taken on behalf of a vulnerable or abused people and where such action is blocked despite being desperately needed.

Why should this kind of veto have been conferred on those states whose adherence to international law is most important if the UN system was ever to become effective and legitimate? The same diplomats who were scorned as idealists for their dedication to the overall UN framework and vision were also attacked for giving large countries a realist reassurance of the veto as an enticement to become members without jeopardizing their geopolitical freedom of maneuver. After the Cold War, the assault on UN legitimacy was less because of the veto than due to the newly claimed hegemonic authority of the United States as the sole surviving superpower. When George W. Bush in the lead-up to the Iraq War in 2003 told the Security Council that the UN risked becoming irrelevant if it did not support the American-led attack on Iraq he was articulating this hegemonic understanding, insisting that the UN would lose credibility if it did not endorse an aggressive war that contravened the core norm of the Charter prohibiting recourse to force in an international conflict unless it could be justified as self-defense against a prior armed attack. Fortunately, despite bullying tactics by Washington, the Security Council withheld its endorsement of aggressive force in this instance, but from an international law point of view this was not a sufficient response with respect to a state wrongly threatened with an attack on its political independence and territorial integrity. The UN Security Council failed to condemn the invasion of Iraq and carry out its supposedly pivotal mission of protecting countries subject to unlawful threats or uses of force. Further, after the American-led attack toppled the Iraq government, the UN established a presence that seemed supportive of the outcome of the aggression. Nowhere in the Charter or in international law is there a rule that states lose their sovereign rights if governing abusively, although in UN practice it is true that if the level of abuse reaches the level of imminent or ongoing genocide, systematic ethnic cleansing and massive crimes against humanity, moral, legal, and political challenges to sovereignty have been made on behalf of the victimized population.[14]

After World War II, surviving Nazi and Japanese leaders were prosecuted for their abusive *international* behavior, and the Nuremberg promise was made at the original legal proceedings in 1945 that the victorious powers sitting in judgment of the defeated Germany would in the future subject their own conduct to a similar constraining discipline of accountability, a gesture intended to overcome delegitimizing double standards. Not surprisingly, this Nuremberg promise was almost immediately broken, inviting a new phase of the sort of cynicism associated with the apology/utopia dualism so strongly emphasized by Koskenniemi. It should be noted that 12 years before the Iraq War of 2003, the UN Security Council had endorsed an extremely punitive peace imposed on Iraq after the Gulf War of 1991, resulting in extreme harm to the civilian population of the country.[15] There is every reason to view the United Nations as both an instrument of geopolitics and as a site of struggle for the establishment of norms and normative architecture that offer soft power encouragement to an array of struggles against oppression, abuse, and exploitation throughout the world. It would thus be wrong to regard the UN as either only a geopolitical instrument or as exclusively a bastion of law, justice, and peace. For better and worse, it is both. Sometimes, as during the anti-colonial period when the General Assembly was more assertive, the UN seemed more aligned with a politics of liberation and justified resistance, and even global reform. And sometimes, as in recent decades, the UN became more overtly associated and identified with a power-driven geopolitics and a unipolar world order that tended to reflect the priorities of American foreign policy, which included consolidating the centrality of the Security Council in matters of peace and security, and marginalizing the General Assembly. This was true whether the issue was regime change in Iraq or subsequently imposing sanctions and threats of a military attack against Iran. In both of these recent instances, the UN seems to have abandoned the foundational mandate of the Charter to save succeeding generations from the scourge of war.

The relationship of the UN to international law in the context of the Israel–Palestine conflict is also emblematic of a split organizational personality. With normative zeal, the idea of a 'responsibility to protect' (R2P) was endorsed as a world community responsibility in the face of severe abuses by a state of human rights, ethnic cleansing, or genocide. The R2P ethos was a diplomatic effort to give 'humanitarian intervention' a post-colonial orientation, but so far this linguistic trope has not overcome the well-founded suspicions that accompany such selective and geopolitically driven uses of force.[16] In mid-2007, Israel responded to the Hamas takeover of the governing process in Gaza by imposing a comprehensive blockade, denying food, medicine, and fuel to the 1.5 million inhabitants, more than half of whom are classified as children. This blockade has been widely condemned as a form of collective punishment in flagrant violation of Article 33 of the Fourth Geneva Convention governing belligerent occupation. This prolonged deprivation in Gaza certainly appears to pose a dramatic challenge to the supposed R2P norm, but the geopolitical circumstances of Israel's posture of non-cooperation, and America's willingness to support whatever Israel does, makes any kind of meaningful UN response not even seriously discussable, much less form the basis for action needed to provide protection to an acutely vulnerable and long suffering people who have endured continuing crimes against humanity for several decades.

But this UN failure is not the whole story. If the conflict is looked at differently, it can be seen that the UN lends significant support to the Palestinian struggle for self-determination, especially in light of the more recent shift in emphasis within the Palestinian resistance movement to a soft power, non-territorial strategy that seeks to do two things: exert coercive nonviolent pressure upon the Israeli government by recourse to such measures as boycott, divestment, and sanctions (the BDS Campaign) and through civil society militancy designed to break the Gaza blockade.[17] The BDS Campaign definitely was strengthened by UN initiatives of the last several years, especially the Goldstone Report on alleged war crimes associated with Israeli attacks on Gaza in the period between December 27, 2008 and January 18, 2009, and in the Human Rights Council's formal inquiry into the lawfulness of the Israeli attack of May 31, 2010 on the Mavi Mamara Freedom Flotilla carrying humanitarian assistance to Gaza.[18] Ideally, these condemnations of Israel's behavior as being in violation of international criminal law would induce intergovernmental and UN sanctions, censure, and mechanisms to impose accountability on those responsible for shaping and implementing the policies, but a geopolitics of impunity continues to shield Israel and its leaders from any kind of negative effects despite these clear and authoritative UN findings.[19] It is misleading to view this result as a reflection of something deeper and more general than geopolitical priorities (even if distorted from a realist perspective by the strength of the Israeli lobby) as is implied by the phrase often used of 'a culture of impunity'. When geopolitical priorities fall on the accountability side of the balance sheet of interests, then vigorous efforts will be made to impose responsibility as in a reverse setting, where evasion of accountability is mandated.[20] The criminal prosecutions of Slobodan Milosevic and Saddam Hussein illustrated this pro-active, selective approach to criminal accountability of heads of state.

The conclusion in relation to Israel is that there is no requisite political will on the intergovernmental level of state-centric diplomacy to hold the Israeli officialdom accountable under international law, but at the same time there does exist sufficient political will within UN circles to determine *whether* Israel should be held accountable. In other words, try as it might, the United States cannot completely insulate Israel from the adverse normative consequences of its policies that affront the conscience of the world, but it can limit these consequences by blocking efforts to implement normative expectations at the UN or in most intergovernmental circles, although far less so with respect to global civil society.

A mid-way, relatively underutilized and controversial, option to implement international criminal law is afforded by some national courts, especially in Western Europe, which allow complaints about violations of international criminal law to be made under the rubric of 'universal jurisdiction'.[21] There have been, as yet, no dramatic results with respect to Israeli accountability achieved by way of universal jurisdiction, although on several occasions Israeli political leaders and military commanders have canceled travel plans to countries where courts possess this potential authority on their law books, for fear of being detained to face criminal charges. Even this low level of informal accountability, a mildly intimidating concern about the possibility of prosecution, undoubtedly adversely affects the comfort level of those Israeli leaders closely associated with policies widely viewed as involving serious violations of international criminal law. Israel has responded to these kinds of tactics, whether involving international criticism or the use of national courts to assess accountability, by relying on a politics of deflection, complaining about the bias of the messenger or the auspices being used to pass judgment rather than addressing the substance of the charges, as well as by mounting a major public relations campaign to present Israel in favorable terms.

Looking at this experience in the ever unfolding Israel–Palestine conflict through the Kaldor lens of 'new wars' accords a much more important political role for these delegitimizing and legitimizing narratives and related undertakings that have proceeded under UN auspices than would be the case if a mainstream state-centric or geopolitical lens was the main optic. Their high profile character gives societal plausibility to the main accusations of criminality associated especially with the expansion of settlements in the West Bank and East Jerusalem and the blockade of Gaza, and this in turn invigorates efforts to organize various civic forms of boycott and divestment activities, as well as to develop a variety of civil disobedience initiatives with the purpose of breaking and discrediting the blockade of Gaza. In other words, the Goldstone Report and the UN Human Rights Council's report of the fact-finding mission on the Gaza Flotilla are important for mobilizing purposes, but the non-implementation of their recommendation gives the contention that international law matters a rather hollow sound. Israel defies international law, enjoys impunity, and can only be stopped by concerted action by the peoples of the world taking and sustaining action on a global scale. There is significant evidence that Israeli leaders view what they call 'the delegitimation project' as now a more serious threat to Israeli security than hard power Palestinian armed resistance. The Israeli ordeal of enduring a wave of 'suicide bombings' during the 1990s helped maintain the Holocaust imagery of Jewish victimization, and denied the Palestinians, despite enduring a systematic abuse of their fundamental rights associated with the post-1967 occupation of Palestinian territory, access to the high moral ground.

The shift in the normative equilibrium of the conflict has taken place since 2006, starting with the Israeli tactics of bombarding civilian centers of population in the Lebanon War, accentuated by the brutality of the 2008–9 Gaza War involving the same tactics on a more intense scale directed at the entrapped civilian population of Gaza, and culminating in the attacks of May 31, 2010 on the civilian flotilla carrying humanitarian goods to Gaza and challenging the blockade.[22] These developments have allowed the Palestinians to take, for the time being at least, control over the moral heights in relation to the conflict, putting Israel on the defensive with respect to the crucial struggle for symbolic soft power ascendancy. I have labeled this new approach to the struggle for Palestinian self-determination as the non-violent reliance on a 'legitimacy war' strategy. The Palestinians are currently winning most battles on this global symbolic battlefield. Whether this use of coercion without reliance on violence, taking full advantage of the high moral ground, will be sustained, and if so, will be enough to alter the balance of political forces in the conflict to achieve a just and sustainable peace for the two peoples, remains highly uncertain. Whatever the outcome, the legitimacy war track offers the Palestinians and other embattled peoples far more promise under most circumstances than either armed resistance or reliance on traditional state-centric diplomacy. However, it is important to draw distinctions among various Palestinian elements in waging legitimacy wars. It is also far from certain that reliance on soft power will continue if there are no signs of substantive progress toward attaining the overriding goal of Palestinian self-determination.

The world of organized diplomacy, in contrast, has been offering the Palestinian people less than zero through its periodic convening of a 'peace process' involving negotiations between governmental representatives of the two embattled parties as mediated by the highly partisan United States. These negotiations are the most cynical imaginable inversion of justice, erecting a facade of pseudo-accommodation that forthrightly excludes any reference to the rights of the Palestinians under international law, while seeking validation of the main unlawful and deliberate features of Israel's encroachment on Palestinian territories during more than 45 years of occupation, that is, legalization of the unlawful Israeli settlement blocs, separation wall, and a total rejection of Palestinian refugee rights. As many observers have commented, there can be no just and sustainable peace, as distinct from a ceasefire disguised as 'peace', until fundamental Palestinian rights and Palestinian security are accorded respect.[23] The current framework of official negotiations has no hope of achieving, or even pretending to proceed in a manner respectful of Palestinian rights, a process that alone would offer some prospect of justice. At present, negotiations are undertaken and promoted without the long abused people of Gaza even being represented in any formal or appropriate manner.[24] What has been argued in relation to Israel/Palestine applies with equivalent force to the differing situations in Kashmir, in the Kurdish struggle for fundamental rights in Turkey, and in many other conflicts around the world, although in each setting the originality of context is crucial. No one template fits all of these situations.

Generalizing these comments makes it evident that transnational civil society initiatives, whether the BDS Campaign or the Free Gaza Movement, are focused on two principal goals: peace and reconciliation based on justice and rights for both peoples under international law; and urgent action to alleviate the daily suffering of the Palestinian people and avert this further unfolding of a humanitarian catastrophe.[25] In this respect, the United Nations can be viewed as a necessary component in the prosecution of a legitimacy war, although not directly through its decisions or behavioral impacts, but indirectly as the world's most influential source of moral and legal authority, a legitimizing and delegitimizing arena that provides guidelines and sets limits on and gives visibility to permissible civil society approaches to conflict resolution. Prospects for a just world order depend on this reliance on peace and justice from below, a kind of nonviolent and populist form of geopolitics that seeks to neutralize the violent and governmental forms of traditional statecraft that continues to rely mainly on hard power calculations in shaping its approach to conflict resolution, which often entails downplaying the rights at stake of the weaker side and disregarding the limits set by international law on territorial gains achieved by force. The experience of the Palestinians since 1948 is extreme in these respects, but the pattern of marginalizing the relevance of international law is paradigmatic in any conflict situation in which the imperatives of geopolitics are allowed to guide diplomatic initiatives.

And this disappointing assessment is not confined to the peace and security agenda of world politics, but applies whenever international law and the authority of the UN are at odds with geopolitical pressures. The same sort of disillusionment with both state-centric diplomacy and the UN as problem-solver has resulted from the failures of the 2009 Copenhagen Conference on Climate Change to achieve the kind of obligatory agreement urgently needed to keep global warming from reaching even more dangerous and irreversible levels than at present. In this policy context the explanation of failure is similar in its generality and different in its particularities. On the latter, there are several distinctive structural flaws in the operation and organization of world order in relation to the sort of globally constituted challenge posed by global warming, and its harmful effects, that call attention to the distinctiveness of the climate change problematic.

Three of these flaws are particularly relevant: short-term cycles of accountability governing the behavior of political leaders of national governments that work strongly against responding to longer-term challenges that require expensive economic adjustments; a spatial disconnect between those most responsible for the buildup of greenhouse gases and the generally distant locus of harm being produced, illustrated by the unevenly high temperature rise and associated droughts in sub-Saharan Africa, a region whose countries are trivial emitters of CO_2 and other greenhouse gases; and the well orchestrated and financed campaign of climate skepticism aimed at discrediting the *scientific* consensus established by the overwhelming majority of climate scientists as most authoritatively expressed by the periodic reports of the UN's Intergovernmental Panel on Climate Change. A heavily funded skeptics' campaign organized by the oil and coal industries has been very effective in discouraging the formation of a *political* consensus needed to shape a viable policy that is just and sensitive to the claims of future generations.[26]

As was vividly dramatized at Copenhagen, the governments could not achieve any appropriate agreement, and used police and naked force to keep the representatives of civil society confined to the outer margins of the negotiations. It seems difficult to envision a solution to these challenges without the emergence of a transformative political consciousness, giving weight to patterns of thinking and acting on behalf of humanity and of future generations as opposed to thinking on behalf of states and corporations, and the present, with most citizens remaining captive of a consumerist mentality that demands maximum short-term satisfaction and is easily confused as to the gravity of ecological dangers. A similar confusion was generated by the tobacco industry with respect to the harmful effects of smoking, delaying restrictions on the sale and use of cigarettes by decades, but here in relation to climate change delay imperils the whole future of humanity.[27] It should be understood that global warming and its effects are currently already inflicting collective harm in various natural settings. The disastrous effects of climate change have not yet been fully experienced and perceived globally, especially, with irony, by those societies where industrialism has given rise to the problem in the first instance by emitting more carbon than the oceans and forests of the world can absorb.

A jurisprudential point is being made to the effect that state-centric international law is incapable of generating systemic norms when the perceptions of responsibility and the experience of harm are geographically so unevenly distributed. Climate change appears at its early stages to have the perverse characteristics of being most dangerous for those low-carbon producing parts of the planet with the least capability to adapt to or mitigate the harm, such as sub-Saharan Africa and Asian coastal and island communities. As a result the more wealthy and technologically capable countries have little current incentive to agree to a necessary *global* approach, since for the near future the worst national effects can be often avoided or mitigated by self-reliance, and any enactment of global norms would seem to involve the acceptance by the richest countries of disproportionate burdens of adjustment. The overall perceptions of how much common interest in reducing the emission of greenhouse gases exists is itself very uneven, with Europe far more willing to accept significant burdens than the United States, and China far readier to invest in alternative energy sources than the rest of the world. Unfortunately, the climate change clock continues to move toward a kind of midnight climax, and the longer appropriate responses are deferred the more dangerous and expensive it will be to respond constructively. Not only are governments being tested, but also civil society, as to whether societal forces can become strong enough to overcome corporate resistance, by creating a political climate that exerts timely pressures on major states, especially the United States, to ensure that the existing robust scientific consensus is converted into a policy consensus that establishes a needed global framework of sufficiently rigorous regulation at the earliest possible time.

International law supplies the markers of the impermissible at a time when the formal annals of state-centric politics are being simultaneously (mis)shaped by the hubris of hegemonic geopolitics and ambiguously resisted by people-centered politics from below. In the varied enactments of this bearing of witness, international law helps parties to put contested behavior within a historical and ethical context, but leaves responsibility for action mostly in the hands of the mobilized peoples of the world and their governmental representatives. In this respect, international law contributes to an ongoing vital discourse, and should whenever possible be invoked and relied upon by those struggling to promote global justice, while at the same time remaining opposed to demystifying claims that international law vindicates this or that use of interventionary violence. This world order bromide of a necessary hegemon is likely to persist unless there is a global justice movement that safeguards and envisions the future from a people-centric viewpoint.[28]

What emerges from this analysis of a changing global setting, underscoring the illuminating and prophetic importance of engaged scholarship that creatively conceptualizes the state/society/planet interaction, are two momentous, not generally appreciated, conclusions: first, violent resistance for an embattled people is being displaced, although not everywhere or consistently, by reliance on soft power instruments of resistance and coercion, including the force of law, morality, and nonviolent militancy; second, the traditional conflict resolving modalities associated either with hard power domination or state-centric diplomacy, whether under UN auspices or independently, are proving increasingly incapable of fashioning humane and effective problem-solving solutions.[29] As a result, there exist expanding opportunities for civil society initiatives, especially as the symbolic battlefields in legitimacy wars are non-territorial and often borderless in scope. If these dynamics are activated, as occurred during the anti-apartheid campaign of the late 1980s and early 1990s, then the UN and states can play a crucial role in encouraging just and sustainable outcomes to conflict. In effect, the war system has become increasingly dysfunctional for both strong and weak potential actors, with a few exceptions, and the future of world order now heavily depends on the extent to which political elites around the world, especially the leaders of major states, absorb and adjust to this indispensable understanding of altered geopolitical realities in the early twenty-first century.

Notes

1 This enumeration of human rights accepts the categorizations and boundaries set forth in the two covenants of human rights, binding international treaties, that were negotiated in 1966 as a sequel to the Universal Declaration of Human Rights. It is important to appreciate that some leading democracies, most notably the United States, while ratifying the Covenant on Civil and Political Rights have failed even seriously to consider the Covenant on Economic, Social, and Cultural Rights. To a degree the two covenants split the unity of human rights as a reflection of the Cold War encounter between the liberal West as advocate of individual rights and the socialist East as champion of collective rights. It should be recognized that such an approach to global justice sets up a clash between the juridical idea of territorial supremacy of a sovereign state that is the foundation of the prevailing Westphalian conception of world order and the protection of human rights, which to the extent that it is externally implemented, is subversive of a statist structure of world order.

2 In fact, moral imperatives and political opportunities may point in one direction, while law points in the opposite direction. For instance, when a government abuses its citizenry to the extent of committing crimes against humanity, an external attempt to protect such vulnerable people may run up against the legal prohibition on recourse to the threat or use of force by states except in circumstances of self-defense rather narrowly defined or under the authority of the UN Security Council. If the Security Council refuses to mandate the use of force, then the tension between respect for law and the humanitarian urge to protect an endangered civilian population is made manifest. This tension was at the root of the debate about whether humanitarian intervention in Kosovo under NATO auspices was appropriate in 1999 without Security Council authorization. The Independent International Commission on Kosovo attempted to resolve this tension by suggesting that in this specific case considerations of legitimacy (moral imperative plus political feasibility) took precedence over legality. See Independent International Commission on Kosovo, *The Kosovo Report: Conflict, International Response, Lessons Learned*, Oxford: Oxford University Press, 2000; for more theoretical exploration of these issues see R. A. Falk, M. Juergensmeyer, and V. Popovski, eds, *Legality and Legitimacy in Global Affairs*, New York: Oxford University Press, 2012.

3 Perhaps the clearest expression of this perspective is still associated with the work of L. Henkin, notably: L. Henkin, *How Nations Behave: Law and Foreign Policy*, New York: Columbia University Press, 2nd edn, 1979; for a view along the same lines although contextualized as a diatribe against the lawlessness of the Bush presidency, see P. Sands, *Lawless World: America and the Making and Breaking of Global Rules from FDR's Atlantic Charter to George W. Bush's Illegal War*, New York: Viking, 2005.

4 This role of international law communicative interaction was memorably articulated by C. A. W. Manning, *The Nature of International Society*, New York: Wiley, 1975; for a somewhat similar contemporary emphasis see D. Kennedy, *Of War and Law*, Princeton, NJ: Princeton University Press, 2006.

5 Latin American jurists took the lead in trying to use international law in such a defensive posture, successfully placing legal constraints on the use of force to collect economic debts or protect the rights of foreign investors in the Western Hemisphere. Such a perspective is well formulated in relation to the development discourse by B. Rajagopal, *International Law from Below: Development, Social Contemporary Movements, and Third World Resistance*, Cambridge: Cambridge University Press, 2003.

6 See M. Koskenniemi, *From Apology to Utopia: The Structure of International Legal Argument*, Helsinki, Finland: Finnish Lawyers' Publishing Co., 1989; also see sympathetic, yet

critical outlook in M. Koskenniemi, *The Gentle Civilizer of Nations: The Rise and Fall of International Law 1870–1960*, Cambridge: Cambridge University Press, 2001.

7 See Hans Kelsen, *Principles of International Law*, 2nd revised edn (R. W. Tucker, ed.), New York: Holt, Rinehart, and Winston, 1966; also H. Kelsen, *The Law of the United Nations*, New York: Praeger, 1951.

8 My views here are heavily influenced by M. Kaldor, *New and Old Wars: Organized Violence in a Global Era*, Cambridge: Polity, 1999.

9 This distribution worldwide of small arms in the period following World War I and continuing throughout the century was an important source of empowerment for colonized peoples. Such a dispersion of weaponry did not nullify hard power disparities, especially as technologically advanced states continued to improve the lethality of their weaponry, but it did provide some means to carry on armed struggle, especially if accompanied by appropriate tactics. The Vietnamese opposition to American intervention was an exemplary instance of waging successful hard power resistance from a position of military inferiority.

10 I have elaborated on this appraisal in R. A. Falk, *The Declining World Order: America's Imperial Geopolitics*, New York: Routledge, 2004, esp. 3–44, 67–103.

11 See R. A. Falk, *Human Rights Horizons*, New York: Routledge, 2009, for an assessment along these lines.

12 M. Kaldor, *Human Security*, Cambridge: Polity, 2007; also détente from below; what was empowering and disempowering in the decolonizing struggles was reproduced in relation to the demand for human rights in the Cold War settings of Eastern Europe. See also: M. E. Keck and K. Sikkink, *Activists Beyond Borders: Advocacy Networks in International Politics*, Ithaca, NY: Cornell University Press, 1999.

13 It should be recalled that the League could neither induce some important states to join in the first place, most notably the United States, nor retain the membership of several important states. In contrast, the UN has retained the membership of all major states despite severe strains at times, and entry into the Organization is seen as a vital sign of legitimate sovereign status for governments and states seeking diplomatic acceptance at a global level.

14 With respect to Iraq, these conditions were not present, despite past abuses that might at the time have justified intervention from a legal and moral perspective. In 2003 the reasons for intervention seemed overwhelmingly strategic, and moral arguments about liberating the Iraqi people from tyranny, while plausible, have little legal weight, and would constitute a dangerous UN precedent. It needs to be remembered that the UN was formed with war prevention as its primary mission, conditioned by assurances of non-intervention in domestic life (Article 2(7)). Human rights emerged during the operation of the Organization, and did erode the UN commitment to unconditional respect for territorial sovereignty, but always problematically.

15 On the general issues of a punitive peace, see R. A. Falk, *The Costs of War: International Law, the UN, and World Order after Iraq*, New York: Routledge, 2008, esp. 37–51; and on the civilian impact of sanctions, see J. Gordon, *Invisible War: the United States and the Iraq Sanctions*, Cambridge, MA: Harvard University Press, 2010.

16 See important critique of these humanitarian pretensions, and the interweaving of neo-liberal and imperial priorities, in: A. Orford, *Reading Humanitarian Intervention: Human Rights and the Use of Force in International Law*, Cambridge: Cambridge University Press, 2003.

17 This shift can be questioned as to its depth and breadth. There is no way to be sure that various Palestinian factions will not in the future revert to their former reliance on hard power tactics, and it is evident that not the whole of the Palestinian opposition is persuaded to pursue a soft power approach. Hamas is still labeled as 'a terrorist organization' by many governments, although its diplomacy since its 2006 electoral victory has emphasized peaceful coexistence and its willingness to find a political solution to the conflict with Israel.

18 For some assessment of these developments see R. Falk, 'The Goldstone Report: Ordinary Text, Extraordinary Event', *Global Governance* 16, 2010, 173–90; M. Bayoumi, ed., *Midnight on the* Mavi Mamara: *The Attack on the Freedom Flotilla and How It Changed the Course of the Israel/Palestine Conflict*, New York: OR Books, 2010.

19 The unconditional support given to Israel by the United States has been sharply and persuasively criticized from a realist perspective, suggesting that it distorts the fulfillment of American strategic priorities in the region, most prominently by J. Mearsheimer and S. Walt, *The Israeli Lobby and U.S. Foreign Policy*, New York: Farrar, Straus, and Giroux, 2002. Two qualifications need to be added: even if foolish from a realistic perspective, the use of American leverage in the UN is an instance of geopolitics; after the Israeli victory in the 1967 Six Day War the Pentagon and Washington think tanks increasingly treated Israel as an important strategic asset in the region, a position further strengthened by the Iranian Revolution in 1979, which deprived the United States of its strongest and most dependable regional ally.

20 As Mary Kaldor has so significantly argued over the years, a statist focus provides an inadequate understanding of contemporary conflict situations, as the roles of civil society actors need to be increasingly taken into account. The Israel–Palestine conflict also illustrates the political importance of controlling the narrative about how to describe the conflict and attribute blame for its origins and persistence, which influences attitudes towards what would be a reasonable and acceptable outcome, and under what conditions resolution and reconciliation would be possible. For a recent example of the Kaldor approach, see S. D. Beebe and M. Kaldor, *The Ultimate Weapon Is No Weapon: Human Security and the New Rules of War and Peace*, New York: Public Affairs, 2010; see also: Kaldor, *New and Old Wars*, op. cit., and Kaldor, *Human Security*, op. cit.

21 See S. Macedo, ed., *Universal Jurisdiction*, Philadelphia, PA: University of Pennsylvania Press, 2004.

22 On the Lebanon War of 2006 see N. Hovsepian, ed., *The War of Lebanon: A Reader*, Northampton, MA: Olive Branch Press, 2008.

23 See V. Kattan, *From Coexistence to Conquest: International Law and the Origins of the Arab-Israeli Conflict, 1891–1949*, London: Pluto, 2009, esp. xv–xx, 248–61.

24 See the still relevant prophetic critique of the peace process by E. W. Said, *The End of the Peace Process: Oslo and After*, New York: Pantheon, 2000.

25 The BDS Campaign was initiated by a coalition of Palestinian NGOs in 2005, but has recently strengthened dramatically, especially in response to the Gaza War and the flotilla incident. BDS tactics are modeled on the anti-apartheid campaign that contributed to the downfall of the racist regime in South Africa in the early 1990s. The Free Gaza Movement was organized initially by Israeli peace activists to deliver symbolically needed medical and other humanitarian supplies to the unlawfully blockaded population of Gaza, relying on civil society donated funds and using unarmed small boats to defy the Israeli blockade. The rationale relied upon was that the failure of the UN or governments to lift the blockade meant that it was appropriate for civil society to expose both the futility of traditional statecraft and the relative vitality of global civil society in its role of responsiveness to a humanitarian catastrophe.

26 See N. Oreskes and E. M. Conway, *Merchants of Doubt: How a Handful of Scientists Obscured the Truth on Issues from Tobacco Smoke to Global Warming*, New York: Bloomsbury, 2010; H. Friel, *The Lomborg Deception: Setting the Record Straight About Global Warming*, New Haven, CT: Yale University Press, 2010.

27 For representative warnings from highly respected commentators, see G. Dyer, *Climate Wars: The Fight for Survival as the World Overheats*, Oxford: One World, 2010; C. Hamilton, *Requiem for a Species: Why We Resist the Truth About Climate Change*, London: Earthscan, 2010; J. Lovelock, *Revenge of Gaia: Earth's Climate in Crisis and the Fate of Humanity*, New York: Basic Books, 2006.

28 For a still relevant assessment of hegemonic stability, see R. Gilpin, *War and Change in World Politics*, Cambridge: Cambridge University Press, 1981.

29 More than any other single person, through her writings and citizen engagement, Mary Kaldor has given tangible expression to these assessments of fundamental historical changes: see the references in Note 20 above. For an attempt to assess these same tendencies from the perspective of international law, see R. A. Falk, *Law in an Emerging Global Village: A Post-Westphalian Perspective*, Ardsley, NY: Transnational, 1998.

5

THE FUTURE OF INTERNATIONAL LAW

A conceptual introduction

Addressing the UN General Assembly on September 25, 2012, President Barack Obama made the following unqualified observation: 'We know from painful experience that the path to security and prosperity does not lie outside the boundaries of international law and respect for human rights.' In my judgment this is a perceptive historical assessment of the contemporary situation, but unfortunately it is only inconsistently reflected in the foreign policy of the United States and many other leading countries. In effect, there is a wide gap between the public *rhetoric* of respect for international law and human rights and the *behavior* of states within and beyond their borders undertaken on behalf of national and global security. The extent of this gap is one way of depicting the contours of global insecurity that exist in this historical era.[1] The shortcomings of response to global insecurity are particularly evident in the inability of international law to implement restraints on threats and uses of force, to establish under UN auspices an effective rule-governed process for protecting vulnerable peoples from humanitarian catastrophe, and to negotiate an agreed framework of obligatory limits on greenhouse gas emissions.

The essential explanation of these failures to achieve acceptable levels of global security, as measured by the common good, relates to the structure of world order as continuing to be state-centric in relation to the global policy agenda. Despite acknowledging the relevance of globalization, most governments continue to proceed on the basis of maximizing their national interests, whether or not such actions can be reconciled with the promotion of global interests, especially when perceived security interests are at stake. So ingrained is this nationalist outlook on the shaping of foreign policy that relationship to a global perspective is rarely even mentioned. Due to the unevenness of sovereign states, with respect to capabilities, size, resource endowments, stage of development, perceptions, information, and policy priorities, it is usually difficult to achieve a multilateral agreement on appropriate behavior if vital national interests of important states or groups of states are diverse. Because the absence of constraints has had such a devastating effect in the recent past and threatens grave dangers in the future, there is a deceptive engagement with rhetoric that acknowledges the requirements of global security, but no commensurate willingness to do what is necessary to make the standards operative as effective regulators of behavior. Thus such legal instruments as the Universal Declaration of Human Rights or the United Nations Charter set forth lofty goals that are ritualistically endorsed by governments, but there are often many strings attached and big loopholes, making the whole far less than the sum of its parts. For instance, the UDHR was expressed in declaratory form so as to give governments an assurance that no enforcement was intended, leaving respect for human rights where it had been for decades, if not centuries, to the untender mercies of the territorial sovereign state. The same pattern of promising without performing can be associated with the refusal to deliver on the pledge by nuclear-weapons states in Article VI of the Nuclear Nonproliferation Treaty to pursue in good faith nuclear disarmament or in acting to uphold the grand commitment of the UN Charter to 'save succeeding generations from the scourge of war'.

State-centrism is built into the constitutional structure of the United Nations, especially by way of giving the victorious powers in World War II permanent membership of the UN Security Council with a right of veto. If we appreciate that the Security Council is the only organ within the UN system that possess a power of decision, it becomes clear that the pursuit of global security is made subject to the approval of those few states playing geopolitical roles in the shaping of world history. These states, or at least some of them, have their own grand strategies for projecting influence and upholding a particular version of world order, but this orientation is not shaped by any sense of allegiance to human security or to the promotion of the human interest, which at most are claimed as incidental benefits of a benevolent pursuit of national interests. Depending on the vagaries of national leadership and shifting domestic public opinion, these patterns may be more or less congenial with the imperatives of global security. For instance, the presidency of George W. Bush was more destructive of global security (and also the national security of the United States) than was that of Barack Obama, although neither leader showed any willingness to defer national policy to assessments of what would most benefit humanity in the long run or to show consistent respect for international law.[2]

Putting the issue more abstractly, state-centric problem-solving mechanisms are not consistently capable of promoting the collective goods of humanity at this stage of history. In earlier periods of less interdependence among states, such concerns mattered less as global interests were seldom at issue. Such a lack would still not be of great concern if there had not arisen a strongly felt need for the protection of a variety of specific collective goods. The development of nuclear weaponry highlights both the importance of a global perspective and the difficulty of implementing the vision of a world without nuclear weapons articulated from time to time by world leaders as morally imperative and politically prudent.[3] Arguably, with nuclear weapons even national security interests are held hostage to entrenched bureaucratic and economic interests, what Eisenhower evidently had in mind when he warned about the insidious influence of 'the military–industrial complex' half a century ago. What was done to address the dangers posed by the existence of nuclear weapons is deeply revealing and disturbing. Instead of eliminating these weapons of mass annihilation, their possession was confined to powerful state actors while other states were tied to the mast of nonproliferation. In the resulting two-tier, discriminatory system of global security, nuclear-weapons states adapted balance of power logic to the new situation by relying on a sophisticated version of 'deterrence', while using their leverage to keep the weaponry from falling into unwanted hands, an approach with its own pattern of inconsistencies, known as 'nonproliferation'.

In other words, the peoples of the world have been burdened by a geopolitical definition of global security that struck an unstable compromise between the dangers posed by these weapons and the refusal of the most powerful sovereign states to give up these most formidable instruments of destruction and deterrence. In the last analysis, the threat to global security posed by the retention of nuclear weapons, with hundreds still kept on alert status by the United States and Russia, and maybe other states, is one of catastrophic warfare, with spillover effects of radioactivity and clouds of smoke causing 'nuclear famine' on earth for a period of a decade or more. As world order is structured, despite a widespread acknowledgement of these risks, no major steps beyond the limits of the geopolitical consensus have ever been taken.[4] The fact that none of these weapons have been used in warfare since 1945 has contributed to complacency about the risks, as well as a normalization of the morally intolerable idea of resting the security of large states on their credible willingness and capacity to kill tens of millions of innocent persons living elsewhere.

But the other side of the conflict spectrum is almost equally unable to address the problems of sustained violence and abuse by governments in relation to their own people or to persecuted minorities trapped within national borders. As Ken Booth influentially pointed out 20 years ago, the Westphalian state has provided a sanctuary for 'human wrongdoing'.[5] The rise of international rights since 1945 is a notable achievement, but as with nuclear weaponry, compliance is more a function of geopolitics than of the recognition that global security would be strengthened by governments that effectively and comprehensively implemented agreed standards of international human rights. As matters now stand, even the most extreme patterns of abuse, associated with persistent and massive crimes against humanity, are not addressed unless the geopolitical climate is sufficiently unified to support a shared response. The international law approach of treating equals equally is not operative when it comes to taking constraints on territorial governance seriously. It is notable that Nazi and Japanese war criminals were prosecuted after World War II, an apparent challenge to the impunity of leaders of sovereign states, and a potential precedent for the future, but experience has abundantly demonstrated that criminal accountability is still confined to the weak and defeated, and is not invoked to address the crimes of the large states, which from a global security perspective pose the most dangerous threats and do the most serious harm.

The organized international community in the aftermath of the Kosovo War of 1999 tried to come up with a new approach to the balance between protecting vulnerable populations from humanitarian catastrophes and respecting sovereign territory. The response to the threat of ethnic cleansing in Kosovo was controversial for several reasons, including the absence of a UNSC mandate, but the fact that 'a coalition of the willing' had the backing of NATO and almost the whole of Europe, as well as the background of Serbian genocidal tactics in Bosnia, gave the intervention on behalf of the endangered Albanian majority population widespread backing, but also occasioned sharp criticism.[6] The most influential result of this debate was the formulation of a Responsibility to Protect (R2P) norm, endorsed by the UNSC, and operationalized to an extent in the 2011 UN-authorized NATO military operations in Libya. What emerged remains controversial. R2P is subject to geopolitical constraints, as well as to the Security Council procedures, which means that some highly vulnerable peoples are outside the orbit of international protection (e.g. Palestinians under occupation; Chechens; Kurds) regardless of the severity of threats directed at them.[7] What it is possible to affirm is that the normative and psycho-political global setting can no longer shut itself off from 'new wars' that are waged within territorial boundaries merely by invoking early Westphalian notions of unconditional territorial sovereignty, but neither can such concerns be consistently addressed due to the persisting primacy of geopolitics. As a result, the nature of global security in relation to these conflict patterns occupies a law/no law space that is subject to contradictory interpretations.

There are new questions being asked about the role of civil society in producing global security. Can humanitarian NGOs promote conflict resolution in situations where traditional statecraft, even as abetted by the UN, is at a loss? The war in Syria that has raged since early 2011 is illustrative of this potentiality, suggesting possible multiple civil society roles, ranging from the delivery of food and medicine to the civilian population, providing auspices for the negotiation of local ceasefire arrangements, compiling the evidence to support charges of war crimes and crimes against humanity, and offering antagonists ideas for limiting or ending the violence.[8] States, despite their sense of futility in relation to such conflicts, are reluctant to yield political space to civil society initiatives, and jealously guard traditional prerogatives exclusively reserved for states. Even the United Nations has not accommodated the rise of global civil society by giving non-state actors a more robust role within the Organization.

Global security, use of force, and international law

Much of the controversy and uncertainty about the relevance of international law to the foreign policy of sovereign states has over the years involved threats and uses of force, and related issues associated with the application of law to war and its aftermath. Due to such preoccupations we tend to forget how dependent the peoples and nations of the world are upon the generally reliable legal framework that governs routine transnational relations, whether in trade, diplomacy, maritime and air safety, tourism, communication, or transportation. There is a widespread recognition among governments and citizens that international law is crucial to the maintenance of routine cross-border stability that is of great benefit to all peoples and establishes relatively high standards of global security under *normal* conditions. International law reinforces this framework of stability by providing participants in international life with flexible dispute settlement procedures by way of arbitration and adjudication that generally keep conflicts within bounds similar to those that exist in well ordered domestic societies. Where the society is poorly governed and internally lawless, then the maintenance of stability for transnational relations of all kinds with outsiders is likely to be seriously weakened.

Why then the inability to find solutions for the governance of the use of force? After World War II the political leaders of the victorious countries were unusually receptive to confining the military option as they were acutely conscious of how devastating a future war was likely to be in the aftermath of the atomic bombings of Hiroshima and Nagasaki as augmented by rocketry and precision guidance. The founding states of the UN were able to agree on four far-reaching ideas: (1) the creation of the United Nations based on a UN Charter that unconditionally pro-hibited threats and uses of force except in instances of self-defense narrowly defined, supplemented by (2) a responsibility of the organized world community to protect states that were victims of aggression by measures of collective security; (3) the imposition of individual criminal responsibility on leaders who waged, and even threatened, 'aggressive wars', and (4) the norm that territory of a sovereign state could not be validly acquired by force.[9] We must inquire as carefully as pos-sible why this seemingly humane, sensible, and ambitious agreement never fully materialized. The result has been a confusing tension between constitutional guidelines for the maintenance of international peace and security provided by international law and the continued reliance by states on self-help mechanisms (defense capabilities, alliances) restrained by countervailing power and prudence rather than by an acceptance of the constraints of international law. When George W. Bush told the US Congress that the United States would never seek a per-mission slip from the UN to use force when its security interests were at stake, it was an assertion of hard power defiance repudiating the authority of law, which is the essence of soft power. It was also a reminder to the world body that leading states consider their geopolitical status as conferring discretion that takes precedence over accountability to law in relation to its security agenda. Although the United States is the most outspoken among the current group of leading states, all of these governments in practice treat their national security priorities as overriding contrary legal obligations. Of course, when international law supports a security claim, or undercuts the behavior of an international adversary, then it will be invoked with the solemnity of a preacher. The realist orientation of government respects international law governing force so long as it is convenient to do so, and departs as necessary without any qualms, although with public rationalizations and justifications couched in moral/legal language.[10] For instance, when the US government in the aftermath of the 9/11 attacks authorized 'torture' – unconditionally prohibited by international law – government lawyers called torture 'enhanced interrogation techniques'.[11]

Two broad lines of assessment can add to our understanding of the character of global security: ideological and structural. Governments, especially of leading countries, continue to be mainly guided by *ideological* adherents of political realism who believe that history is shaped by the outcome of military confrontations, that military superiority is positively correlated with national and global security, and that neither nuclear weapons nor international law have changed this fundamental situation.[12] The structure of world order reinforces this realist consensus by fragmenting political consciousness on the basis of separate and distinct sovereign states that are oriented around the promotion of *national* interests often at the expense of *global* interests.[13] Beyond this, there is a challenge to territorial sovereignty that combines the emerging authority of human rights with the geopolitical capability and willingness to intervene selectively to protect human rights. There exists a widespread view, especially influential in the West, that in an interconnected world, the insulation of the internal political life of sovereign states should not be exempt from international accountability under extreme circumstances that put the people of a country at great risk due to governmental abuse or incompetence. The structural perspective continues to mean that global security is achieved, or not, at the level of the state, and that reliance on collective security mechanisms depends principally on alliance relationships rather than on rule-governed undertakings of the UN and regional actors.[14]

Nuclear weapons

The interplay of these factors produces a distinctive diplomacy that is more complicated than what existed until the last half of the twentieth century. The existence of nuclear weaponry makes war avoidance among powerful states a high priority for realists, but their choice is not the renunciation of the weaponry but its 'use' in a threat mode called 'deterrence'. The efforts to challenge such reliance on massive threats of indiscriminate warfare produced an advisory opinion by the International Court of Justice that concluded that this weaponry could be provisionally retained despite the seeming inability to find lawful uses for it in warfare, except conceivably if the survival of a state was credibly threatened. Unanimously, also, the ICJ contended that the nuclear-weapons states had an obligation under the Nuclear Nonproliferation Treaty to enter nuclear disarmament negotiations in good faith.[15] What is most revealing is that this carefully reasoned assessment of the status of nuclear weapons has had no discernible impact on the behavior of those governments that possess nuclear weapons. It confirmed, on this matter of the greatest potential relevance for global security, that there is no willingness whatsoever on the part of leading states, including those that have the strongest liberal credentials, to allow international law to supplant geopolitical calculations.

When it comes to what can be identified as 'second order legality', then international law is employed to manage the geopolitical regime as by way of the Nonproliferation Treaty and its implementation.[16] The NPT relies on the authority of an international treaty instrument to obligate non-nuclear states that become parties to forego the weapons option in exchange for receiving assurance of gaining the benefit of peaceful uses of nuclear energy. The diplomacy adopted by nuclear-weapons states toward those states seeking to obtain nuclear weaponry, including Iraq, North Korea, and Iran, is suggestive of geopolitical procedures put to work in the service of de jure nonproliferation obligations.[17] The Iraq War of 2003 was alleged at the time to be undertaken as a means of preventing a future acquisition of such weaponry by a rogue state, creating a geopolitical claim to override the constraints of international law. By way of contrast, Israel, and to a lesser extent India and Pakistan, states that remained outside the NPT framework, were given a pass to enter the club. There was initial discomfort about India and Pakistan, but it was quickly overtaken by an entry into nuclear technology-sharing arrangements between the US and India; Israel in contrast has been allowed to fly under the radar of accountability while acquiring and developing an arsenal of nuclear weapons over the course of several decades. In other words, international law is appropriated to make effective a legal regime that reflects an approach to nuclear weaponry that rejects the fundamental legal principle of treating equals equally. Its implementation enshrines double standards and generates a violent geopolitics that has meant in the aftermath of nuclear weaponry a dubious connection between genocidal threats and global security, as conceptualized during the Cold War in the doctrine of deterrence.[18]

Recourse to threats and uses of force

The core commitment of the UN Charter is contained in Article 2(4): 'All Members shall refrain in their international relations from the threat or use of force against the territorial integrity or political independence of any state.' It is important to note that in the Charter threats are as prohibited as are uses of force, which in effect legally disallows what is sometimes called 'coercive diplomacy'.[19] But in state practice actual uses of force are at least scrutinized, as was the case in relation to the 2003 attack on Iraq, but threats are not even treated as legally problematic. For instance, the frequent allusions by the United States to keeping the military option 'on the table' and Israeli-leaked stories about war games involving attack scenarios on Iran's nuclear facilities and speculation about the location of red lines with respect to the Iranian nuclear program, are clearly articulated in the form of 'threats' that would on the face of it violate the prohibition in Article 2(4). But here the legal sphere has given way altogether to the political sphere, and threats have come to be regarded an acceptable mode of diplomatic interaction that accords de facto deference to prevailing patterns of geopolitics. Again, the efforts of international law to confine reliance on force to situations of genuine self-defense have not been integrated into responsive behavioral patterns.

The prohibition on force as means of territorial expansion has been reasonably well respected since the UN was established in 1945, and even implemented, when massively violated. The UN responded to the North Korean attack on South Korea in 1950, the Suez operation of France, Israel, and the United Kingdom in 1956, and the Iraq attack on Kuwait in 1990. In all of these instances, the norm prohibiting aggressive warfare was upheld, although some degree of controversy exists in each setting. The 1967 War between Israel and its Arab neighbors resulted in the expulsion of Jordan from its administrative role in the West Bank and East Jerusalem, and the prolonged occupation of these portions of historic Palestine by Israel, although without the seal of international legitimacy. The United Nations in Security Council resolution 242 (1967) set forth the expectations that Israel would withdraw forthwith from occupied Palestine, invoking explicitly the norm against the acquisition of territory by force of arms. More than 45 years later these expectations, generally considered expressive of international law, have not been fulfilled; on the contrary, Israel has taken steps by way of establishing settlements, building a network of settler roads, constructing a separation wall that encroaches on occupied Palestine, and shows no signs that it has any intention of ever implementing the withdrawal obligation at the heart of resolution 242.[20]

Another important situation arose in 1974 when Turkey intervened in Cyprus, supposedly for the protection of the threatened Turkish minority, with a resulting division of the island. The Turkish intervention was censured at the UN and denied any legal effect. Turkish Cyprus remains diplomatically isolated after almost 40 years. Several attempts have been made by third parties to negotiate a solution for Cyprus that would reunify the island, most notably the so-called UN backed 'Annan Plan' that was approved by a referendum in Turkish Cyprus, but rejected by the people of Greek Cyprus. Turkish Cyprus remains in a twilight zone of legality, with formal recognition being given only by Turkey, and a strong conviction on the Greek side that Turkey had unlawfully seized territory by force without suffering adverse consequences. Again, geopolitics probably helps explain the neutralization of international law: the United States, in particular, was caught between its support for two members of NATO, and Turkey, the transgressor state in the eyes of the world, was crucial to Western strategy in the Cold War era.[21]

Although the record of compliance with the prohibition of aggression is on balance impressive, the story is somewhat more clouded in relation to the use of force to carry out military interventions designed to alter the dynamics of self-determination within the borders of sovereign states. Although the norm of self-determination is not made obligatory in the UN Charter, it has subsequently become a primary principle of international law. Respect for self-determination was one of seven principles agreed upon in the influential 1970 UN General Assembly resolution 2625 with the title 'Declaration of Principles Concerning Friendly Relations and Co-operation Among States', as well as being affirmed in

Common Article 1 of the two major UN human rights covenants that were signed in 1966.[22]

Interventions to achieve regime change tend to be justified either by humanitarian claims or to protect the international community from dangers associated with the acquisition of nuclear weapons by states branded as 'outlaw states'.[23] Despite a major effort by the United States government to obtain authorization for the use of force in 2003, the Security Council refused to grant it, and the subsequent American invasion and occupation of Iraq was widely viewed as unlawful under the UN Charter and international law.[24] The perspectives of international law were only clearly developed by the Iraq War Tribunal, a civil society initiative, organized on a worldwide basis culminating in a 2005 session in Istanbul.[25] Civil society actors have tried in recent decades to fill this void left by the refusal of geopolitical actors to abide by international law, having organized essentially *symbolic* events in the form of peoples' tribunals, which have no *substantive* capacity to implement their findings. At the same time, the proceedings of these tribunals have often provided the most comprehensive and accurate legal assessments of the challenged behavior of geopolitical actors.[26] The mainstream media tend to ignore these civil society events because they are seen as without legal weight since not backed by governmental or intergovernmental authority. In a few instances, the finding of such undertakings have had a mobilizing effect on public opposition to authoritarian governance.

Humanitarian intervention or R2P is more controversial, and as earlier suggested is widely viewed with suspicion in the non-Western world, where vivid bad memories of colonialism remain. The underlying legal idea is expressed by the status of the norm of non-intervention, which can be understood as a natural byproduct of territorial sovereignty. It is also asserted in Article 2(7) of the UN Charter that affirms that there is no authorization for 'the United Nations to intervene in matters which are essentially within the domestic jurisdiction of any state or shall require Members to submit such matters to settlement under the present Charter'. This principle of international law is a central feature of the social contract struck between sovereign states and the UN, and is, in effect, a commitment to respect the internal authority of small states. Larger states by their size and capabilities are not, as a practical matter, subject to intervention, nor are smaller states that enjoy clear geopolitical backing. Russia, China, the United States, and Brazil are examples of respect for non-intervention on the basis of size, while Israel, Turkey, and Bahrain illustrate the same phenomenon on the basis of geopolitical patronage and size. Deference to non-intervention has been eroded by the rise of human rights as a challenge to unconditional sovereignty, by a global media that calls attention in real time to crimes against humanity and other humanitarian catastrophes, and by some moves in the direction of reformulating sovereign rights by reference to 'responsible sovereignty'.[27]

The struggle in Syria dramatically demonstrates the dilemmas of intervention and non-intervention. As the French statesman Talleyrand insisted long ago, non-intervention can act as a form of intervention. This is especially true, as in Syria, where states are lending material support to both sides in an ongoing civil war. There is an underlying rule of world order that legally allows states to discriminate in favor of the established government faced with a domestic insurgency. But what if the government is guilty of atrocities or unable to protect its population from famine and disease? In effect, governments have wide discretion to determine their relations to internal conflict in foreign countries, and the UN responses to such conflicts depend on whether a geopolitical consensus can be achieved. The authorization to use force in Libya reflected such a consensus, although a weak one, while the inability of geopolitical rivals to agree about the situation in Syria has effectively neutralized the UN, limiting its role to seemingly futile pleas for compromise and negotiations put forward by UN/Arab League special envoys. In effect, international law is flexible, but dependent on a political climate that generates a consensus. The political climate registers the frequently antagonistic views of geopolitical rivals and the world order tensions of a post-colonial global setting.

There are also issues involving capabilities and tactics. Military intervention, especially if carried out to minimize the human costs to the intervening side, is a very crude instrument, and unless reinforced by a lengthy commitment to economic and political reconstruction, can lead to political frustration and fatigue even if overwhelming military superiority has brought initial success. This questionable efficacy of military superiority to offset the dynamics of self-determination should have been one of the primary lessons of the Vietnam War, rather than overcoming the 'Vietnam Syndrome' by the redesign of counterinsurgency warfare.[28] The United States has had further negative experiences along similar lines in relation to Iraq and Afghanistan, but shows little willingness to rethink the viability of the underlying mission. The latest move is to shift from traditional combat operations to a mixture of covert undertakings by 'special forces' and reliance on the attack drone, both highly interventionary, without any foundation in international law, but adaptations to the non-territorial nature of 'the long war' carried out against al Qaeda and its affiliates on a global battlefield that seeks 'consent' from the territorial government, but when it is not forthcoming, as in Pakistan, goes ahead with its attacks in any event.

The opportunities for civil society interventions in ongoing internal wars is an under-explored subject that relates ambiguously to the role of international law in relation to global security. Part of the difficulty is the reluctance of governments to cede space to civil society actors with respect to conflict mitigation and conflict resolution. Where trust is absent, there would seem to be important opportunities for independent civil society actors to propose compromises to both sides, to provide a presence in areas under the control of opposition forces, and to provide the kind of monitoring capabilities that could help to sustain a truce, facilitate a transition from war to peace, and provide parties with a means of indirect communication that tests whether grounds for agreements exist. Should international law venture onto this hitherto off-limits terrain? One can imagine an agreed code of conduct for civil society activities in internal war situations that was formulated and agreed upon by an assembly of civil society actors. Such a development, although seemingly a challenge to state-centric lawmaking, would be innovative in the best sense, an instance of international law, perhaps better understood as 'global law', negotiated from below.

Climate change and other global challenges

As earlier suggested, state-centric international law has been remarkably successful in providing a stable framework for a wide spectrum of transnational relations. It has had a measure of success in addressing global collective goods problems in the past, including management of the global commons and polar regions. Perhaps the most impressive achievement along these lines is the Law of the Seas Treaty (1982) negotiated over the course of a decade, and involving significant tradeoffs and compromises for the sake of reaching a maximum level of agreement. Ironically, the United States was instrumental in brokering the process, but to this day has been unwilling to ratify the treaty due to opposition from sovereignty-oriented members of the US Senate. Global security has been benefitted by these arrangements, and it is suggestive of the degree to which global leadership by dominant states can put the lawmaking process beyond the scope of narrowly conceived national interests. Management of the global commons for the sake of the common good suggests that in some situations national interests and global interests are perceived to converge, even by realist-oriented representatives of government.[29]

Yet there are important instances where national and global interests diverge, and these concerns have become more serious under contemporary conditions. I have earlier referred to the inability to work out an agreed scheme of nuclear disarmament, which actually ignores the NPT legal obligation to do just that. In the setting of hard power, the divergence is too great in situations where perceived security interests are at stake, and is heightened by the overestimation of the use value of hard power in the present global setting.[30] Although nuclear weapons have not been used since 1945, the apocalyptic effects of some future use, together with the error-prone nature of governmental institutions and the suicidal character of extremist politics, suggests that over time humanity is irrationally subjecting itself to a risk of immeasurable gravity by not taking all possible steps to eliminate nuclear weaponry. The failure to do so underscores a fundamental crisis of world order associated with insufficient mechanisms for the promotion and protection of the global and species interests.

Climate change highlights this deficiency in world order, as it has proved impossible to find a sufficient response to the challenge of global warming to protect either global security or the human interests. And this deficiency is already causing severe harm to societies and the environment, and is unresponsive to the warnings issued by a well-documented consensus among climate scientists.[31] Why has international law been so unable to move toward establishing a regulatory framework that protects human interests, given its ability to do so in other domains of concern?[32] There are several reasons for this world-order failure. First of all, states are pursuing national interest in a setting where restraints on GHG emissions are seen as impediments to economic growth, which is the priority of almost every government. This impediment is made more serious because states disagree about the proper way to apportion responsibility for the buildup of greenhouse gases: aggregate present volume of emissions, historical contributions dating to the Industrial Revolution, per capita level of emissions. These complications are further aggravated by a well-funded campaign of climate skeptics, those scientists who question whether global warming is actually occurring, or is a result of GHG emissions, or merely reflects natural cyclical weather behavior.[33] Such well-financed challenges to the scientific consensus create public confusion and, especially in the United States, strengthen the position of rightist opposition to environmental and other forms of international regulation, which in turn erodes the global leadership role of the United States, and makes the negotiation process very much associated with the promotion of distinct national interests. Under these circumstances it is hardly surprising that international law has not been able to respond to the challenge, and seems unlikely to do so until tipping points have been passed that make the restoration of favorable climate conditions almost impossible.[34] While climate science seems almost certain that average earth temperature rises of 2°C at most would be manageable, although with some disruptive developments (increases in extreme weather, polar melting, ocean acidification), the dynamics of rising energy use, rising standards of living, and increasing population are producing conditions that seem likely to result in the disastrous result of a 4°C average temperature rise, or possibly even more, by the end of the century.

Concluding comment

In effect, the mechanisms of law making to serve the global interest exist, as does the diplomatic rhetoric that acknowledges the gravity of global challenges; but the structures of world order create a situation in which the policy outcomes are dysfunctional from the perspective of achieving sustainable development and equitable burden-sharing. It does not seem coincidental that Europe by way of the European Union has been the most forthcoming political actor in relation to climate change because its policies seem less beholden to narrowly defined national interests. On a global level international institutions are too weak to overcome the effects of political fragmentation with respect to climate change, and the system depends on a benevolent hegemon to overcome the authority deficit. The United States played this role to a certain extent in the last half of the twentieth century, but not in relation to nuclear weaponry, and always with certain self-serving limitations.[35]

As scholars in international relations have argued, the plural order of sovereign states was capable of promoting cooperative relations and maintaining order that served the community of states until the prior century. It became evident that the military technology was undermining the viability of such a decentralized world order a century ago, with the huge mutually destructive costs of World War I. From that time on efforts were made to strengthen international law, weaken sovereignty, and construct international institutions dedicated to global security, dispute settlement, conflict resolution, and the human interest. But the political will on the level of the state to make these procedures, norms, and institutions effective enough to cope with global challenges of great magnitude has not been forthcoming. The United Nations has in some respects been far more successful than its predecessor, the League of Nations. It has achieved universal membership, presided over the dismantling of colonialism, facilitated the rise and implementation of human rights, and helped to promote peaceful resolution of many conflict situations. At the same time it has not been able to protect vulnerable peoples from abuse by territorial governments, rid the world of nuclear weapons, or establish an obligatory framework for constraints on GHG emissions. One way of expressing this limitation on international law is to insist that *some* global challenges require mechanisms of 'global law', and these are not currently available for many pressing problems.

The plan B of world order is reliance on what used to be called Great Powers as playing managerial roles that combined self-interest with the promotion of global security. This has been most evident in relation to the global commons, especially the oceans. Here there were early tensions between advocates of the territorializing of the oceans and those states supportive of 'freedom of the high seas', which was of greatest benefit to maritime states with strong navies. Shared interests were strong enough to create tolerable conditions in the global commons until recently, and lent support to the view that a plural structure of world order was preferable to a unified structure that posed risks of global tyranny, unnatural uniformity, and the like.[36]

The emergence of a unipolar world after the collapse of the Soviet Union created an opportunity for the United States to use its dominance on behalf of global security for the sake of sustainable development and world peace and justice. Instead, it emphasized a predatory form of neoliberal globalization that accentuated inequality and environmental irresponsibility, without seeking to diminish the role of military power and building up the capabilities of the UN.[37] After 9/11 there occurred a major resecuritization of the global agenda, and American leadership relating to the global common good essentially evaporated.[38]

The plan C of world order is associated with global multilateralism by way of the UN General Assembly and related activities pointing toward the establishment of global democracy. For instance, the mechanisms for addressing climate change come by way of the UN Framework Convention on Climate Change, which organizes annual meetings of all parties to produce global policy that will protect the peoples and states of the world from the ravages of global warming. Such mechanisms have proved unwieldy when important and divergent economic interests are at stake, especially if there is no strong leadership by geopolitical actor(s) that perceive a strong enough self-interest to press for a regulatory approach that will both uphold global security and seem fair in its allocation of burdens. At the 2009 Copenhagen UN conference on climate change, the United States undermined the multilateral approach seeking obligatory controls over GHG emissions by proposing, in concert with an ad hoc coalition of state actors, a voluntary approach based on national pledges that are at most unilaterally determined statements of good faith.

The plan D of world order is associated with the degree to which transnational civil society activism can mobilize a constituency for the promotion of global security by way of the development and implementation of international law.[39] There is no doubt that such civil society activism has been effective in a number of specific contexts, including exerting pressures supportive of lawmaking in relation to human rights, some forms of environmental protection, prohibition of anti-personnel landmines, and the establishment of the International Criminal Court. But as has been obvious, at the level of implementation, the *vertical* dimension of the state system means that implementation will be subject to geopolitical control, with resulting patterns of non-compliance and double standards. For instance, the implementation of criminal accountability is illustrative: it is imposed only on losers in conflicts or on the leadership of weak and marginal non-Western countries, while Western leaders enjoy unlimited impunity.[40]

Civil society initiatives have sought to overcome the failure of international law to protect the human interest in relation to criminal accountability, climate change, and nuclear disarmament, but have not had the capability to generate global law responsive to the challenge or to alter the understanding of national interests on the part of dominant states. For instance, I would argue that the United States government would better serve its national interests by adhering to international law, which would have avoided the several disastrous involvements in interventionary diplomacy ever since Vietnam; but such a view is not influential at the level of governmental policymaking, where traditional realist thinking prevails, as reinforced by an array of special interests. Each realist failure is attributed to symptoms rather than underlying causes, encouraging efforts to remove the symptoms with renewed confidence. But since the causes of failure remain, the outcome will be another disappointment attributed to different symptoms that are subject to removal, and so the cycle of repeated failures is not challenged.

Notes

1 See J. H. Mittelman, *Hyperconflict: Globalization and Insecurity*, Stanford, CA: Stanford University Press, 2010; also for limits of law in relation to uses of force, see M. J. Glennon, *Limits of Law: Prerogatives of Power: Intervention After Kosovo*, New York: Palgrave, 2001.
2 P. Sands, *Lawless World*, New York: Viking, 2005; M. Cohn, *Cowboy Republic: Six Ways the Bush Gang Has Defied the Law*, Sausalito, CA: PoliPoint Press, 2007, explicates the refusal of the Bush presidency.
3 Barack Obama articulated such a vision early in his presidency, but took no steps to exhibit an intention to bring it about. Prague, June 2009.
4 See warnings of Jonathan Schell and many others: J. Schell, *The Fate of the Earth*, New York: Knopf, 1982; R. A. Falk and D. Krieger, *Path to Zero: Dialogues on Nuclear Danger*, Boulder, CO: Paradigm, 2012.
5 See seminal article of K. Booth, 'Human Wrongs and International Relations', *International Relations* 71, no. 1, 1993, 103–26.

6 See N. Chomsky, *The New Military Humanism: Lessons from Kosovo*, Monroe, ME: Common Courage Press, 1999; for an analysis and argument in support, see Independent International Commission on Kosovo, *The Kosovo Report: Conflict, International Response, Lessons Learned*, Oxford: Oxford University Press, 2000; for more general critique of humanitarian intervention, see A. Orford, *Reading Humanitarian Intervention: Human Rights and the Use of Force in International Law*, Cambridge: Cambridge University Press, 2003.

7 A. Orford, *International Authority and the Responsibility to Protect*, Cambridge: Cambridge University Press, 2011; A. Francis, V. Popovski, and C. Samford, eds, *Norms of Protection: Responsibility to Protect, Protections of Civilians and their Interaction*, Washington, DC: Brookings Institution Press, 2013.

8 See S. Beebe and M. Kaldor, *The Ultimate Weapon Is No Weapon: Human Security and the New Rules of War and Peace*, New York: Public Affairs, 2010; M. Kaldor, *New and Old Wars: Organized Violence in a Global Era*, Stanford, CA: Stanford University Press, 2nd edn, 2006.

9 It is useful to recall that prior to the outlawing of aggressive war, peace treaties validated territorial expansions resulting from the use of force; there are still arguments about whether territory acquired in the course of exercising a right of self-defense must be relinquished. Security Council resolution 242, adopted after the Six Day War in 1967, decided that Israel must withdraw from the territory it had acquired. The fact that Israel has failed to do so is illustrative of the gap between international law and its implementation in situations where geopolitical factors support non-implementation.

10 For an exposition of such realist orientations, see H. Kissinger, *Diplomacy*, New York: Simon and Schuster, 1994, esp. 218–45; G. F. Kennan, *American Diplomacy, 1900–1950*, New York: New American Library, 1952; for realism from the perspective of international law experts, see A. C. Arend and R. J. Beck, *International Law and the Use of Force: Beyond the UN Charter Paradigm*, London: Routledge, 1993; A. M. Weisburd, *Use of Force: The Practice of States since World War II*, Philadelphia, PA: University of Pennsylvania Press, 1993; M. S. McDougal and F. P. Feliciano, *The International Law of War: Transnational Coercion and World Public Order*, New Haven, CT: Yale University Press, 1994.

11 The issues are usefully explored in M. Danner, *Torture and Truth: America, Abu Ghraib, and the War on Terror*, New York: NYRB, 2004; for range of views, see S. Levinson, ed., *Torture: A Collection*, New York: Oxford University Press, revised paperback edn, 2008.

12 I have tried to challenge this presumption on empirical and normative grounds, contending that respect for international law rules governing the use of force is more likely as of the twenty-first century to serve the national interest than is their rejection.

13 See Robert. C. Johansen, *The National Interest and the Human Interest: An Analysis of U.S. Foreign Policy*, Princeton, NJ: Princeton University Press, 1980.

14 There is legal ambiguity as to whether regional actors can undertake 'enforcement' without receiving the prior approval of the UNSC. Article 53 of the UN Charter has some rather clear language to the effect that 'no enforcement shall be taken under regional arrangements or by regional agencies without the authorization of the Security Council'. But what is 'enforcement'? And is NATO an alliance or a regional organization?

15 See text of 'Legality of the Threat or Use of Nuclear Weapons', advisory opinion, International Court of Justice, 1996.

16 First-order legality refers to rules governing the weaponry itself, not agreements that prohibit access; in contrast to nuclear weaponry, biological and chemical weapons are prohibited to all states as a result of first-order treaty law regimes.

17 Categorizing these states as an 'axis of evil' was particularly provocative and self-serving, as well as misleading; North Korea and Iran and Iraq have no linkages, much less an 'axis'.

18 There is in the NPT a nod toward a negotiated bargain based on 'sovereign equality' in Article VI mandating nuclear disarmament, but its implementation was left to the goodwill of the nuclear-weapons states, while the nonproliferation obligations are enforced, although selectively, by geopolitical managerial procedures.

19 See R. A. Falk, 'Threat Diplomacy in World Politics', in Deen K. Chatterjee, ed., *The Ethics of Preventive War*, Cambridge: Cambridge University Press, 2013, 87–99.

20 These encroachments on occupied Palestinian territories also seem in direct violation of Article 49(6) of the Fourth Geneva Convention (1949) governing occupation in accord with international humanitarian law.

21 It should also be observed that the Turkish narrative of the case for intervention due to the imminent threat directed at the Turkish minority has not received as much sympathetic attention as it deserves.

22 There are significant ambiguities regarding the principle of self-determination, including the idea that its exercise should not have the effect of fragmenting the unity of existing states; in other words, the idea of self-determination was formulated with the primary idea of supporting movements against alien rule, most prominently the European colonial system, but it was *formally* not intended to encourage minorities to seek political independence by challenging the territorial unity of an established state. The Kosovo case is controversially situated at the interface, as arguably Serbian rule was 'alien', but the result was the dismemberment of Serbia, a UN member. In the background is the question as to whether Serbia forfeited sovereign claims by gross violations of human rights. In practice, claims of self-determination are validated if the movements so dedicated are successful, regardless of whether dismemberment occurs, as happened after the collapse of Yugoslavia and the Soviet Union; the political outcomes create legitimate secessionist states provided the result is endorsed by the international community, especially as reflected in membership of the United Nations.

23 The Bush presidency developed two related ideas that were relied upon to justify the attack on Iraq in 2003: that Iraq possessed chemical weapons of mass destruction and was pursuing a program to acquire nuclear weapons and that force could be used preemptively and preventively to avert a future credible threat, given the realities of the post-9/11 world.

24 Ambiguity surrounds the legal status of the Iraq War, as the UN immediately after the fact cooperated with the American-led occupation of Iraq and failed to condemn the attack or to make any effort to protect a state threatened by aggressive war.

25 See proceedings and expert testimony in M. G. Solkmenn, ed., *World Tribunal on Iraq: Making the Case Against the War*, Northampton, MA: Olive Branch Press, 2008.

26 For the proceedings of the Russell Tribunal, see J. Duffett, ed., *Against the Crime of Silence: Proceedings of the International War Crimes Tribunal*, New York: Simon and Schuster, 1968.

27 See F. Deng, S. Kimaro, T. Lyons, D. Rothchild, and I. W. Zartman, *Sovereignty as Responsibility: Conflict Management in Africa*, Washington, DC: Brookings Institution Press, 1996.

28 See F. Kaplan, *The Insurgents: David Petreus and the Plot to Change the American Way of War*, New York: Simon and Schuster, 2013.

29 See related argument on disaggregated sovereignty in A-M. Slaughter, *The New World Order*, Princeton, NJ: Princeton University Press, 2004; another important example is the Antarctica Treaty, suspending sovereignty claims and mining operations.

30 In the nineteenth century, hard power was a rational instrument for territorial gains and access to resources, but that changed in the mid-twentieth century with the normative rise of self-determination, reinforced by renewed confidence in the combination of soft power and national resistance.

31 See e.g.: IPCC; 'Turn Down the Heat: Why a 4°C Warmer World Must be Avoided', A Report for the World Bank by the Potsdam Institute for Climate Impact Research and Climate Analytics, November 2012, Washington, DC: The World Bank; for a view that corporate obstruction of climate change adaptation is endangering the human future, see B. McKibben, 'Global Warming's Terrifying New Math', *Rolling Stone*, July 19, 2012.

32 E.g. agreements to sustain fisheries, protect whales; ozone depletion.

33 N. Oreskes and E. M. Conway, *Merchants of Doubt: How a Handful of Scientists Obscured the Truth on Issues from Tobacco Smoke to Global Warming*, New York: Bloomsbury Press, 2010.

34 See A. Giddens, *The Politics of Climate Change*, Cambridge: Polity Press, 2009, especially the 'Giddens Paradox', which suggests that by the time there exists a political will sufficient to address climate change it will be too late to take effective action, at 2–3; for a helpful overview of the potential political consequences of global warming, see G. Dyer, *Climate Wars: The Fight for Survival as the World Overheats*, Oxford: Oneworld Publications, 2010.

35 For instance, the United States has failed to ratify the Law of the Sea Treaty despite its strong support from national interest perspectives by the executive branch because of sovereignty-oriented concerns and its overriding interest in maintaining freedom of navigation for naval vessels.

36 Perhaps most compellingly argued by H. Bull, *The Anarchical Society: A Study of Order in World Politics*, New York: Columbia University Press, 1977.

37 R. A. Falk, *Predatory Globalization: A Critique*, Cambridge: Polity Press, 1999.

38 Obama made some idealistic statements in 2009 relating to nuclear weapons and to Palestine/Israel, but was revealingly unable to deliver.

39 On transnational activism, see M. E. Keck and K. Sikkink, *Activists Beyond Borders: Advocacy Networks in International Politics*, Ithaca, NY: Cornell University Press, 1998.

40 The horizontal dimension of world order is based on juridical equality, while the vertical dimension of world order reflects the hierarchy of political influence and the exercise of geopolitical leverage.

PART II
The global imperative

6

CLIMATE CHANGE AND NUCLEAR WEAPONS

Situating the world order challenge

The very character of world order, which served elites well during the modernizing and colonizing project initially in Europe, and then after decolonization stimulated hyper-development in Asia, is now dysfunctional so far as serving fundamental human needs is concerned.[1] The problematic character of world order premised on the interplay of territorial sovereignty and hegemonic geopolitics (that is, its horizontal juridical aspect of the equality of states, and its vertical political aspect of control exerted by the leading state actors) is unable to address in satisfactory fashion any of humanity's most urgent challenges: climate change, nuclear weaponry, global poverty, unregulated world economy, pandemics, genetic engineering, preserving biodiversity.

Reduced to fundamentals, the deficiencies of world order can be summarized as the fragmenting of a unified approach to problem solving by allowing unevenly situated states to pursue their distinct national interests at the expense of the overall human interest. Beyond this, the political life of the planet is preoccupied with short-term priorities, which are incapable of addressing concerns that require much more longer-term planning than is now possible, a reason to be pessimistic about the capacity of the intergovernmental system, including the United Nations, to provide solutions.[2]

A further reason for concern arises from the seemingly unreformable character of the Westphalian world order system as those state actors favorably situated refuse to adjust to a shifting reality, and even the hegemonic actors continue to be selectively deferential to sovereignty of otherwise subordinate states. There is a widening gap between what is feasible given these constraints on global problem-solving and what is necessary to safeguard the future health and wellbeing of the peoples of the world. Or as Winston Churchill expressed the same idea: 'It's not enough that we do our best; sometimes we have to do what is required.'[3]

In the past, those kinds of entreaties were directed at distinct polities or, at most, aligned or threatened civilizations, but since the advent of nuclear weaponry the scope of what is required is systemic in character. The Westphalian political reality, having demonstrated an impressive degree of resilience in addressing intra-systemic challenges, shows a lemming-like refusal to acknowledge, much less adapt to systemic crises, even if threatening to human survival.[4] At present, there is no prospect that the states, collectively or through benign hegemonic leadership, will manage to act responsibly on behalf of long-term human interests, or by relying on the normative guidance of human solidarity.[5]

The best that can be hoped for is a marginally more enlightened pursuit of national interest as perceived by governmental representatives, and even this palliative is far from assured. The United States, still claiming hegemonic stature, hovers between the pursuit of greed and a posture of denial as to the need for drastic downward adjustments in both its wildly excessive claims on the world's energy capacities, its overall per capita contribution to the build up of atmospheric greenhouse gases, and its self-destructive misplaced reliance on military adventurism in pursuit of twenty-first-century security. Such an example set for the rest of the world is a spectacular illustration of irresponsible leadership that is likely to become standard operating procedure for many less influential actors in the system unless offset by countervailing forces that seek systemic adjustments. It is reasonable to expect that as the severity of the multidimensional crisis impact on public awareness increases, there will arise some strong pressures from below that will alter the political calculus of elites representing states.

Such a possibility calls attention to the only hopeful scenario for humane governance in a post-Westphalian globalizing world – namely, the further awakening of global civil society to the dangers that lie on the road ahead. Only the mobilization of transnational forces, globalization-from-below as an initial expression of opposition to the policy and normative failures of an outmoded Westphalian framework, can create a new public consciousness that gradually infiltrates, and reconstitutes, elite thinking and action. It remains to be seen whether market forces that constitute capitalism are capable of self-interested long-term visions that exert pressures on governments to do more of what is required for the sake of stability, if not justice. But the main responsibility will need to be discharged by the organized transnational initiatives of civil society militants promoting human solidarity, and global public interests, even at the expense of certain national interests. It will be up to civil society to create a new equilibrium between the local, the regional, the global, and the universal, as well as between the immediate, the intermediate, and the long term. In effect, the Westphalian world order logic of statist pluralism and fragmentation, privileging the part over the whole, needs to give way to a post-Westphalian emergent framework that recognizes the urgency of fashioning policies that promote the wellbeing of the whole. To explore these general issues, from the standpoint of the deepening global crisis, this chapter will pay particular attention to two salient dimensions: the seemingly futile struggle to abolish nuclear weaponry that has gone on since 1945, and the newer, equally futile struggle to take steps to reverse the disastrous global warming trend. As this introduction has argued, this futility is an expression of the anachronistic ineptitude of the entrenched world order system, and sets the stage for a revolutionary transformative eruption of societal energies as awareness grows of the onset of this world order emergency.

Depicting the world order challenges

The two greatest world order challenges of a structural character over the course of the past 75 years have been, first, nuclear weaponry and, more recently, global climate change.[6] On nuclear weaponry it can be argued that the challenge has been successfully met (so far) because no nuclear weapons have been used against cities or hostile targets since the atomic bombs were dropped in 1945.[7] This seems unconvincing over time as the possession, deployment, development, proliferation, and doctrinal readiness to use these weapons suggests a very precarious firewall protecting humanity from a war fought with nuclear weapons.[8] The basic accommodation of nuclear weapons has been based on containing their spread to the extent possible through a regime that embodies a bargain in which non-nuclear-weapons states give up their option to acquire the weaponry in exchange for assurances of beneficial access to nuclear energy for peaceful purposes, and a pledge by the nuclear-weapons states to pursue in good faith nuclear disarmament.

The record of past decades also supports the conclusion that the challenge posed by the existence of nuclear weapons has not been met.[9] There has been a slow, yet steady, increase in the number of states that possess nuclear weapons and that have the knowledge and the technological capacity to produce nuclear weapons. The nonproliferation regime has not been able to prevent determined states from crossing the nuclear weapons threshold. Furthermore, the effort to restrict access to the weaponry or impose sanctions on proliferators has been selective and discriminatory, and driven more by geopolitical priorities than by counter-proliferation goals. The silent acquiescence by the West to Israel's covert acquisition of nuclear weapons was one expression of double standards, while the 2003 invasion of Iraq was illustrative of the use of a counter-proliferation rhetoric to obscure other strategic motivations and to excuse an unlawful recourse to aggressive war making. Rewarding India with access to nuclear technology after it had crossed the weapons threshold is another regime-eroding expression of selective implementation of a nonproliferation ethos. Although proliferation of nuclear weapons is a derivative problem arising from the evident unwillingness of the nuclear-weapons states to eliminate this weaponry of mass destruction, it nevertheless adds to the dangers embedded in present world order. Autocratic states, and those animated by extremist ideology, such as North Korea and Iran, seem likely to have the capabilities, and possibly the will under certain conditions, to ignite wars fought with nuclear weapons. Beyond this, a country such as Pakistan, which could easily become captive of extremist leadership – an eventuality frightening to its Indian neighbor – and could produce a regional nuclear war of great destructiveness, whose effects due to radioactive fallout and economic dislocation are felt far beyond the borders of the adversaries, and the release of huge quantities of smoke could damage agricultural productivity in many parts of the world for as long as a decade.

There is also a persisting, and many would argue, an increasing risk that the existing restraints on use are fraying. Of particular concern are the apparent efforts of extremist political networks to acquire such weaponry.[10] An organization such as al Qaeda cannot be deterred by retaliatory threats, offering no suitable targets for large scale weaponry. Such a condition has given rise to both preemptive and preventive war claims and practice as the only means to safeguard against attack, but also to the revival of the visionary goal of a world without nuclear weaponry that had been quite prevalent immediately after the atomic attacks on Japanese cities and then during the early stages of the Cold War.[11]

Yet the most revealing failure involves the reluctance of the nuclear-weapons states to pursue in good faith agreed nuclear disarmament goals while weapons arsenals were still small. It seems in retrospect that the leading nuclear-weapons states never were politically willing to disarm except possibly on terms that were clearly disadvantageous to their adversaries, although there was some initial willingness by the United States and the Soviet Union to express diplomatically their shared embrace of the goal of 'general and complete disarmament'.[12] It was especially disheartening that, after the end of the Cold War when the deterrence rationale for this weaponry evaporated, there was no move whatsoever toward exploring abolitionist prospects. The triumphal celebrations of the fall of the Berlin Wall and the collapse of the Soviet Union were accompanied by a deplorable lack of American leadership with respect to long-term global stability and security. A definite window of opportunity for disarmament, as well as for a strengthened United Nations, existed between 1989 and 2001, and was never exploited. Instead, American leadership during the 1990s was focused on expanding the world economy, fostering a minimally regulated and predatory form of neoliberal globalization.[13]

On the contrary, these states, led by the United States, have continuously tested and developed new, more sophisticated types of weaponry of mass destruction, and have recently explored a variety of battlefield uses for such weapons, as well as continuing to rely on their deterrent and retaliatory roles. In effect, the nuclear-weapons states lack the political will to eliminate nuclear weapons from their military arsenals. This constitutes noncompliance with Article VI of the Non-proliferation Treaty, but more fundamentally, interprets the world order challenge of nuclear weapons as not requiring their elimination, or in some versions, as making their elimination imprudent because of the risk of cheating or impossible because the knowledge of how to make the weaponry exists and therefore cannot be safely eliminated.[14] It is important to treat these lines of argument as morally, legally, and politically unacceptable rationalizations for nuclearism. There are no compelling reasons to suppose that a phased, verified process of nuclear disarmament is not both attainable, and far safer, as well as less inhumane, in its implications for security policy than continuing to target the largest cities in the world for a potential omnicidal attack. What do we learn about world order from this failure to address the challenge of nuclear weaponry in a more satisfactory manner? Mainly, that there exists on the part of ruling elites a deep attachment to military power, reinforced by economic and bureaucratic interests, and accompanied by a strong reluctance to part with the most powerfully destructive weaponry ever developed.[15] There is the closely related populist sentiment that having this weaponry is an important status symbol; after all, the first five members of the nuclear weapons club were also the five permanent members of the UN Security Council. Beyond this, in the nuclear-weapons states, especially the United States, there are strong pro-nuclear establishments, an integral segment of the 'military–industrial complex' that opposes moves toward denuclearization from deep within the governmental structures of sovereign states.[16] Also, when it comes to war and the use of force, governments as political actors are essentially amoral, seemingly ready to sacrifice the lives of millions of citizens while being prepared to launch genocidal, even omnicidal, attacks to avoid a strategic defeat or to reach some other strategic goal such as permanently disabling a global rival.[17]

This assessment is particularly disturbing when it is recognized that global ethics, public reason, and long-term security reinforce the worry that without nuclear disarmament a humanitarian catastrophe will result at some point. It was this worry that led observers to assume immediately after Hiroshima and Nagasaki that governments would uniformly quickly understand that their survival would now be dependent on the total abolition and repudiation of this weaponry. There was nothing in the structure of international relations that prevented achieving complete nuclear disarmament. Governments representing states could have negotiated verifiable agreements, and established trustworthy compliance mechanisms if the political will had been present, which would have meant overriding the logic and habits of several centuries of statecraft.[18]

When it comes to the other great world order challenge, accommodating global climate change, the prospects seem at once better and worse. They are worse because it is harder for the political imagination to comprehend the dangers posed by climate change and take appropriate action in a timely manner. The causation is more hidden and contested, and there exists no model of ecological catastrophe that is comparable to the charred urban landscapes of the two Japanese cities hit by atomic bombs.[19] Beyond this, most of the world's governments will have to act collaboratively to meet this challenge, substituting policy guidance on the basis of the global public interest for a long-held practice of shaping global policy by reference only to narrowly conceived national interests. More difficult, governments accustomed to very short cycles of accountability, often equated with electoral intervals of 3–6 years, will have to construct policy, major resource allocations, and domestic regulation on the basis of far longer cycles of 10–50 years or more. Also difficult is the investment in future wellbeing in ways that impose considerable financial burdens on present government budgets, requiring added taxes, restrictions on market operations, and likely to lead to increased budget deficits and lower corporate profits in some market sectors. The extent of the burdens will almost certainly grow as time passes, but at each point short of tangible effects on the health and wellbeing of powerful countries, the likelihood is that costs of adjustment for the sake of the future will not be deemed politically acceptable. This political resistance to paying now to avoid severe harm much later is accentuated by the current global economic crisis in which the combination of high unemployment and stagnant growth exert pressure on fiscal policy without taking into consideration adverse economic consequences of rapidly reducing the emission rates of greenhouse gases. This pressure is heightened by the fact that competitiveness and growth in the global marketplace could be negatively affected by placing extra burdens on industrial and consumer activities.[20]

At the same time, global climate change seems to have slightly better prospects than nuclear weapons for several reasons. Regulation involves constraints on industrial and societal activities, but it does not intrude directly upon the security domain that has remained resistant to public accountability even in the most democratic of sovereign states. Furthermore, it is possible to calibrate adjustment responsibilities to negotiated levels taking account of differential capabilities, resources, and emission levels, that is, fixing and distributing obligations in a flexible manner. There is also the sense that reducing these emissions has no downside, nothing comparable to the alleged fear of cheating in the context of nuclear disarmament. International society has exhibited a strong commitment to act cooperatively in meeting the challenge, as evidenced by the 1997 Kyoto Protocol, and by follow-up conferences leading up to the much heralded 2009 sessions in Copenhagen that aimed to put forward a global climate change framework treaty, which is supposed to set the stage for the unprecedented levels of future cooperation that will be needed to deal with such a fundamental threat to the global commons. It was also expected that a fund would be established by the developed industrial world to enable the less developed and more disadvantaged countries to reduce their carbon emissions, and although there is agreement on principle, there is much skepticism as to whether the contributions will produce a fund of sufficient size to accomplish its goals. The world community has in the past displayed such a cooperative capacity, despite differential interests and capabilities, in relation to the public law of the oceans, the governance and environmental protection of Antarctica, and meeting the threat to the ozone shield posed by reliance on chlorofluorocarbons (CFCs).[21] These are positive and relevant precedents, but in each instance far less costly adjustments have been required of the parties.

In each of these two exemplary tests, the structure of world order seems incapable of generating a satisfactory solution, at least without the transforming impact of either a catastrophic event or of the rise of a global social movement that dramatically alters the political climate. The failure to address the challenge of nuclear weapons in a satisfactory manner has gone on now since 1945, but because no weapons of mass destruction have been used in wartime the challenge is not currently perceived to be serious.[22] Also, the absence of intense inter-state rivalry of the sort that existed during the Cold War appears to have reduced the perception of danger on the part of the public. In fact, this perception is misleading. More than previously there is a real possibility that nuclear weapons might be used in an

Indo-Pakistan or Middle Eastern war. There are also anxieties that a nuclear weapons black market ('loose nukes') is operating in the world, and then there is the new threat of acquisition and use by an extremist network. The current global setting has given rise to some serious interest in exploring the possibilities of eliminating nuclear weaponry. President Obama's identification with such a goal has temporarily encouraged the belief that maybe for the first time a real push to achieve nuclear disarmament will take place in the second decade of this century.

From a certain perspective, the modern world order system based on sovereign territorial states has demonstrated extraordinary resilience. Until the challenge of nuclear weaponry global problems were either trivial or addressed through the mechanisms of common practice, agreed rules and regimes, and hegemonic self-discipline. The main deficiencies were war and oppression, but until nuclear weapons neither threatened the system as distinct from its parts, although the destructiveness of World War I gave rise in civil society to widespread systemic concerns, which were effectively deflected by sovereign states. In relation to oppression, the normative energies associated with human rights, including the right of self-determination, scored many impressive victories: decolonization, anti-apartheid, and the liberation of Eastern Europe. What is distinctive about nuclear weaponry and global climate change is that the system of world order as a whole is at risk, and seemingly incapable of generating durable and ethically acceptable responses within its framework of governmental representation reflective of distinct state interests. The remainder of this chapter explores whether this presumed statist incapacity will control human destiny, or whether there is a way forward that will emerge that further mobilizes global civil society and leads to the emergence of new world order paradigms of thought and action far more responsive to challenges of global scope.[23]

Deficiencies of world order to address global climate change

There are several structural obstacles to adaptive policies that depend on significant cooperative action on the part of a large number of governments. With respect to climate change there is a firm consensus on the part of the scientific community that dangerous levels of global warming have been reached as a result of human activity, and far worse is to come, as a result of human activities (especially, the burning of fossil fuels and deforestation). In effect, according to the scientific consensus, ever higher temperatures will have increasingly severe adverse impacts on human wellbeing, including rising sea levels, ocean acidification, extreme weather events, increased incidence of drought and floods, desertification, and deforestation.[24] Part of the consensus includes the recognition that the adaptation costs will be significantly lower if paid sooner rather than later, and also that the burden of these costs should be distributed equitably to take account of differential responsibilities for causing global warming and varying capabilities for addressing the challenge due to different stages of development, degrees of wealth, and extent of vulnerability. The question then arises: why, in light of this level of consensus, has there been such difficulty in establishing a regime that is more responsive to the challenge? As mentioned above, the international system has demonstrated the capacity to act collectively for the global common good in a number of different settings. It was also argued that the failure with respect to nuclear weaponry can be explained by the degree to which the realist consensus that has controlled governmental thinking of leading states since World War II is skeptical of constraints on military power, and this skepticism is reinforced strongly in leading states by a domestic military–industrial complex that would lose status and economic benefits if nuclear disarmament took place. Such resistance to disarmament is strongest in the United States, and is further inhibited by a refusal to embrace the moral argument in light of the American reliance on the weaponry in World War II, and throughout the Cold War. Undoubtedly, the largest obstacle in the somewhat different policy context governing climate change is the power and resolve of the huge fossil fuel industry worldwide, which seeks to prolong oil and gas dependence and profitability as long as possible with a seemingly minimal regard for adverse human consequences.[25] In many respects, despite the absence of the security dimension, there are important similarities in our two test cases of world order capacity.

I United States

In both circumstances it is impossible to contemplate a solution that does not rest upon US leadership. And in both instances the US government, despite espousing lofty rhetorical commitments from time to time, has blocked progress toward more ambitious goals. The United States is not a party to the Kyoto Protocol, and even if the Bush presidency had submitted the agreement to the US Senate for ratification, it is almost certain that it would never have been ratified or respected. Similarly at the Copenhagen conference, the US government opted for the lowest common denominator rather than pressing forward toward the sorts of policies that might give hope that obligatory reductions in greenhouse gas emissions will stabilize the global climate over the course of the next two decades. Aside from the usual reluctance to devote major resources to risks that are deemed to fall mainly well beyond the electoral cycle of accountability, there are ideological and normative inhibitions that push American leaders toward a regressive posture on climate change.

There exists strong ideological opposition in the United States to increased government regulation and spending designed to influence market behavior. With respect to climate change, there was a legislative effort of questionable value to adopt a 'cap and trade' approach, which is insufficient even if it had been accepted, rather than rejected. It is doubtful that if it had been adopted it would have been fully implemented in such a way to avoid 'the worst impacts of climate change'. According to calculations, parties to the Kyoto Protocol must agree to pledge steps that 'are expected to result in aggregate emissions reductions of 16–23% below 1990 levels by 2020'. The inclusion of the American legislative commitment means 'the aggregate reductions would fall to 10–23% in one estimate, and 11–18% in another'. This is not an encouraging prospect, as it is widely believed that '[i]f the worst impacts of climate change are to be avoided, stabilization levels of 450 ppm[26] of CO_2 and a reduction target of 25–45%' would need to be adopted by the developed countries.[27] A growing number of climate change specialists regard the figure of above 400 ppm as the appropriate threshold, noting that the current level of carbon density in the atmosphere is already at 390 ppm of CO_2, and that the best that can be hoped for at present is that the US government can be pulled along to uphold a Copenhagen consensus; but that will only be possible if the consensus scales back its approach to emission reductions to a point where what is required falls well below stabilization requirements as defined by 1990 emission levels, and even then are not imposed as obligations as distinguished from voluntarily pledged targets. And then, assuming the American government seeks to fulfill its pledge, there is still a high risk that Congress will resist even these informal commitments, and the public will support such a regressive reaction.

This ideological opposition to managing the market for the public good expresses, in part, a lingering societal optimism that all genuine risks can be addressed down the line by technological fixes that obviate any need for economic sacrifices. Indeed, the approach preferred by far is reliance on market-based solutions that actually create opportunities to turn carbon reductions into either a source of profits or as a cost passed on to consumers.[28] It is an opposite turn of mind to that embodied in 'the precautionary principle', which argues that it is dangerous to defer responses because of faith in technological rescues. The rejection of the precautionary principle goes along with a corresponding distrust of calls for burdensome action now that is based on pessimistic trend analysis. The state of the American economy will also work against a positive role for the United States in the climate change policymaking dynamic – high unemployment, trade and budgetary deficits, a falling dollar, and faltering competitiveness all add to the pressure to minimize any kind of regulatory burden on the American economy. These elements are present in other developed countries but with somewhat less ideological reinforcement, although the rightwards drift in Europe suggests that despite European positive leadership at Kyoto, and later at Durban, there appears to be a growing readiness to allow American minimalist leadership to set the pace of adjustment at Copenhagen. There exists during this period an enormous set of missed opportunities to facilitate a transition to reliance on greener technologies, for example, in relation to the troubled American auto industry or by investing in mass transit in the cities of the world.[29]

II Statism

In distinct ways, the persistence of the Westphalian system of sovereign states greatly complicates the formation of effective responses to global policy challenges requiring large scale adjustments in thought, action, and allocation of resources. An essential feature of this world order arrangement is the dominance of the part in relation to the whole, which privileges state-centric attitudes toward problem solving. Such circumstances are aggravated by an unwillingness to govern external behavior relating to vital security and economic interests by deference to either considerations of law or ethics. That is, there is little confidence in legal constraints and an extremely limited willingness to subordinate national interests to the wider claims of international law or international morality. This posture is exhibited in part by the prevalence of the realist consensus in governmental circles, which is identified by its skepticism about the relevance of ethical and legal perspectives in the formation of foreign policy. This skepticism is heightened in the American case by its hegemonic status and a tradition of 'exceptionalism' that has been extended since 1945, and even more so since 1989, by its imperial or hegemonic role. The problems associated with seeking a normatively acceptable approach to climate change are rendered far more difficult by the multiple dimensions of unevenness that characterize the 195 or so states that currently exist. This unevenness relates to both objective conditions and to perceptions, and helps explain a variety of views as to what course of action is rational, equitable, and responsible.

Unevenness inevitably raises problems of both distributive and corrective justice, involving differentiating between present capabilities and emission levels, and vastly unequal past responsibilities for the global buildup of CO_2. How should this unevenness be reflected in global arrangements? Who decides? There is much discussion of stakeholder democracy to ensure representation and participation by those affected by environmental policymaking, but the dynamics of decision continue to be dominated by governments, hobbled by special interests heavily weighted to benefit corporate and financial power at the expense of the wellbeing of society, future generations, and the global human public interest. One way to understand this deplorable situation is to treat it as a symptom of a deepening crisis of global governance; another is to emphasize the global democratic deficit; and still another is to pin the blame on neoliberal capitalism. These issues were at the core of the dissatisfaction with the Copenhagen process for shaping global policy on climate change, and call attention to the potential opportunities for non-governmental organizations (NGOs) and a worldwide social movement for achieving an equitable and effective regime to regulate carbon emissions under circumstances of ecological emergency.

This unevenness is probably greatest in relation to the least developed low-lying island states and several African countries that are confronted by near-term survival threats. From their perspective, there is an immediate condition of urgency that would justify a far higher level of worldwide reduction of emission levels than seems rational and politically feasible for many of the richer and larger states, including especially the United States and much of Europe. The countries less immediately and seriously threatened are more tempted to postpone large-scale adjustment burdens in the rather vain hope that technological innovations will lower the costs of or need for accommodation, or that in any event they will not be around when the increased damage of current inaction is experienced. If there existed a more centralized form of global governance then adjustments could be made on a priority basis to take far more account of those most vulnerable geographically and economically disadvantaged spaces in the world. The Washington response to Hurricane Katrina in 2005 revealed that even centralized national governments in a fully developed country may fail to protect those harmed by environmental disasters, failures that appeared in New Orleans to be aggravated by the race and class identities of the principal victims. Such an experience dramatized for many the racial and class dimensions of what can aptly be described as 'climate change injustice'.[30]

Of course, states do cooperate to promote common interests, and have displayed some willingness in certain situations to accommodate various aspects of unevenness. The Law of the Seas Treaty made special provisions for landlocked countries to ensure outlets to the ocean. The Montreal Protocol on Ozone subsidized the phasing out of CFCs by developing countries. The Antarctica Treaty overlooked different degrees of territorial occupation and suspended sovereign claims by states through the negotiation of an overarching agreement establishing a protective regime. In all of these instances, national interests were compromised to a limited extent to serve wider collective interests, but in each instance there was no encroachment on the security role of the state, nor any economic burden imposed that would diminish the standard of living in richer countries.

III Presentism

A predisposition in favor of the present as over against the future is deeply embedded in the cultural outlook of the developed countries. This outlook reflects partly the belief deeply embedded in the modern psyche that technological innovations have often in the past emerged to reduce the seemingly menacing prospects of present trends. Perhaps the most relevant example is the dire Malthusian predictions associated with the alleged negative interplay of a projected arithmetic growth in food supply as compared to an anticipated geometric growth in the population. More recently, in the 1970s, a wave of neo-Malthusian alarmism swept across modern industrial society.[31] There remain a variety of climate change skeptics who contend that the climate change challenge is being similarly exaggerated, and that accommodation efforts should be moderated.[32] This presentist bias is neglectful of the prospects of future generations.[33] It does not, with very few exceptions, view the present as having responsibilities toward the future except rhetorically. As a result, the short time horizons associated with political accountability are not offset in situations such as exist for climate change where periods of 20–100 years should be treated as relevant for the formation of global public policy. In other words, deficient recognition of human solidarity relates to time as a result of presentism, as well as pertaining to space due to political fragmentation (that is, statism).

IV Ideology

There are certain reinforcing elements embedded in the dominant ideological outlook, especially associated with market driven economic globalization and state-centric nationalism. The ascendancy of historically contingent neoliberal economic policy means that governmental policy is guided by special interest groups and by degrees of profitability rather than by global public interests or by taking into account the perspectives of human solidarity. Only if a very long-run perspective informs policy and decisions would it be possible to take due account of global warming pressures. This is not likely to happen until tangible harm for richer countries occurs on a massive scale. One effect of this type of globalization is to outsource production and investment to minimize costs and maximize profits, which again places a premium on keeping wages low and on avoiding expensive regulation for the public good. That is, other things being equal, the primacy of market criteria for policymakers works against serving the global public interest in the manner that will address the challenge of global climate change. Similarly, the strength of nationalism implies a reluctance to bear burdens for the wellbeing of those situated outside of territorial boundaries. It provides an emotive reinforcement to statism, which could according to idealistic projections produce an inclusive political culture informed by a Buddhist ethos of universal compassion.[34] Statism (conjoined with secularism, a modernist sequel to religion as the source of societal cohesion) historically has nurtured nationalism as an exclusivist basis of loyalty, and has viewed the outsider as an 'alien', if not an 'enemy'. The kind of political culture most conducive to meeting global-scale challenges of large magnitude would produce a far better balance between the selfish pursuit of nationalist goals and the more empathetic embrace premised on both human solidarity and taking the suffering (present, past, and future) of all humans seriously.[35]

V Reform and transformation in response to global-scale challenges

Part of the world order dilemma posed by global-scale challenges of large magnitude can be expressed as a gap between what is feasible and what is necessary.

For reasons set forth in the prior section, the limits of feasible reform to take account of regional and global public interests preclude adaptive responses within the Westphalian framework of global policymaking and problem solving, especially when the proposed adjustments encroach on the militarist domain of national security, on the consumptive habits of society, and on the profit margins of corporations and financial institutions. There are no exceptions to this generalization about the potentialities of reform through collaborative behavior by states in the Westphalia era of world order. It is the case that wartime alliances are the most impressive instances of intergovernmental collaboration for shared goals, but rarely with reformist motivations in mind.[36] It might appear that the establishment of the United Nations, and before it the League of Nations, were exceptions, but the lofty goals set for such innovations were never matched by appropriate transfers of power, authority, and resources or public expectations in major states that would have been required if a serious challenge was to be mounted to the control exercised by sovereign states over the use of force as legally mandated by the UN Charter.[37] Indeed, the grant of a veto power to the permanent members of the

Security Council and the geopolitical insulation of the dominant states from international accountability confirms the substantial continuity of this inability to institute global-scale reforms that go beyond the horizons of feasibility as set by the realist consensus. This intergovernmental inability to promote and protect adequately global human public interests is a complex compound of statism, neoliberal capitalism, hegemonic geopolitics, presentism, militarism, and nationalism. To be sure, a modest reformist potentiality does exist. It involves pragmatic and small-scale global adjustments that can be managed, reflecting a genuine, if weak, relevance of global public interests and human solidarity. For instance, natural disasters caused by tsunamis, hurricanes, and earthquakes elicit tangible empathetic responses from rich and powerful countries. Managing the war system by prohibitions on certain weapons systems (biological and chemical weapons) or by restricting the size of nuclear weapons arsenals are illustrative of feasible undertakings that prevent matters from getting worse for the world as a whole. When President Obama articulated a vision of a world without nuclear weapons in 2009, he signaled its utopian (that is, non-feasible) character by situating the attainment of such goals as likely beyond his lifetime, but still generated some angry realist backlash sentiments on the part of those who thought, perhaps, that he might be seriously (and in their view dangerously), embracing a transformative political project that was responsive to his understanding of what was necessary (and desirable).[38] In the environmental area, certain regional anti-pollution and conservation regimes have been effective because the economic costs have been either isolated to specific sectors of the economy without sufficient leverage to resist (e.g. commercial whaling) or not so burdensome as to generate a strong political backlash (e.g. the phasing out of CFCs).[39]

Climate change resembles nuclear weaponry to the extent that it is difficult to deny that risks of severe harm to the wellbeing of all peoples and societies, including those that are rich and powerful, are at stake. These risks are already responsible for significant harm, and worse is certain to come in the future unless drastic action is taken that is not dismissed as unfeasible by political leaders and the media. In this regard, there currently exists a raised consciousness about this challenge that exerts some pressure on governments to act more constructively in response. The governments challenged are doing their best to manage this pressure given their belief that the adjustments needed are not politically palatable to their main constituencies. This pressure is augmented, and will be further intensified in the future, by transnational civil society actors motivated by considerations of necessity, and to varying degrees, of desire, as well as by their adherence to universally shared values.[40] The present degree of mobilization of societal pressure seems now unable to push the intergovernmental framework sufficiently hard to produce policies that exceed prevailing ideas as to the limits of feasibility, including what the citizenry in rich countries, especially the United States, is prepared to accept. Sadly, George H. W. Bush was probably accurately reflecting political constraints, at least back in 1992, when on the eve of the Rio Earth Summit he declared that 'the American way of life is not negotiable'.

There is some basis for believing that 2012 is not 1992, and that the publics of many states are far more willing than in the past to make material sacrifices for the sake of avoiding catastrophic global warming. This encouraging development is not matched by a comparable willingness on the part of an array of economic special interests or market forces generally (and their many governmental allies). Politicians are wary of pushing the climate change agenda too hard if large burdens are to be placed on the national economy. Political leaders continue to worry about their capacity to govern, and do seem highly unlikely to survive in the present political atmosphere if they ignore these limits by favoring large carbon emission cuts or imposing taxes on activities with high emissions. The outer limit on regulation is set by these elite perceptions of feasibility, which are, at best, likely to slow down somewhat the global warming trends, deferring the days of reckoning somewhat further into the future. Almost certainly, the Copenhagen outcome fell far short of reduction restrictions and funding arrangements that correspond to even the lower end of the scientific consensus that pertains to doing what is necessary to stabilize CO_2 levels by 2030 or so. It is true that there are subjective variations as to the identification of the spectrum of feasibility that accounts for debates among reformers, and as to the spectrum of necessity, which explains the lack of uniformity with respect to degrees of disappointment with governmental responses. The Copenhagen results were treated by the mainstream media as modest steps forward despite their extremely unsatisfactory achievements as measured by the mounting seriousness of climate change or the views of environmental NGOs.

What can be anticipated, then, is a certain reformist satisfaction if Copenhagen produces agreements that seem too little and too late. As often happens in the setting of dramatic gatherings of the governments of the world, more is claimed than achieved, and even what little is achieved is not fully implemented, with compliance being treated as an essentially voluntary matter. Failure with respect to climate change is ascertained by moving far too slowly toward imposing adequate emission reductions on countries differentiated by wealth and stage of development, by not establishing a sufficient fund to subsidize efforts to slow the rate of deforestation and to provide mitigation in developing countries, and by not creating a sufficient fund to provide the poorest and least developed countries with assistance in their efforts to deal with the most immediate challenges associated with climate change. At the same time, depending on whether these reformist efforts are regarded as falling at the upper or lower end of the spectrum of feasibility, there are likely to be constructive expressions of disappointment and even anger among civil society actors convinced that what has been agreed upon falls alarmingly short of what it is necessary to do. Hopefully, this disappointment will generate a new cycle of environmental activism rather than take refuge in passive enclaves of despair.

There is an opportunity for a radicalization of transnational efforts that can build on the realization that waiting any longer for governments to do what is necessary will produce human tragedy. This realization can encourage citizens throughout the world to appreciate their own responsibilities to participate in the struggle for a robust and equitable set of responses to the challenge of global climate change. Such a populist movement is also more likely to focus attention on the complicated issues of environmental justice that underlie the distribution of duties relating to a comprehensive, holistic, and planetary approach to climate change that is people-centered, rather than state-centric and market-oriented. There is also the question of what is desirable in the sense of being intrinsically beneficial. The desirable merges with the politics of feasibility and necessity, and also raises distinct additional issues. The merger results from the need for global or near-global participation to achieve the managerial control that feasible reform entails. This was evident in the attempted structuring of emission reduction obligations contained in the Kyoto Protocol based on a generalized idea of 'differentiated equality'. This quest for a political consensus on the allocation of emission duties will again be evident in the arrangements discussed at Copenhagen. Putting this in world order terms, it means that statism and nationalism gives way to considerations of equity so as to secure voluntary participation; without differentiating degrees of burden poorer and less developed countries would not participate. The perspectives of necessity are not directly responsive to considerations of global justice so much as preoccupied with building support for solutions that address the underlying problem at a level of appropriate commitment, which may or may not rely on adding incentives for the poorer societies to participate more fully, and could be prepared to adopt coercive or even authoritarian and hegemonic approaches to implementation as the pressure mounts.[41]

As earlier, the nuclear weapons analogy seems illuminating, given the control choice shifting from disarmament to nonproliferation thereby accepting a coercive approach to risk management, conceding agency to hegemonic governments as in the US reliance on military interventions and threats to control the spread of nuclear weapons to states deemed hostile (for example, Iran and North Korea). This view of necessity in the nuclear weapons context overlaps with considerations of feasibility. For climate change at some future point, the managerial imperatives of feasibility might merge with the transformative claims of necessity, leading to centrally mandated and enforced emission limits that may or may not be sensitive to considerations of equity. One of the features of adaptive dynamics within a Westphalian framework is the degree to which considerations of equity are understood in statist terms. Whether the particular state allocates internal burdens equitably is treated as totally a matter for national policy. Past experience with respect to environmental regulation suggests that the poor and marginal are made to bear disproportionate burdens and risks as, for example, with respect to the location of toxic waste disposal sites.[42] The protection of such human security interests will depend mainly on societal vigilance and local grassroots activism.

Conclusions

The world order argument of this chapter has been that the challenge of global climate change will not be effectively addressed by the response of governments seeking to negotiate an agreement that will stabilize the levels of greenhouse gases in the atmosphere at sustainable levels. As a result, human societies around the world will suffer intensifying harmful effects from continuing emissions, and the various consequences of global warming. Intergovernmental efforts to fashion a response have been continuing for more than a decade, and have been reinforced by citizen and NGO activism.[43] This degree of raised consciousness has already produced some encouraging extensions of the horizon of feasibility with respect to controlling emissions, subsidizing forest maintenance, and financing climate change initiatives in the poorest countries, but it will not come close to reaching the minimal goals as specified by considerations of necessity – minimum stabilization levels of 350–400 ppm CO_2 and reduction targets of between 25 and 40 percent of 1990s levels for the thirty-seven most developed countries attained by 2030, and a complete phase-out of carbon emissions by 2050.

In the past, most major social adjustments within and between societies have been a result of sustained struggles against the established order arising from societal mobilization taking a variety of forms. The long struggles against slavery and racism, as well as on behalf of the rights of women, are emblematic. Reflecting on the period since World War II, decolonization, the Anti-Apartheid Movement, the Civil Rights Movement, and the rise of human rights have succeeded against the odds because of mounting symbolic pressures based on law and morality exerted on governmental actors. I would regard these various struggles as 'legitimacy wars' in which the social movement is politically strengthened by seizing the high moral ground. Over time these commanding moral heights expose the limits of coercive dominance, demonstrating that nonviolence and resistance, even if weaker in terms of military capabilities, can often, but not always, prevail.[44] Unfortunately, the anti-nuclear movement has been winning the legitimacy war for decades without being able to come any closer to achieving its primary goal of eliminating these weapons from military arsenals. Similarly, Tibet has prevailed in its legitimacy war with China, and yet seems unlikely as ever to achieve its objectives of self-determination, or even autonomy within the Chinese state. At present, the Palestinians are winning the legitimacy war being waged against Israel, but it remains unclear as to when, or even whether, such a victory will yield corresponding political results with respect to Palestinian self-determination in either one state or two.

When it comes to climate change this background is certainly relevant, but there are additional considerations at stake as well. A series of pressing immediate societal problems make it difficult to focus sufficient mass attention on the climate change agenda either from the perspective of necessity or justice. Presentism, statism, and nationalism pose obstacles when seeking to form a transnational consensus in global civil society as to how best to proceed. Also the forces of market, geopolitical, and class opposition, strengthened by a generally passive mainstream media, further complicate activist efforts to overcome current dispositions to limit adjustments to the realm of the feasible. And yet these difficulties are not meant to offer a rationalization for resignation in the face of such ominous trends and political tendencies. Even within the gridlocked world order system there are possibilities for reform from below, abetted by collaborators from above. Consider, for instance, the global coalition of hundreds of NGOs and moderate governments (non-players in the great games of geopolitics) that led to the surprising establishment of the International Criminal Court in 2002. Before it happened, such an undertaking could easily have been written off as utopian, challenging the most precious prerogative of sovereign states to confer impunity on their leadership. Such an uncertainty as to outcomes should encourage a suspension of disbelief by responsible citizens throughout the world and a willingness to engage in a struggle for a sustainable and healthy climate, despite the absence of an assurance in advance that the outcome will be favorable.[45]

In short, as far ahead as can be envisaged, it seems highly unlikely that the existing world order system will find an acceptable response to the global climate change challenge even if it were pushed much harder by the growing militancy of civil society activism that has yet to materialize. Perhaps, a populist dynamic of reform, especially if abetted by some governmental collaboration (as helped bring the International Criminal Court into being) will lengthen the time interval available for necessary adjustments. One daunting element in the climate change context is ignorance as to the precise location of thresholds of irreversibility, which once crossed, make stabilization of carbon levels either impossible or significantly more burdensome. At the same time, the many unexpected happy endings of legitimacy wars over the course of the last 75 years make it rational to lend maximal support to the struggle for a global climate insulated from damage caused by human activities. It is also important to think beyond substantive reform, and consider the case for the transformation of world order so as to achieve a just, democratic, and effective form of global governance.[46]

The argument for paradigm change results from three intersecting propositions. First, the state system, even if making full use of its maximal capacity for reform, seems unlikely to make the adjustments necessary to avoid carbon levels that produce global warming above 4 degrees centigrade, which are projected by an overwhelming scientific consensus to cause several varieties of severe harm to human and societal wellbeing, and catastrophic damage to particularly exposed communities (for instance, low-lying habitations on shores and islands). As argued, it needs to be understood that current carbon levels, especially as abetted by the lag between use and atmospheric effect, is already responsible for a variety of serious planetary harmful developments, including polar and glacial melting, rising sea levels, drought, desertification, human displacement, environmental refugees, and extreme weather. Second, even if such restraint were to be achieved by concerted intergovernmental collaboration, it would not be in a form that was fair to the more vulnerable societies or to various marginalized human communities within states. Third, the possibility of a humane form of global governance is dependent on democratizing participation and accountability, as well as on transcending nationalism and statism, which means a form of global governance that is post-Westphalian, privileging people over market and state, which is to say, the emergence of a new structure and normative mandate for world order. This visionary future seems increasingly embodied in the hopes, actions, and dreams of civil society activists throughout the world.[47]

Notes

1 Whether it ever served the masses well is far more doubtful. For thoughtful explorations of this theme from a contemporary political economy perspective see the final two books of the trilogy authored by M. Hardt and A. Negri: *Multitude: War and Democracy in the Age of Empire*, Paris: La Decouverte, 2004; and *Common Wealth*, Cambridge, MA: Belknap Press of Harvard University Press, 2009.

2 For a journalistic assertion of the same point, but set in terms of changed evolutionary priorities, see A. Gore and D. Blood, 'Time Is Up for Short-term Thinking in Global Capitalism', *Financial Times*, 27 November 2009, 11. The article argues that for primitive human society the preoccupation with short-term thinking contributed positively to survival prospects, but no longer.

3 Quoted in Gore and Blood, op. cit., 11.

4 J. Schell, *The Fate of the Earth*, New York: Knopf, 1982, posed this question eloquently in the setting of the Cold War.

5 For a consideration of the alternatives to Westphalian world order, as well as an argument that supports adopting a post-Westphalian perspective in light of overall globalizing impacts, see R. A. Falk, *The Decline of World Order: America's Imperial Geopolitics*, New York: Routledge, 2004, 3–44.

6 These two concerns are given this salience because of their structural resistance to fashioning a satisfactory response within a statist framework of world order, thus posing an overall threat to systemic stability and survival; from a contrasting normative perspective of human values, great challenges to human dignity have been accommodated within the Westphalian system since its inception, including poverty, war, oppression, even genocide. These challenges under conditions of modernity have been insulated from wider concern by deference to state sovereignty, including its imperial extensions. See an important article by K. Booth, 'On Human Wrongs and International Relations', *Journal of International Affairs* 71, no. 1, 1995, 103–26; also T. Dunne and N. Wheeler, eds, *Human Rights in Global Politics*, Cambridge: Cambridge University Press, 1999.

7 Even this claim overlooks the 'use' of nuclear weapons in numerous test explosions that have been conducted in the atmosphere, oceans, and underground since the 1950s, including detonations of a magnitude many times greater than the bombs dropped on Japanese cities, causing various degrees of radioactive fallout. Additionally, some weaponry such as warheads tipped with depleted uranium have been used in a variety of conflicts, with some health impacts alleged.

8 It is also an exterminist firewall with deeply corrupting consequences for any society that prepares for such an eventuality as E. P. Thompson (*Beyond the Cold War*, Pantheon: New York, 1982) powerfully argued decades ago. See also R. J. Lifton and R. A. Falk, *Indefensible Weapons: The Political and Psychological Case Against Nuclearism*, New York: Basic Books, 1982.

9 On this generally disappointing failure to move toward the nuclear disarmament stage, at least as a matter of aspirational policy, see R. A. Falk and D. Krieger, eds, *At the Nuclear Precipice: Catastrophe or Transformation*, New York: Palgrave Macmillan, 2008; and D. Krieger, ed., *The Challenge of Abolishing Nuclear Weapons*, New Brunswick, NJ: Transaction, 2009, 227–42. On April 5, 2009, President Barack Obama delivered a speech in Prague announcing a commitment to seek a world without nuclear weaponry, but situated the attainment of the goal as possibly beyond his lifetime.

10 President George W. Bush based the preventive rationale for the Iraq War on such a perceived connection between weapons of mass destruction and the resolve of global terrorists. See Bush's West Point speech of 2002 for initial exposition of this doctrinal response to the 9/11 attacks. Expressed in more authoritative terms in the White House

document, 'The National Security Strategy of the United States of America', 2002; especially chapters 5, 13–16. On 'Climate Change and the Threat of Nuclear Weapons', see p. 145. For a sophisticated application of this doctrine to a broad conception of American security in a global setting shaped by the terrorist challenge, see P. Bobbitt, *Terror and Consent: The Wars for the Twenty-First Century*, New York: Knopf, 2008.

11 For such rearticulations, see Barack Obama's 'The Rome Declaration of Nobel Laureates', 7th World Summit of Nobel Peace Laureates, 2006; and an influential realist call for abolition by former US secretaries of state and defense and a former senator with stature as a defense specialist: G. Shultz. W. J. Perry, H. A. Kissinger, and S. Nunn, 'A World Free of Nuclear Weapons', *Wall Street Journal*, January 4, 2007.

12 There was an earlier period in which the goals of general and complete disarmament, as well as nuclear disarmament, were officially endorsed by the two Cold War antagonists. This shared public position was most prominently contained in the so-called 'McCloy–Zorin Statement', named after the negotiators. It was more formally named 'The Joint Statement of Agreed Principles for Disarmament Negotiations'. For a useful overview of the global setting as applied to disarmament discourse, see R. Rydell, 'Nuclear Disarmament and General and Complete Disarmament', in D. Krieger, ed., *The Challenge of Abolishing Nuclear Weapons*, New Brunswick, NJ: Transaction, 2009.

13 For an interpretation, see R. A. Falk, *Predatory Globalization: A Critique*, Cambridge: Polity, 1999. For important critical studies of American militarism and decline, see C. Johnson, *The Sorrows of Empire: Militarism, Secrecy and the End of the Republic*, New York, Metropolitan Books, 2004; C. Johnson, *Nemesis: The Last Days of the American Republic*, New York: Metropolitan Books, 2006 and T. E. Paupp, *Exodus from Empire: The Fall of America's Empire and the Rise of the Global Community*, London: Pluto, 2007.

14 Prominently argued by J. S. Nye Jr., *Nuclear Ethics*, New York: Free Press, 1986; see also A. Carnesale, P. Doty, S. Hoffmann, S. P. Huntington, J. S. Nye Jr., S. D. Sagan, and D. Bok, *Living with Nuclear Weapons*, New York: Bantam, 1983.

15 For a deep analysis of this militarizing of conflict resolution, see J. Mittelman, *Hyperconflict: Globalization and Insecurity*, Stanford, CA: Stanford University Press, 2010; also M. Klare, *Resource Wars: The New Landscape of Global Conflict*, New York: Metropolitan Books, 2001.

16 The domestic obstacles to disarmament are formidable, including a deeply embedded nuclearist bureaucracy that has roots in Congress, the market economy, the scientific and academic establishments, the mainstream media, and in Beltway think tanks. There are various inquiries into this rarely discussed societal and governmental underpinning for nuclearism, and more generally, militarism.

17 The reliance on exterminist weaponry for security may reflect the amorality of realist policy advisors, but its implications for use are flagrantly immoral. See E. P. Thompson, *Beyond the Cold War*, New York: Pantheon, 1982; R. J. Lifton and E. Markusen, *The Genocidal Mentality: Nazi Holocaust and Nuclear Threat*, New York: Basic Books, 1988; R. J. Lifton and R. A. Falk, *Indefensible Weapons: The Political and Psychological Case against Nuclearism*, New York: Basic Books, 1982.

18 For one projected 'solution' that depends on an ideational paradigm shift from realism to 'global republicanism', see the pioneering book by D. Deudney, *Bounding Power: Republican Security Theory from the Polis to the Global Village*, Princeton, NJ: Princeton University Press, 2007, 244–77. See also R. Rydell, op. cit., 'Nuclear Disarmament and General and Complete Disarmament', 227–42 for a consideration of various moves toward nuclear disarmament, which were in all instances undercut by nuclearist domestic forces. For a trenchant assessment, see R. J. Barnet, *Who Wants Disarmament?*, Boston: Beacon, 1960.

19 Recent futurist films have treated these possibilities, including *The Day After Tomorrow*, *The Road*, *2012*, and a whole range of documentaries of which the most widely known is *An Inconvenient Truth*, narrated by Al Gore, and winner of an Academy Award. There is also a book version (A. Gore, *An Inconvenient Truth*, New York: Rodale, 2008).

20 There are several contested issues. First, the economic costs of delay. Second, the divergence between states as to the appropriate allocation of emission reduction targets. Third, domestic resistance in democratic states to agreed emission reductions.

21 See the Montreal Protocol on Substances that Deplete the Ozone Layer (1987).

22 But there has recently been some renewal of concern, especially associated with worries about the erosion of the nonproliferation regime, but also flowing from President Obama's Prague speech (see Note 9). The Nuclear Age Peace Foundation has maintained a steady focus on the menace of nuclear weaponry in all of its manifestations.

23 T. E. Paupp, *Crumbling Walls. Rising Regions*, New York: Palgrave Macmillan, 2009; J. Attali, *A Brief History of the Future*, New York: Arcade, 2006, esp. 255–78; D. Archibugi, *The Global Commonwealth of Citizens: Toward Cosmopolitan Democracy*, Princeton, NJ: Princeton University Press, 2008; J. Stevens, *States without Nations: Citizenship for Mortals*, New York: Columbia University Press, 2010; R. A. Falk, *On Humane Global Governance: Toward a New Global Politics*, Cambridge: Polity, 1995; and Mittelman, *Hyperconflict*, and 'Crisis and Global Governance', 157–72.

24 See Deudney, *Bounding Power*; Rydell, 'Nuclear Disarmament and General and Complete Disarmament', 227–42; Barnet, *Who Wants Disarmament?* B. Gills and J. O. Osthoek, *The Globalization of the Environmental Crisis*, London: Routledge, 2007; World Development Report, *Development and Climate Change*, Washington, DC: The World Bank, 2010.

25 See P. Maass, *Crude World: The Violent Twilight of Oil*, New York: Knopf, 2009. For a more general assessment of the end time of the petroleum age, see J. H. Kunstler, *The Long Emergency: Surviving the Converging Catastrophes of the Twenty-first Century*, New York: Atlantic Monthly Press, 2005.

26 Many recent assessments suggest that even 450 ppm is far too high to avoid severe dislocations from global warming, and the maximum tolerable level is 350 ppm, which could only be achieved if more rigorous constraints on emissions were imposed to reduce GHG levels below their current level estimated to be at 390 ppm. See B. McKibben, 'As the World Waits on the US, a Sense of Déjà vu in Denmark', *Environment* 360, 3 December 2009.

27 L. Raj Amani, *The 'Cloud' over the Climate Negotiations From Bangkok to Copenhagen and Beyond*, New Delhi: CPR Climate Brief, Centre for Policy Research India, October 2009.

28 J. Kurtzman, 'How the Market Can Curb Climate Change', *Foreign Affairs* 88, no. 5, 2009, 114–22.

29 These issues of transition are provocatively discussed, as are the severe adverse consequences of deferral, in Kunstler, *The Long Emergency*.

30 A public forum with this focus was organized at the 2010 annual meeting of the International Studies Association, appropriately in New Orleans.

31 D. H. Meadows, J. Randers and D. L. Meadows, *The Limits to Growth: A Report for the Club of Rome's Project on the Predicament of Mankind*, 2nd edn, New York: Universe Books, 1974; B. Commoner, *The Closing Circle: Nature, Man, and Technology*, New York: Knopf, 1971; R. A. Falk, *This Endangered Planet: Prospects and Proposals for Human Survival*, New York: Random House, 1972.

32 For example, see B. Lomborg, *The Skeptical Environmentalist*, Cambridge: Cambridge University Press, 2002; and the sensationalist bestselling fictionalized account by M. Crichton, *The State of Fear*, New York: Avon, 2004.

33 Depicted in prescient manner in E. Brown Weiss, *In Fairness to Future Generations: International Law, Common Patrimony, and Intergenerational Equity*, Dobbs Ferry, NY: Transnational, 1988.

34 An influential example of this tendency to overlook the obstacles to such universalism is found in the work of H. Küng, for example, *A Global Ethic for Global Politics and Economics*, New York: Oxford University Press, 1998.

35 For a valuable inquiry, see A. Sen, *The Idea of Justice*, Cambridge, MA: Harvard University Press, 2009; D. Moellendorf, *Cosmopolitan Justice*, Boulder, CO: Westview, 2002;

R. A. Falk, *The Decline of World Order*, op. cit.; T. W. Pogge, *World Poverty and Human Rights: Cosmopolitanism, Responsibilities, and Reforms*, Cambridge: Cambridge University Press, 2002.

36 But see G. J. Ikenberry, *After Victory: Institutions, Strategic Restraint, and the Rebuilding of Order after Major Wars*, Princeton, NJ: Princeton University Press, 2001, for a valuable analysis of post-war efforts in the twentieth century to restore stability to liberal international order.

37 The Nuremberg experiment of holding political leaders and military commanders legally accountable for recourse to war as well as for its conduct seemed to be a gesture in the direction of establishing a regime of law that transcended the geopolitical regime of exception. But with the benefit of further experience, encompassing even the establishment in 2002 of the International Criminal Court, it is clear that such a regime of law is meant to be applied only to subordinate states and leaders, or to the losers in a war. For a classic justification for acknowledging a modest role for international law, as essentially a mode of cooperation, while upholding the primacy of the geopolitical regime and repudiating advocates of a more ambitious role for international law in a war/peace setting, see H. Bull, 'The Grotian Conception of International Society', in *Diplomatic Investigations*, ed. H. Butterfield and M. Wight, Cambridge, MA: Harvard University Press, 1966, 50–73.

38 For explanation of the distinctions between horizons of feasibility, necessity, and desire in the context of proposed reforms of the United Nations, see R. A. Falk, 'Illusions of Reform: Needs, Desires, and Realities', in K. P. Clements and N. Mizner, eds, 'The Center Holds: UN Reform for 21st Century Challenges', in *Peace and Polity*, vol. 12, New Brunswick, NJ: Transaction Publishers, 2008, 19–30.

39 See illuminating profile of James Hansen, prominent NASA official, who initially believed that the same rationality that led to a solution of the ozone depletion problem would serve to address the climate change challenge, and his subsequent disillusionment in E. Kolbert, 'The Catastrophist: NASA's Climate Change Expert Delivers the News No One Wants to Hear', *New Yorker*, June 2009, 40–41.

40 See J. Garvey, *The Ethics of Climate Change: Right and Wrong in a Warming World*, London: Continuum, 2008.

41 Cf. G. Hardin, *Exploring New Ethics of Survival: The Voyage of the Spaceship Beagle*, Baltimore, MD: Penguin, 1972; V. Shiva, *Earth Democracy: Justice, Sustainability, and Peace*, Cambridge, MA: South End Press, 2005.

42 See J. Ebbesson and P. Okawa, eds, *Environmental Law and Justice in Context*, Cambridge, MA: Cambridge University Press, 2009; also Shiva, *Earth Democracy*, 2005; and Garvey, *The Ethics of Climate Change*, 2008.

43 See A. Gore, *An Inconvenient Truth*, New York: Rodale, 2008; and range of NGO activism, including Greenpeace, Friends of the Earth, Climate Chaos, Climate Justice Coalition, World Social Forum, and demonstrations associated with the 2009 Copenhagen climate change conference. For valuable overview of the role of activism in the context of resistance to inequitable globalization, see R. Broad, ed., *Global Backlash: Citizen Initiatives for a Just World Economy*, Lanham, MD: Rowman and Littlefield, 2002.

44 See important argument along these lines in J. Schell's *The Unconquerable World: Power, Nonviolence, and the Will of the People*, New York: Henry Holt, 2003, an important book drawing heavily on the inspirational writings and practices of Henry David Thoreau and Mahatma Gandhi.

45 See N. N. Taleb, *The Black Swan: The Impact of the Highly Improbable*, New York: Random House, 2007.

46 See, among others, D. Held, *Global Covenant: The Social Democratic Alternative to the Washington Consensus*, Cambridge: Polity, 2004; also J. A. Camilleri and J. Falk, *Worlds in Transition: Evolving Governance Across a Stressed Planet*, Cheltenham: Edward Elgar, 2009.

47 M. Hardt and A. Negri, *Multitude: War and Democracy in the Age of Empire*, New York: Penguin, 2004.

7

9/11 & 9/12 + 10 = THE UNITED STATES, AL QAEDA, AND THE WORLD

Setting the stage for 9/11

The 9/11 attacks were one of six transformative ruptures that have occurred over the course of the last 30 years: the Iranian Revolution; the end of the Cold War and the collapse of the Soviet Union; the 9/11 attacks and the American initiation of a global war on terror, called 'the long war' by Pentagon strategic planners; the realization that climate change was posing unprecedented challenges to the global environment, which if not met with a sense of urgency and commitment would lead to a series of catastrophic developments that were both local and global in their effects; doubts about the viability and desirability of neoliberal globalization, generating a crisis for global capitalism that has produced a series of formidable and specific challenges for regional and national actors; and the uprisings of 2011 throughout the Middle East, known collectively as 'the Arab awakening'. These ruptures are interrelated and are expected to exert a persisting influence. Also, each of these concerns centrally involves the global role of the United States and initially was experienced as a surprise, catching government problem-solvers unprepared and ill-equipped to fashion effective solutions. Other crucial global developments during this period were less obviously linked to 9/11 and the American response, and will not be addressed here. These include the rise of China, Brazil, and Turkey as geopolitical players, the introduction of drone technology as a global killing machine, and the catastrophic humanitarian emergency confronting sub-Saharan Africa that exists in its most extreme form in Somalia, but is bringing violence and suffering to many African countries.

The end of the Cold War was an almost universally unexpected development at least until the Berlin Wall fell in November of 1989. When the Soviet Union imploded a few years later it heralded a new phase of international relations associated with the ascendancy of the United States as global actor and as the uncontesed source of ideological orthodoxy. Triumphalist American voices arrogantly announced 'the end of history' and 'the unipolar moment', trumpeting the claim that not only had the Soviet Union fallen, discrediting Marxist-Leninist alternatives to capitalism, but that the American star was shining more brightly than ever, lighting up the geopolitical skies with its ideology of 'market-oriented constitutionalism', that is capitalism + constitutional democracy. Various pundits insisted that the twenty-first century was likely to become even more 'an American century' than was the twentieth given military dominance, control of the world economy, technological innovativeness, the worldwide appeal of its popular culture, and global diplomatic leadership. In the early 1990s there seemed to be no significant obstacles to this image of an Americanizing world on the road ahead, and the global hegemonic ambitions of government policymakers seemed realistic and reasonable.

As the tenth anniversary of 9/11 fades from view we should keep these two seemingly opposed features of the preceding decade or so in view: first, that the most transforming developments were not anticipated, nor did they follow from projecting trends into the future. This should make us modest about the human capacity to assess political reality. And second, from the perspective of the 1990s the United States seemed like the unassailable model of success and influence in the world. Its multiple vulnerabilities that have emerged in the decade following 2001 should also not be presumed to provide reliable insight into future American developments at home and globally.

Even in the 1990s not all commentary coming from the United States in this period was as positive about the future as the mainstream celebrations of the end of the Cold War would suggest. There were signs of nervousness about whether the future was so supportive of America's hopes and goals. Samuel Huntington's inflammatory formulation of an emergent 'clash of civilizations' was by far the most influential insistence that there were dark clouds gathering on the horizon, and for some his analysis was a prefiguring of 9/11 with its emphasis on 'the West against the rest'. Huntington's musings were also conceptually provocative, as he predicted that the future world order would be shaped by civilizational groupings more than by the interplay of sovereign states, as had been the case ever since the states system evolved in the mid-seventeenth century, its birth generally linked to the Peace of Westphalia. What Huntington foresaw, largely in negative terms, was an encounter between civilizations, and especially a mounting and coordinated challenge to the West from resurgent non-Western civilizations, including the Confucian rising under the leadership of China.

There were other forebodings of a radical character about global developments. For instance, a perceptive journalist, Robert Kaplan, foresaw 'a coming anarchy' as African failed states spiraled out of control due to their lack of capacity to govern effectively. Shifting the focus beyond the Eurocentric optic that shaped most commentary on the international scene, Kaplan understood both the dangerously fragile post-colonial political arrangements that existed throughout Africa, and their potential to generate problems for the West, and specifically for the United States.

Even though Afghanistan, not Africa, provided the base area for al Qaeda, Kaplan's assessments were prophetic to the extent that he understood that failed states led to the emergence of national enclaves of discontent that could be mobilized to inflict severe harm on geographically distant centers of wealth and power in the world, in which the United States seemed responsible for the most extreme grievances of those enduring poverty, injustice, occupation, displacement, and the ravages wrought by predatory globalization. What Kaplan didn't address was the degree to which these failed states were in large part legacies of colonial abuses and subsequent geopolitical ambitions that disrupted the traditional domestic balance of forces.

From the American perspective, then, there were in the period between the end of the Cold War and the 9/11 attacks a major theme of what might be called 'inviting opportunities' and a minor theme that could be described as 'ominous prospects'. The public mood in the United States and elsewhere was mainly infatuated with the opportunities, especially those provided by expanding trade and investment on a world scale and a global security system administered from Washington. The more liberal part of the American establishment put its emphasis on taking advantage of economic globalization while the rising conservative mood in the country was more interventionary in its prescriptions for American success, with a particular focus on reconfiguring the governing regimes in the Middle East in directions more congenial to the national economic and political interests of the United States and its Western allies. In the 1990s economistic geopolitics prevailed; while starting with the election of George W. Bush in 2000, a more militarist geopolitics with its sights set on fulfilling Middle East objectives shaped American foreign policy, but it was a purely statist outlook that faulted the Clinton leadership of the country for its timidity with respect to projecting American power and derided its humanitarian ventures in Somalia and Kosovo. This militant neo-conservatism failed to perceive, due to its conventional realist understanding of world politics, the future *geopolitical* challenge of non-state transnational violence, nor the diminished geopolitical utility of military dominance. This shift during the last decades was dramatic, and its most extreme undertakings were made politically possible in the aftermath of the 9/11 attacks, which in the United States raised public concerns about distant threats to fever pitch.

There were several facets of this new global setting in the early 1990s that shaped the road to 9/11:

American military dominance throughout the world, combined with the de-securitization of world politics due to the withering away of strategic rivalries after the Soviet collapse, meant that credible threats of an outbreak of a war of global proportions evaporated as a concern for foreign policy analysts; regional conflicts persisted, as did internal wars for control of the governmental structures and political destiny of particular states, but for the first time in the modern era there seemed to be neither incentives nor prospects for warfare between core states in the West.

This rise of the American empire, seemingly unopposed by states yet viewed by many around the world as responsible for acute suffering and injustice, gave rise to a variety of critical and extremist responses of which Osama Bin Laden's letters and statements, including a declaration of war against the West, turned out to be the most historically consequential.

A related shift of governmental priorities was expressed through an emphasis on economistic geopolitics associated with a neoliberal push in the direction of deregulating and privatizing international trade, investment, and financial markets, a process that led to governmental policies of uncritical support for 'globalization-from-above' during the 1990s that brought incredible wealth to transnational corporations, bankers, and currency traders, but also gave rise to continually widening gaps between rich and poor within and among countries.

There dawned a new realization of the relevance of cultural and religious tensions to the conduct of international diplomacy, which reflected in part a deferred recognition of the serious ideological challenge posed to the region by the Iranian Revolution of 1979, given this provocative post-Cold War geopolitical twist by the Huntington warnings about the challenge to Western interests and values posed by a resurgent Islam. Aside from this central preoccupation with an incipient encounter between Islam and the West, there was a growing awareness that religion throughout the world was an emergent political force increasingly challenging the complacent assumptions of secular politics that science, technology, and rationality had permanently superseded religion in the modern world, at least in the public sphere of governmental behavior. This reassertion of religion as a renewed and vital dimension of political and moral life became part of the national background that helps explain the mindless rush to war by the United States immediately after 9/11, as well as the reliance on a religiously resonant description of the conflict as a struggle between 'good' and 'evil'. Both the United States and al Qaeda shared this polarized view of their adversary, ruling out compromise and concession, and making the elimination of the other the only acceptable solution. In this sense, as Tariq Ali and others argued, 9/11 and its aftermath should be regarded as a 'clash of fundamentalisms', reworking Huntington's theme from the orientation of extremism and sameness rather than as a manifestation of civilizational identity and difference.

Why 9/11 was a revolutionary event

The 9/11 attacks on the World Trade Center and the Pentagon, the prime architectural icons of American ascendancy in the domains of market and war making, were a criminal instance of mega-terrorism from the perspective of the states system, but a new type of just war given the outlook of the attackers. These attacks exhibited the expanding ambition, ingenuity, and capabilities of extremist anti-system, non-state actors and exposed American vulnerability to severe symbolic and substantive harm. The most militarily powerful sovereign state on the face of the earth could no longer ever again feel secure against the possibility of a devastating terrorist strike carried out within its own borders, but organized and arranged from anywhere on the planet. It seemed that the military capabilities of the modern state were of little use in responding to the source of such attacks, although this acknowledgement continues to be resisted and denied by many governments and their advisors, and most definitely by a United States that keeps upping its effort to construct the most massive, versatile, and dominant global military machine in all of human history. The perspective of 9/12, that is, the response to the attacks, is a poignant demonstration of the failure of a military approach conceived along statist lines to address effectively security threats posed by hostile and aggressive non-state political actors.

9/11 should have prompted an immediate rethinking of the nature of power in political conflicts taking place in the contemporary world. Such rethinking would be preoccupied with the relevance of the rising capabilities of low technology tactics as accentuated by the declining effectiveness of high technology weaponry in providing defensive security for territorial political entities. This new relation of forces did prompt a search for an appropriate military approach to the 9/11 type of adversary and its reliance on tactics designed to exploit the soft underbelly of the modern state. War planners and military strategists concentrated their efforts on what they called 'asymmetric warfare', that is, warfare between states and non-state actors in which the tactics and capabilities of the two sides are dramatically different in their nature and style of fighting. The choice of terminology was to point up the differences with prior forms of *international* warfare that were 'symmetrical' in the defining sense of being between territorial sovereign states. Of course, many *internal* wars in the course of modern history were inherently asymmetrical to varying degrees, pitting armed movements of discontented citizens against the militarized and policing capabilities of the state. Such encounters were recently dramatically relied upon to achieve unimagined successes in contesting the dictatorial structures of rule in several Arab countries. The cases of Tunisia and Egypt are the clearest instances, with Libya being the most clouded example as the overthrow of the Qaddafi regime depended on NATO's intervention, a classic use of military power by an alliance of states.

It is worth observing that no foreign state could have survived a retaliatory attack if it had inflicted comparable harm on the United States to that achieved by al Qaeda on 9/11. The response to a state carrying out such a surprise attack would have been instant and overwhelming. In contrast, this non-territorial terrorist network with its hidden presence in dozens of countries seemed invulnerable to normal retaliatory responses. This made al Qaeda a formidable and illusive adversary that shook the statist foundations of a structure of world order that had been stably sustained for several centuries on the basis of the relative autonomy of sovereign states. After 9/11, even the most powerful of states had to address its own realization of a vulnerability that military capabilities could never overcome, and at the same time come to the disturbing realization that the non-state opponent could not be destroyed by traditional war making. Military capabilities of governments were also unable to offset statist vulnerability nor allay the accompanying rise of acute societal feelings of outrage, fear, and frustration that caused insecurity at home. This combination of effects is what made 9/11 seem revolutionary, especially this first impression that military power was of little use against such an enemy and that restoring confidence of the citizenry in the ability of the government to provide internal security was a daunting challenge, especially considering that protecting all the soft targets in a large complex state is impossible even if the structure of civil democracy was to give way to authoritarian rule. Even the effort to protect society from future attacks after 9/11 has led to a disturbing series of legalized encroachments on the liberty of the citizen in the United States, which have brought particular strains and hardships to the Muslim minority living in the country, and inconveniences and uncertainties into the lives of all citizens.

What was done in response to 9/11 by the neoconservative leadership provided by the presidency of George W. Bush unleashed two distinct intersecting redirections of foreign policy that must both be taken into account to avoid confusion: first, there was featured a reflexive reliance on conventional war making despite the non-state adversary, which meant in practice treating the governing regimes in Afghanistan and later in Iraq as if responsible for 9/11; and second, taking advantage of the belligerent mood in America after the attacks to activate a pre-existing, yet until 9/11 politically dormant, neoconservative grand strategy that was formed without concern about international terrorism, and was mainly intent on aggressively projecting US military force to reconfigure the political landscape of the Middle East with several traditional statist objectives in mind: satisfying Israeli regional priorities and countering their worries; gaining secure control over Gulf oil reserves by establishing military bases in nearby Iraq additional to those that already existed in the region, and countering anxieties about the proliferation of nuclear weapons within the Middle East, especially regarding Iran.

The first set of influences led to the still unresolved Afghanistan War, while the second generated the Iraq War that is undergoing a bloody epilogue after the occupying American forces had claimed that the objective of a stable political order in Iraq based on human rights had been finally achieved. The Afghanistan War seemed initially responsive to future security threats raised by the 9/11 attacks, considering the large al Qaeda presence in the country, while the Iraq War from its outset seemed a war of choice undertaken for essentially non-defensive and imperial goals that used the enveloping patriotic belligerent mood in the United States to build support for an aggressive war that had nothing to do with the dangers posed by al Qaeda. The American and British leading proponents of the Iraq War invoked the global counter-terrorist rationale, reinforced by the false contention that Iraq possessed an arsenal of weapons of mass destruction (WMD), to drum up international support for the approval of a preventive war at the UN and elsewhere. Validating this war by seeking UN authorization seemed mainly motivated by an effort to counter the robust worldwide grassroots opposition to what was widely being denounced by civil society forces around the world as a planned criminal recourse to aggressive war by an unlawful 'coalition of the willing'. The February 15, 2003 anti-war protest demonstrations held in eighty countries unsuccessfully sought to head off the Iraq War some weeks before it was actually launched. These protests were the largest and most global of peace efforts in all of human history. The magnitude and globality of the demonstrations created the fleeting impression of a new global populism that was mounting a strong challenge to the established order, what might be called a democratizing force, expressive of 'globalization-from-below' as an emergent peace and justice transnational move- ment potentially capable of countering the corporatist priorities and militarist ten- dencies of globalization-from-above (market forces plus leading states). The *New York Times* referred at the time to this civil society activism as 'the second super- power', but this assessment proved to be journalistic hyperbole, as this challenge from below quickly dissipated, and has not been reasserted, except fleetingly in the Occupy Movement of 2011. It is relevant conceptually to note that globalization- from-below is another way of undermining the credibility and questioning the competence and legitimacy of the states system of world order.

This suspect interaction between recourse to allegedly defensive wars and the pursuit of imperial foreign policy goals has contributed to a widespread distrust of the official version of the nature of the 9/11 attacks, a lingering deep suspicion among large sectors of the public shared by some former government officials, which put forward the startling claim that this spectacular terrorist assault on the United States was either pre-arranged in some way or allowed to happen by those in authority. There were other causes of this atmosphere of societal suspicion and anti-government radicalism that has led defenders of the established order to adopt a posture of extreme defensiveness. Anyone daring to question the official account of 9/11, for instance, is immediately branded as 'a conspiracy theorist' without making an accompanying attempt to provide convincing answers to the now considerable body of evidence advanced by the 9/11 doubters.

Added to the re-securitization of American foreign policy since 2001 on a global scale, there has been added uncertainty and this aura of illegitimacy surrounding the governing process in the United States, which has eroded its ability to provide global leadership that is generally regarded as benevolent. Such distrust has been reinforced strongly by totally independent developments within the United States. The outsourcing of American manufacturing to take advantage of cheap and skilled labor and low regulatory standards in the global South has generated populist anger toward Washington, further intensified by the wrenching experience of rising unemployment and home foreclosures which was brought to an alarming climax by the financial meltdown in 2008 and its seemingly endless aftermath of deep and continuing recession. The economic policies pursued in response to the meltdown by the American government were widely criticized for soliciting the guidance of the same neoliberal economic advisors who were instrumental in encouraging the bubble that burst. Their guidance to the Bush and Obama presidencies seemed only responsive to the worries of the rich ('too big to fail') while refusing to insist upon help for the poor and most vulnerable people suffering daily throughout America ('too small to save'). Huge bailout subsidies were given to leading banks and insurance companies that quickly recovered their profitability while letting market chips fall where they may when it came to jobs and home foreclosures. What has ensued, spurred by technological innovation substituting capital for labor, has vindicated the views of Joseph Schumpeter, the Austrian economist, that capitalism regularly overcomes its recurrent crises by processes of 'creative destruction', leaving behind a path littered with ruined lives and livelihoods so that economic masterminds could proceed to the next phase of wealth creation and capital accumulation. So far the destruction has been evident, but not yet the creative side of how Schumpeter envisioned the process of correction endemic to capitalist enterprise.

This pattern of societal distress stemming from hostility to government in the United States has given rise to another unexpected trend − the rise of the radical right as a formidable mainstream cultural and political influence. The evangelical Christian churches and the Tea Party have been the main organizational expressions of this shift to the right. The ideological center of gravity here projects extremist rhetoric and recommendations that constitute a new and serious presence in the American public order. It possesses a composite identity that tends to be ardently anti-government and pro-military, a political identity that seems best described as 'libertarian militarism', although there are some participants in these new political formations who are anti-government and anti-militarist, emphasizing the imperative of fiscal downsizing above all else, with an impassioned distaste for all forms of taxation. This movement has a unifying social agenda of hostility to such traditional liberal policies as support for immigrant rights, public education, progressive taxation, and welfare programs. This is the militant ideological background that lends unwavering support for years to failed wars, although also giving a new visibility to anti-intervention isolationist convictions. Overall, this new religious and libertarian politics is generating a shrill and demoralizing national debate in the United States that seems more animated by calls to prayer and patriotic excess rather than by ideas, national ideals, and problem-solving. As such, a decade after 9/11 there seems to be a populist current of influential opinion in the United States that refuses to heed a series of basic challenges to the future security of the country and the world, and instead gives a measure of respectability to Islamophobic diversionary explanations of national distress and global turmoil.

This observation is most dramatically illustrated in relation to climate change. As of 2007 when the respected Intergovernmental Panel on Climate Change issued its authoritative report on the dangers, there has existed a consensus among climate scientists that the world must reduce greenhouse gas emissions quickly and significantly or suffer a series of devastating adverse effects. The longer the delay in response, the more costly and painful the adjustment costs. Arguably, sub-Saharan African droughts and famines, as in Darfur and Somalia, as well as the alarming frequency of extreme weather events throughout the entire world, reflect the present impact of global warming. Such a conclusion cannot be conclusively demonstrated, as almost all forms of environmental deterioration have multiple causal explanations and are over-determined. This makes connecting the dots joining climate change to environmental problems a controversial conjecture rather than the outcome of a scientific proof. In light of this, climate change policy, while enjoying the support of a scientific consensus, is also subject to cynical refutation by those with a vested interest in resisting the evidence. This confuses the public and, especially in times of economic decline, makes it difficult to induce politicians to act responsibly, and so greenhouse gas emissions continue to accumulate beyond safe levels, and the process of their reduction grows ever more expensive and even questionable. The world has responded to the warnings of the scientific community and environmental activists with some gestures of concern, which although insufficient at least acknowledge the gravity of the challenge. These efforts include the Kyoto Protocol of 1997, but the United States and some other important countries have been unwilling to go along with even these minimal adjustments, much less consider commitments that involve a carbon tax or serious encroachments on current industrial practices causing carbon emissions. My contention here is that 9/11 dysfunctionally diverted public attention from addressing urgent challenges to human wellbeing, including this strengthening of religious politics that is skeptical of both scientific claims of knowledge and any initiative that calls for government spending and bureaucratic oversight.

These rightest political trends in America are further abetted as a result of the anxieties generated by the recession, inhibiting politicians from taking responsible, knowledge-based positions with respect to environmental regulation, as well as to a host of other issues involving the material fundamentals of modern societal wellbeing. The UN attempt at Copenhagen in 2009 to fashion a global regulatory framework that was seriously responsive to the climate change consensus was stymied by the refusal of the United States, more or less backed by China and India, to accept any commitments that would interfere with corporate profitability and industrial development. Although the UN continues to hold annual conferences dedicated to meeting the challenges associated with climate change, there is absent the political will on the part of leading governments that would be needed to move beyond the rather hollow rhetoric of concern in the direction of a regulatory framework designed to draw down greenhouse gas emissions to prudent levels. It is notable that any public figure who expresses worries about climate change is likely to encounter an irresponsible firestorm of vindictive reaction from 'climate skeptics' on the payroll of oil and gas companies. Tea Party militants, such as Michelle Bachmann, who view the climate change movement as nothing other than an excuse for government spending, seem to be gaining the upper hand in the national debate, reducing those who advocate steps to reduce greenhouse gas emissions to silence or consigning them to the outer margins of political activism.

Such a political atmosphere prevents the US government from pursuing a responsible approach to climate change, and such related issues as transitioning to a post-petroleum economy and dealing with fragile technologies in the energy area that seek to make commercial use of more remote sources of oil and gas as well as to foster reliance on greater use of coal and nuclear power. Both offshore oil drilling and nuclear power have recently disclosed their susceptibility to catastrophic accidents: the Deep Horizon British Petroleum (BP) explosion and oil spill in the Gulf of Mexico and the Toyko Electric Power Company (TEPCO) nuclear meltdown at the Fukushima Daiichi reactor complex as a consequence of the March 2001 earthquake and tsunami in northern Japan. Neither event has prompted adaptive changes in government policy, but instead have led to renewed endorsements from both public and private sector leaders to the effect that these technologies are necessary for energy security and the servicing of consumer demand around the world, including even Japan. Efforts to restore confidence in these risky technologies is usually reinforced by vague pledges to improve safety measures that are intended to reassure the public about the future.

Contextualizing 9/11 in the transformations and challenges of the last two decades helps us evaluate the complex fabric of success and failure generated by the attacks and responses. The main contention of the following two sections is that both al Qaeda and the United States experienced a mixture of successes and failures in relation to their opposed objectives in regard to 9/11, and in the course of fashioning and implementing a response (9/12).

Why al Qaeda failed

The issue of success and failure associated with any appraisal of the 9/11 attacks is filled with ambiguity. If George W. Bush was correct that the objective of the attacks was to change the American political system because 'they hate our freedom', then ironically the attacks must be considered an extraordinary success. America fearful of its newly appreciated vulnerability strained every institutional muscle to deter future hijackers and extremists, subjecting air travelers to increasingly invasive and burdensome searches that threaten privacy and erode dignity. Beyond this, the legislative authority given to the government by way of the omnibus Patriot Act and Homeland Security apparatus has created vast authority to engage in surveillance of ordinary citizens and to treat everyone in the society as a potential terrorist on the basis of mere suspicion, often fueled by nothing other than ethnic and racial profiling. This set of responses to 9/11 disclosed the fragility of democratic freedoms in the United States, which are likely to be much further eroded if subsequent attacks of comparable magnitude ever occur. The slide toward fascism has started in the United States, and is hastened by corporate interests and media manipulation, and if a new security pretext arises due to mega-terrorist incidents, the political survival of democracy will be very much in doubt.

However, this domestic scenario associated with authoritarian responses to mega-terror seems remote from the actual goals of al Qaeda. Their stated goals, which seem genuine, were to challenge the American physical presence and influence in the Islamic world, especially in proximity to religious sites sacred to Muslims, to mount their own Islamic challenges directed at oppressive secular and monarchical regimes throughout the region, particularly in the Arab world, and to inspire an Islamic oriented worldwide renaissance and re-establishment of a Muslim caliphate. It could be claimed that the Arab Spring, with its likely effect of giving an enlarged political role to Islam and Islamic political parties in countries such as Egypt and Tunisia, is in line with the al-Qaeda political program. But there is scant indication at this time that the political uprisings seek to displace the American presence in the region in any dramatic way, but rather aim to release their populations from the bondage of oppressive rule and create national conditions for a fairer and more productive economy that provides opportunity and hope. There is little evidence that the youth leaders of these uprisings were being responsive to the messages of the inspirational voice of the now slain Osama Bin Laden. In fact, the regimes most resistant to the recent wave of popular uprisings have been the Arab monarchies that have withstood political challenges up to this point. In fact, the two most contested situations have arisen in Libya and Syria where the beleaguered leaders have opportunistically blamed the anti-regime uprisings on Islamists as well as outside forces, not due to evidence of their participation in these political events, but to build national support from within and weaken interventionary pressures from without.

Additionally, the operations of al Qaeda have been severely curtailed by the non-war spectrum of responses by the United States and its allies. In other words, not only did the nineteen attackers on 9/11 die in their suicide mission, but the central organizational leadership of al Qaeda has been decimated, highlighted by the execution of Osama Bin Laden in his Pakistan hideout by a team of Navy Seals striking their decisive blow on May 31, 2011. But even before this the global hunt for al Qaeda's inner circle of operatives had required senior al Qaeda figures to run and to hide, curtailing their capacity to mount major terrorist events. This decline was not attributable to the military capabilities of the United States, although the drone attacks across the Pakistani border, as well as Special Forces operations worldwide, were part of what might be described as the global law paramilitary enforcement campaign launched by the US government in response to the 9/11 attacks. This campaign ran roughshod over Westphalian notions of territorial sovereignty, but it was effective in inflicting major losses on the al Qaeda network in a whole series of countries.

Whether al Qaeda can build on recent waves of anti-American resentment to reconstitute itself remains to be seen. What does appear to be the case is that American police and paramilitary capabilities unleashed by 9/11, acting in collaboration with other governments throughout the world, have achieved near victory in relation to the al Qaeda threat. This strengthens the conclusion reached for other reasons that from al Qaeda's perspective the attacks of 9/11 were a critical mistake that has weakened the organization, substantially discrediting its tactics, strategy, and above all, severely diminishing the appeal of its ideology and tactics to Muslims around the world. What is striking about this depiction of al Qaeda's failure is that it occurred despite the fact that the United States' 9/12 response was also a failure, decisively weakening, demoralizing, and discrediting the American global role, as well as releasing regressive political trends within the United States.

The flawed logic of 9/12

The 9/11 attacks, while inflicting extraordinary damage without relying on the extensive sacrifice of blood or treasure of al Qaeda's militant cadres, did not succeed in attaining their objectives, but neither did the American response. Just as al Qaeda miscalculated, so did Washington, failing to adapt sufficiently to the specificities of this mega-terrorist incident. Instead of de-emphasizing the role of international war making despite its extraordinary range of capabilities for waging war anywhere on the planet, the United States subsumed its response under the belligerent heading of the 'global war on terror', and actualized it by launching two major wars. These wars in Afghanistan and Iraq were draining of resources and were reminders that reliance on a war machine to restructure the political life of a non-Western country is rarely successful in this period of history, especially if the foreign intervention generates a robust movement of national resistance. Instead of bringing crushing victories, these wars reached such inconclusive outcomes as to be mainly important as demonstrations of the limits of conventional military superiority. This central feature of the 9/12 day-after approach taken by the United States partly reflected a failure of political understanding, and partly exhibited the pre-existing imperial motivations that pushed toward war for reasons other than counter-terrorism.

The United States missed a great opportunity to transform a difficult and tragic experience into a constructive occasion for an altered approach to global security. In the past, terrorist challenges to state power had always been treated as essentially law enforcement issues unless acquiring a capacity to undermine the stability of the state. Extending police powers and the rule of law globally, with the collaboration of governments around the world and international institutions, would have achieved a restoration of American security at a fraction of the human and political cost, avoided most of the unfortunate and hysterical authoritarian measures internally and recourse to discrediting practices of torture internationally, and generated confidence that even mega-terrorist challenges could be met without undermining the legitimacy of the state or challenging the basic framework of world order premised on a legal commitment to respect territorial sovereignty.

Perhaps, even more important than getting the nature of the threat correctly understood, there was the possibility of correcting American responsibility for some of the hostility in the Islamic world that lent an initial measure of credibility, and even popularity, to this violent pushback by Muslim extremism. There were several grievances widely felt by Arab public opinion in relation to the American role in their region: the US maintenance of a cruel blockade of Iraq during the 1990s was believed throughout the Middle East to be responsible for several hundred thousand Iraqi civilian deaths; and America's unconditional military and diplomatic support for Israel imposed an oppressive colonial/apartheid reality on the Palestinian people. These American policies qualify as legitimate grievances that help explain the intense anti-American sentiments (directed at the US government, and not the American people) that were present throughout the non-Western world, but particularly in the Middle East. Beyond this, as the Arab Spring made clear, the United States had for decades lent strong economic and diplomatic support to authoritarian regimes throughout the region that served its strategic interests, despite the degree to which such leaders were criminally abusing their own populations.

If it had been able to engage in self-criticism and taken corrective measures, the United States might have turned a new page in world history, but it possessed a political culture and leadership that seemed even unaware of alternative strategies of response, much less able to contemplate advocating such an unfamiliar course of action to restore American security after 9/11.

In contrast, the Israeli model exerted a powerful influence on American public opinion after 9/11, and was uncritically accepted as an effective way to respond to terrorist challenges. It is true that Israel in addressing Palestinian resistance used its military machine to inflict disproportionate losses, and to sustain decades of occupation in the face of a restive and hostile Palestinian population. But this approach, by reliance on conventional military power, was confined to a fixed territorial site of struggle, although spilling over these boundaries from time to time. Its imitation seemed to dismiss the European counter-terror model of response relying on enhanced law enforcement, and it was unconcerned about the degree to which the Israeli approach was defiant of international humanitarian law and basic human rights standards, which partly accounts for the growth of an anti-Israeli global public opinion.

There were also tactical difficulties associated with an imitation of the Israeli approach to its Palestinian adversaries. Unlike the Palestinians, al Qaeda had no real territorial presence once it was forced out of its Afghan bases, and thus applying the Israeli model, which itself has not been successful in stamping out Palestinian resistance despite military superiority, was highly inappropriate. The Israeli presence in occupied Palestine has relied on the tactics of state terror to maintain control, which has undermined over time the legitimacy of its policy, leading to a growing global solidarity movement supportive of the Palestinian struggle for self-determination. The American relationship to Iraq and Afghanistan is more marginal, and now seems on the brink of accepting defeat by way of withdrawal as being its best option. As has been suggested, the only winner of the Iraq War has been Iran, which is precisely the opposite of what was intended by the intervention. In Afghanistan, as well, it appears that the political future of the country in all probability belongs to the Taliban, and the regional winner seems likely to be extremist elements in Pakistan, but again the best available option for the United States is a rapid withdrawal signaling an acceptance of political defeat.

It is not convincing to attribute the American-initiated global recession altogether on the misplaying of the 9/12 response, but there are certain reasons to notice some connections. The imperial goals of the Iraq War, as suggested, contributed to a weakening of the dollar and exerted a further strain on America's precarious world financial role. Additionally, the hyper-capitalist mood that prevailed in Washington intensified political alienation that was being caused in any event by the dynamics of capital-driven globalization, and led to intense backlash politics at home and abroad. The 9/12 super-patriotic mood in America dominated the political discourse and imagination, diverting attention from the need to take major regulatory steps to fix market operations in housing and banks, and hastened the drift toward a recession that has yet to have a discernable end point, with some fearing that it may yet take a further nosedive into the dreaded domain of worldwide depression.

Drawing conclusions today

On the basis of the above analysis, several conclusions emerge:

- Al Qaeda on 9/11 and the United States on 9/12 both embarked on policies that produced major defeats for themselves in relation to their expressed goals and values over the course of the decade following 9/11.
- Despite the unprecedented scale of the 9/11 attacks, the most functional response would have involved primary reliance on improved transnational law enforcement, police and intelligence collaboration, and attentiveness to legitimate grievances in the Islamic world vis-à-vis the West, especially the achieving of a just, peaceful and sustainable resolution for the Israel–Palestine conflict.
- The effort to shape the response to 9/11 within a template of asymmetric war, including reliance on what was earlier known as counterinsurgency war, over-looked the central lessons of the Vietnam War, and the extreme opposition to military intervention under Western auspices in the non-West.
- Extremist politics have demonstrated the vulnerabilities of modern technological societies organized around the principles of human rights and political freedom, but so far there has also been demonstrated the resilience of societies to address such threats without losing their political composure; the 9/11 attacks did undermine substantially American political composure, partly because of the shock effect of the vulnerability suddenly exposed, but also because the political leadership made pragmatic use of the fear and anger produced by the attacks to mobilize strong popular support for its imperial agenda, an agenda that had previously lacked a sufficient political mandate in American domestic public opinion.
- The apparent invulnerability of al Qaeda because of its lack of a territorial identity is superficial, as it is vulnerable to a variety of suppressive responses that have weakened the appeal of extremist violent approaches; this weakening was evident in the reliance of all anti-regime movements during the Arab Spring on moderate political programs of change that emphasized inclusiveness, human rights, self-determination, economic reform, and a secular constitutional order.

8

THE PROMISE AND PERILS OF GLOBAL DEMOCRACY[1]

Why global democracy now?

Reading the recent literature on global democracy fills me with admiration for the conceptual and social science rigor, conceptual clarity and sophistication of much of this work, for its illuminating depictions of several ways to frame global democracy as goal, process, and vision, and finally, for the attention given to transition pathways seeking to bridge the gap between global governance as of 2011 and some realization of global democracy at an undetermined, and undeterminable future date. As such, scholarly endeavors relating to global democracy are crafting a superb intellectual tool with which to study present and future international relations from a normative standpoint specified by these shared preoccupations with global democracy. This is a notable pedagogic achievement as it lays claim to an alternative paradigm for study and research that is not completely state-centric, and yet at the same time cannot be dismissed as utopian or mere advocacy. In this respect, the orientation of this global democracy scholarly performance can be described as proceeding from a post-Westphalian consensus that is fully sensitive to the resilience of sovereign states, and to their continuing prominence in almost any achievable global democratic polity.

As reader and sympathizer, I believe there is a significant, and likely illuminating, issue present that does not seem to have been raised clearly in this literature: why has this interest in global democracy flourished now in the early twenty-first century, and rarely earlier except in the marginal literature of utopian critics of a politically fragmented world order that built security and national interests on the foundations of an ever more menacing and expensive war system? World federalists, dreamers and proponents of world government, were the most notable antecedents to the less structurally and constitutionally driven models of global democracy. Unlike the recent writing on global democracy, world federalists were typically amateurs with regard to social science, and almost totally Western in outlook and prescription. Quite often world federalists were unabashedly seeking a world order that generalized the supposedly exemplary American experience with domestic federalism, relying for persuasion on an argumentative logic that was unduly confident about the mobilizing potential of common sense and rationality. It seems only slightly unfair to characterize such advocacy as a legacy of the Enlightenment, culturally provincial and lacking in mass appeal – even in the West – and indifferent to the political obstacles that beset any path from the 'here' of war and sovereign states to the promised land of 'there'.

Let me venture a hypothesis: earlier surges of global reformism were essentially post-war phenomena in relation to the two great wars of the twentieth century. World War I struck many as the death knell of a balance of power world, causing many millions of deaths for no discernible worthwhile human end and prompting Woodrow Wilson and others to insist on finding an institutional arrangement that would put an end to war. The League of Nations was posited as the means to such an end. It turned out to be too much for a state-centric world that was unwilling to participate in such a scheme, with even the United States awkwardly refusing to join the organization that its wartime president had so ardently promoted as the best way to overcome the curse of war and militarism. Contrariwise, the League blueprint was too little for those who believed only a genuine world government could tame the militarist tendencies of sovereign states and a subculture of arms merchants. As we know, the League failed miserably when it came to coping with the re-emergence of war and conquest, and the world drifted toward a disastrous Second World War.

Unlike World War I, World War II seemed to most as if both necessary and desirable, defeating fascism and aggression, and even holding the surviving leaders of defeated Germany and Japan accountable as war criminals. Yet future war avoidance was nevertheless very much part of the political consciousness after 1945, especially catalyzed by the atomic attacks on Hiroshima and Nagasaki, and the resulting widespread belief that a third world war would destroy modern civilization, perhaps permanently. Major warfare had to be prevented for the sake of the powerful as much as for the benefit of the weak. Two elements of this outcome are relevant to the normative narrative of global democracy that lends coherence to this pattern of advocacy. The first was the renewal of the impulse to institutionalize peace and security, giving rise to the United Nations, which also was constituted in such a way as to also be related to sustaining economic stability through the establishment of the so-called Bretton Woods institutions (the World Bank and the International Monetary Fund, with a much later institutionally independent extension to trade, the World Trade Organization). Second, and most relevantly, was the implanting of constitutional democracy in each of the defeated countries with the objective of building stable, moderate, and economically robust political actors on the ashes of Nazi Germany, fascist Italy, and imperial Japan. In most respects, the UN failed, at least if envisioned as the transformative force implied by the preamble to the Charter, which grandiosely promised 'to save succeeding generations from the scourge of war'. To the extent a third world war was avoided, it was mainly a result of old fashioned geopolitics combining prudence, countervailing power, and some good fortune. It was given the new name of 'mutual deterrence' so as to seem responsive to the radical impact on world politics of nuclear weaponry.

Here again the post-war efforts at global reform had a complex relationship to a state-centric world order. The UN was in many respects a child of the Westphalian understanding of global society as constituted by sovereign states, and managed by those states that were dominant in 1945. The importance of granting the victorious powers in World War II a right of veto in the Security Council was a dramatic recognition that the repudiation of aggressive force, the core commitment embedded in the Charter, was not meant to override or do away with the discretionary authority of geopolitical actors to use force and wage wars. In this sense, the primacy of geopolitics was reasserted in the Charter itself, and the danger of nuclear war was either repressed or supposedly managed via the rationality of deterrence, and in this respect, a militarist component of the Enlightenment legacy that was over-confident about the guidance capabilities of instrumental rationality. These five states with a veto power (and their friends) were given a constitutional exemption from the discipline supposedly being imposed on the system as a whole. In the lead-up to the 2003 Iraq War, George W. Bush pushed this geopolitical logic so far in 2003 as to claim that the UN would itself lose relevance if it withheld support from the United States in the latter's unshakeable resolve to wage aggressive war against Iraq. As we know, the US government went ahead, with its flimsy coalition of the willing, and the UN failed to condemn the attack, much less organize collective action in support of Iraq's right of self-defense, and seemed ready to pick up the pieces by cooperating with the occupation of the country as soon as the battlefield phase of the war ended.

But the other reformist undertaking, implanting democracy to achieve a *restorative* peace, had a much more enduring effect that seems also relevant to the growing interest in and support for global democracy.[2] The extraordinarily impressive economic recovery of Germany and Japan fostered the belief that there was a correlation between democracy and sovereignty. Also relevant was the idea that fostering a tradition of *international* human rights was important to discourage the sort of failure by the liberal democracies to do more than they did to oppose the genocidal policies of Nazi Germany. A consensus gradually took shape throughout the world with respect to governance on the domestic level that presupposed both adherence to democracy and respect for human rights. Governments felt obliged to give lip service, at least, to these twin normative pillars, regardless of the often anti-democratic and oppressive patterns of existential governance that persist to varying degrees in all parts of the world. I would argue that 'democracy' became the only legitimate form of governance toward the end of the twentieth century, especially after the fall of the Berlin Wall in 1989, which was quickly followed by the collapse of the Soviet Union. It is also significant that all the successor states to the Soviet Union opted for constitutional democracy, nominally at least, and for the free market, although here too there were regressions and deviations in practice. What emerged from the Cold War outcome was this fusion of democracy and capitalism, openly espoused by such phrases as 'market-oriented constitutionalism' used to identify the only acceptable form of governance.[3] Arguably, as the experience of China during recent decades dramatically underscores, if capitalist economic policies are adopted with respect to trade and investment, the constitutional demands for human rights either disappear altogether or are mostly muted. Another quite different example of this dynamic is Saudi Arabia, which makes no pretensions of democracy, and yet finds its legitimacy as a governing process rarely drawn into question. That is, democracy is rhetorically to be preferred, even demanded, but what seems alone indispensable for political acceptability on the global stage is adherence to neoliberal policies and behavior.[4] It is this economistic shading given to world politics after the Cold War that casts something of a shadow across the ideological triumphalism associated with the privileging of democracy as the only legitimate governing process for a sovereign state. Some scholarly attention was paid to 'democratic peace' theorizing that crudely informed American foreign policy after the 9/11 attacks, underpinning the claim that enlarging the international sphere of democratic governance at the level of the state would correspondingly and automatically extend the international domain of peace.

Despite this enthusiasm for democracy as the basis for economic and political viability of states, there was surprisingly little spillover with respect to world politics. The most liberal of democracies were quite comfortable with the lack of popular participation, transparency, accountability, even the rule of law, when it came to the procedures and decisions of international institutions. In this regard, operative diplomacy never extended democratic values to global arenas of policymaking and contestation. When civil society actors began to attend global policy conferences under UN auspices in large numbers during the 1990s it generally alarmed most democratic states, and especially the important ones. In recent years, such events have been either not held, or if organized, have been sharply criticized or boycotted, as was the fate of the UN conferences on racism held in South Africa. If democracy globally means in part participation from below, more inclusive forms of representation of social forces, greater accountability by those that carry out policy, and increased transparency in the operation of international institutions, then most 'democratic states' are not behaviorally sympathetic to the claims of 'global democracy' no matter what their leaders might say on ritual occasions about the reform of the UN and the Bretton Woods institutions.

Yet, such an assessment does not answer the question posed at the outset, namely, why now is there emerging a serious social science interest in global democracy as a desirable future for world politics? I believe there are three kinds of explanation, each of which could be explored at length, but will only be briefly mentioned here. The first line of explanation has to do with an effort to rediscover a coherent and historically relevant framework for progressive politics, here conceived as dedication to human betterment by actual design rather than by reliance on the automaticity of market forces ('the invisible hand' and the like).[5] Global democracy presents itself as an attractive normative project in the form of a post-Marxist engagement with the classless achievement of a more just social and political order.

The second line of explanation overlaps with the first, but it involves an insistence on *political* agency, and a repudiation of a purely economistic approach to change, reform, and revolution. A central, rarely expressed motive seems to be to disentangle politics from its Marxist and neoliberal immersions that always depict political economy scenarios as the inevitable wave of the future. More vocationally, the motive may also be to reclaim some of the policy-relevant ground from economists who have been so influential in the formation of national policy for the last half century.

The third, and possibly decisive line of explanation, is the political recognition that globalization is generating a need for global authority structures and norms to facilitate effective responses to global-scale challenges such as weaponry of mass destruction, global warming, and world poverty. If these structures are not democratically constituted, then either hegemonic/imperial solutions will be forthcoming, doing severe damage to overall human wellbeing, or a dysfunctional chaos will ensue, also causing devastation and massive suffering. In effect, such reasoning insists that global steering mechanisms are increasingly needed, and it seems preferable that these should be shaped by democratic values and procedures.

My intention is not to insist that there is only one acceptable form of global democracy, and its study and advocacy. There are many diversities in style, substance, and methods, which is overall a strength in presenting global democracy as a rich body of evolving thought that is becoming more nuanced through reliance on empirical observation and a willingness to construct a variety of abstract models of global governance.

Should we privilege global democracy?

In conceiving of a just world order, should we presuppose that it is essential that some form of global democracy must be realized, or do other modes of political belief deserve serious attention from the perspective of global reform? It would be valuable to encounter such inquiries, including a discussion evincing more sensitivity to civilizational and ethical diversity, and either championing the exclusive consideration of global democracy or opting for a wider range of normatively desirable world order solutions.

The recent advocacy of global democracy is sensitive, perhaps over-sensitive, to the perils of global political centralization, even if constitutionally based on separation of powers and maximal decentralization of authority and capabilities. But sensitive or not, there seem to be serious dangers that any realization of global democracy in the near future would fall captive to either world capitalist machinations or to schemes for global empire once power and authority are centralized so as to achieve globally beneficial results. In effect, even if global democracy might be accepted as the most desirable basis of world order, it could be still too vulnerable to appropriation by anti-democratic and exploitative forces to be favored by the risk averse. The same concern arises with respect to regionalism, but less insistently, as it is not based on the organization of the whole. A regional form of world order remains pluralist even if the parts are larger, and likely stronger, and probably provides greater opportunity for political embodiments of 'regional democracy' to give more expression to distinctive regional values, traditions, and priorities.[6]

It is important not to introduce the difficulties associated with democratic states into the consideration of global democracy. At the same time, it seems likely that any foreseeable pathway to global democracy would involve the passive or active participation of leading states, and especially the United States. There are claims that United States global leadership is already a nascent form of global government that provides other governments and the peoples of the world with many global public goods.[7] I find this sort of political agency for global democracy disquieting within the current configuration of world social forces, as it promotes an excessively militarist version of security and predatory capitalist outlook as beneficial for the development of global policy.

In this respect, might it not be important to explore whether for very large political groupings some other form of political organization might not work better even if its actualization presently seems remote? Let's say a Council of Nobel Peace Prize winners providing a kind of global policy oversight within a political framework that could be regarded as a form of 'moral hegemony' or 'normative oligarchy'.[8] And might not it be worth considering a radical localization of power and authority that, in effect, repudiated the assumptions that central guidance in some form was an unavoidable effect of modern technologies and the apparent ineluctable momentum of increasing fragility, complexity, and interdependence?

There seems to me to be a need to draw into critical question the normative horizoning of global democracy from a variety of perspectives: effectiveness, achievability, acceptability, sustainability, community, citizenship, justice, and nonviolence. Such perspectives must color any assessment of global democracy as purportedly the only desirable political future and amounts to a proposal for future inquiry and research.

In search of history and context: the loneliness of the social scientist

As someone trained in law but teaching for decades in a social science environment of a liberal arts college, I appreciate the prodigious efforts in recent years to establish an empirically grounded and conceptually sophisticated epistemology for the study of issues of global scope. Some recent scholarly work confirms the importance of this enterprise, but it also generates some concerns that touch on what sorts of knowledge are useful to achieve the best possible understanding of world order policy options. There are three sets of issues responsive to these concerns that I wish to raise in the spirit of constructive dialogue.

When talking about 'global democracy' the speculative nexus is embedded in analogic reasoning because such a political set of *global* democratized circumstances has never existed. As such the normative advocacy is inherently speculative, that is, without any experience to learn from, either positively or negatively. Derrida often spoke about 'democracy to come' as a way of expressing the unrealized but realizable potential of democratic political arrangements within sovereign states. Of course, he also implied, without using the terminology of 'global democracy' that aspects of benevolent future democracies would show great respect for international law, and particularly for the stigmatization of crimes against humanity in carrying further the ideas of accountability launched at Nuremberg.[9] It seems to me that when, if ever, the leadership of major states are socialized to the extent of submitting their foreign policy to the discipline of international law and the procedures of the United Nations, a major precondition for transition to global democracy will have been satisfied. In effect, since we cannot speak about the future with experiential authority, it is important to be attentive to antagonistic behavioral patterns on the part of the dominant actors that inform international relations practice, particularly geopolitical actors who continue to insist on relying upon unrestricted self-help as the foundation of their security, including even extending to claiming a unilateral and unregulated option to wage preventive wars.[10] We can have an important discourse on the geopolitics to come, but unless we are sensitive to the geopolitics that persists, there will be a utopian disconnect between advocacy of global democracy and the actuality of global militarism.[11]

A second concern in my view insufficiently addressed in the relevant literature has to do with the particularity of global challenges associated with the presently emergent historical moment. The shape of problems such as climate change, proliferation, possession and possible use of weaponry of mass destruction, and pandemics involving deadly disease are substantive contingencies of such a magnitude as to condition the kind of political futures that seem likely and desirable under an array of quite conceivable happenings. In other words, one plausible array of scenarios for a dramatic political rupture from state centrism would involve a response to a condition of global emergency generated by perceptions of an imminent or existing catastrophe that cannot be managed by traditional mechanisms of crisis management. Would a move toward some variant of global democracy be more or less plausible under such circumstances?

A third concern relates to agency, and the unlikelihood that entrenched national elites would voluntarily cede participatory rights and accept accountability procedures implied by the establishment of global democracy on a foundation of global law and constitutionalism. If this concern is particularized to take into account the role of geopolitical actors, insistent on their rights of veto at the UN and resting security on a logic of non-accountable self-help, the prospect of moving toward global democracy, unless possibly in the altered atmosphere of a post-catastrophe global setting, seems currently inconceivable. The prevailing political consciousness of the publics in major states is still infused with such a deep attachment to what continues misleadingly to be called 'realism', but is much better understood as dysfunctional 'militarism'. This background condition makes any mobilization of civil society on behalf of global democracy difficult to envision at this stage of global history.

The main contention here is that theorizing about global democracy needs also to be rooted in the historical experience of change during the past several centuries and to be explicitly attuned to contextual variables that might provoke ruptures, or put differently, the advent of the unexpected. In essence, social science research on global democracy needs to become more substantive, as well as being attentive to empirical testing, normative hopes, and conceptual alternatives.

A concluding thought

Theorizing at the global level is in its infancy. Until very recently serious political theory in the West almost always was state-centric, and was predominantly preoccupied with internal state/society relations. The global realities surrounding the state were regarded as a realm of acute chaos (Hobbes, Machiavelli) or relative anarchy (Bull and 'the English School'), and not viewed as of great intrinsic interest or relevance. Theorizing about global democracy remains ambiguous about whether it is postulating a rupture with the Westphalian framework (as embodied, for instance, in the UN Charter) or some kind of normative extension by way of institutional innovations (world parliament, global taxing system, compulsory participation in the International Criminal Court and International Court of Justice). That is, global democracy, in theory, could come about incrementally, with a cumulative effect that is dramatic, or it could be the consequence of a constitutional leap of faith at a given moment in time, unlikely as a rational coming to terms with globalization but possibly as a trauma-induced adjustment to an emergency or unmanageable crisis.

No matter how the reflections on the global future are situated, the *idea* of global democracy is rapidly becoming more than a manifestation of utopian imaginaries. Global democracy is staking serious claims as to its relevance for political theorizing about the future. Whether global democracy becomes a *project* to be realized in addition to an *idea* to be delimited is essentially unknowable at present. Whether global democracy should occupy the *entire* horizon of desire for humanity deserves debate and further exploration. And whether the horizon of desire can or should be separated completely from horizons of feasibility (what seems politically attainable at present) and horizons of necessity (what seems necessary to address severe global challenges to security, sustainability, and stability) requires both conceptual clarification and ethical judgment. Beyond serious doubt, what can be said with confidence is that as citizens in the troubled early period of the twenty-first century we need to act, think, and feel globally and normatively, whatever we decide to do locally and personally.

Notes

1 This chapter is a revised adaptation of an essay that originally appeared in D. Archibugi, M. Koenig-Archibugi, and Raffaele Marchetti, eds, *Global Democracy: Normative and Empirical Perspectives*, Cambridge: Cambridge University Press, 2012, 274–84.

2 In contrast, after World War I Germany was subjected to a *punitive* peace by way of obligations to pay reparations to the victorious powers and to renounce any option to rebuild its military capabilities. This approach was widely believed to have contributed significantly to the rise of Hitler in Germany. Also, the related view was that authoritarian governments are more inclined toward war. Significantly, in the ceasefire imposed on a devastated Iraq after the First Gulf War (1991), a regime of harsh sanctions maintained for 12 years was a punitive peace, an approach thought to have been discredited on the basis of the failure attributed to the Versailles Peace Treaty in 1919.

3 Undoubtedly, the high point in this ideological trope came during the Bush presidency, clearly set forth in a kind of manifesto: 'The National Security Policy of the United States of America', Washington, DC: US Government Printing Office, 2002. The first sentence of the covering letter signed by the president was particularly revealing in this regard.

4 Such a position was explicitly advocated in several influential books by Thomas P. M. Barnett. See especially T. Barnett, *The Pentagon's New War Map: War and Peace in the Twenty-first Century*, New York: G. P. Putnam, 2004; T. Barnett, *Blueprint for Action: A Future Worth Creating*, New York: G. P. Putnam, 2005.

5 My own effort to think through this puzzle from an angle different than, although congenial with, global democracy is 'Anarchism without Anarchism: The Search for Progressive Politics in the Early 21st Century', *Millenium – Journal of International Studies* 39, no. 2, 381–98, December 2010.

6 For a well developed argument along these lines, see T. E. Paupp, *The Future of Global Relations: Crumbling Walls, Rising Regions*, New York: Palgrave Macmillan, 2009.

7 This position has been most elaborately, albeit rather uncritically, elaborated by Michael Mandelbaum. See M. Mandelbaum, *The Case for Goliath: How America Acts as the World's Government in the Twenty-first Century*, New York: Public Affairs, 2005; M. Mandelbaum, *Frugal Superpower: America's Global Leadership in a Cash-strapped Era*, New York: Public Affairs, 2010.

8 Although it is important to take account of the important argument of Fredrik Heffermehl, who argues that many recent Nobel Peace Prize awardees do not reflect the values of peace or the vision of Alfred Nobel. See F. Heffermehl, *The Nobel Peace Prize: What Nobel Really Wanted*, Santa Barbara, CA: Praeger, 2010.

9 See G. Borradori, *Philosophy in a Time of Terror: Dialogues with Jürgen Habermas and Jacques Derrida*, Chicago: University of Chicago Press, 2003, 110–24.

10 For perceptive exploration of these issues, see M. W. Doyle, *Striking First: Preemption and Preventive War in International Conflict*, Princeton, NJ: Princeton University Press, 2008.

11 For one attempt to depict a geopolitics to come, see R. A. Falk, 'Renouncing Wars of Choice: Toward a Geopolitics of Nonviolence', in D. R. Griffin, J. B. Cobb Jr., R. A. Falk, and C. Keller, eds, *The American Empire and the Commonwealth of God*, Louisville, KY: Westminster John Knox Press, 2006, 69–85.

9

ILLUSIONS AND METAPHORS OF UN REFORM

Metaphor and the politics of despair

In addressing the General Assembly in 2003 on the urgent need for UN reform, the then secretary-general of the United Nations, Kofi Annan, resorted to a frequently quoted metaphorical trope: 'Excellencies, we have come to a fork in the road. This may be a moment no less decisive than 1945 itself, when the United Nations was founded.' He elaborated on this rhetoric by saying '[n]ow we must decide whether it is possible to continue on the basis agreed upon or whether radical changes are needed'. Annan pointed out in the speech that he had earlier drawn attention

> to the urgent need for the Security Council to regain the confidence of States, and of world public opinion – both by demonstrating its ability to deal effectively with the most difficult issues, and by becoming more broadly representative of the international community as a whole, as well as of the geopolitical realities of today.[1]

To build support for the needed radical changes, that is, to ensure that the right road is chosen at the fork, Annan appointed two panels designed to shape an agenda for the General Assembly's reform summit scheduled for the fall of 2005, the 60th anniversary of the UN. Both groups operated according to a realist calculus that tried to take account of what sorts of changes would be acceptable to a majority of states comprising the membership of the United Nations, and especially the rich and powerful states. A less heralded inquiry was carried out by the Panel of Eminent Persons on UN–Civil Society Relations, chaired by Fernando Henrique Cardoso, the former president of Brazil. Its mandate was narrowly framed to encourage proposals that would give civil society organizations somewhat better access and more efficient opportunities for participation, but in an entirely non-threatening form within the existing pattern of the UN system. The thirty recommendations of the Panel were rather technical and managerial in tone, being mainly bureaucratic in nature, and whether implemented or not, unlikely to alter the basic non-impact and peripheral participation of global civil society in important UN undertakings.[2] No consideration was given, for instance, to the initiative widely favored in civil society to establish a World People's Assembly as a new organ of the UN, parallel to the General Assembly representing states. The self-imposed caution of the Cardoso Panel reflected, I believe, the statist atmosphere that dominates the inner workings of the UN, making it almost impossible to consider seriously any innovation in structure that would dilute its Westphalian character.

A more important initiative than the Cardoso Panel was the High-level Panel on Threats, Challenges and Change that issued a widely discussed report entitled *A More Secure World: Our Shared Responsibility*.[3] In the transmittal letter to the secretary-general, prefacing the report, the panel chair, Anand Panyarachun, observes that

> [o]ur mandate from you precluded any in-depth examination of individual conflicts and we have respected your guidance. But the members of the Panel believe it would be remiss of them if they failed to point out that no amount of systemic changes to the way the United Nations handles both old and new threats to peace and security will enable it to discharge effectively its role under the Charter if efforts are not redoubled to resolve a number of long-standing disputes which continue to fester and to feed the new threats we now face. Foremost among these are the issues of Palestine, Kashmir and the Korean Peninsula.[4]

This passage thinly disguises the double bind contained in the mandate given to the Panel: to address threats to peace in the current global setting, but without treading on toes by discussing specific conflicts. As any inquirer knows, the only way to grasp the general with respect to peace and security issues is by attentiveness to the particular, and this is precisely what is precluded. Hidden here in the bureaucratic jargon of the UN is the decisive obstacle to the sort of UN reform that is, indeed, urgently needed if the Organization is to realize the goals of its most ardent supporters and move in the directions encouraged by the UN Charter, especially as set forth in its visionary Preamble. Otherwise it is not possible, even in the spirit of reflection and advocacy, to consider the most serious existing breaches of peace and security, or even the most serious proximate threats.

Despite these restrictions, the Panel does face some of the new realities of the twenty-first century in ways worthy of discussion, especially on several highly contested issues bearing on the use of force. Three aspects of its approach are illustrative of its image of reform. Each is situated within a realist calculus of reformist feasibility, but despite this sensitivity to restraints, still lacks favorable prospects for implementation because of a failure to take sufficient account of the statist minefield that makes even taking a realist road to reform treacherous. The High-level Panel suggests: (1) broadening the idea of security by noting positively the rising support for the concept of 'human security' and treating issues of disease, poverty, environmental degradation, and transnational organized crime as newly falling within the ambit of security;[5] (2) that the new threats to world order associated either with transnational terrorism or crimes against humanity/genocide can be addressed within the existing Charter framework if the right of self-defense as set forth in Article 51 is 'properly understood and applied'.[6] The reformist element here insists that such an extended view of the use of force in self-defense, including controversial justifications for preemption and intervention in internal affairs, *requires prior* UN Security Council authorization; (3) following the influential recommendation of the Canadian International Commission on State Sovereignty and Intervention, an endorsement of

> the emerging norm that there is a collective international responsibility to protect, exercisable by the Security Council authorizing military intervention as a last resort, in the event of genocide or other large-scale killing, ethnic cleansing or serious violation of international humanitarian law which sovereign Governments have proved powerless or unwilling to prevent.[7]

These proposals tread delicately on a series of tightropes. To begin with, the tightrope that allows the broadening of the idea of security to include threats to human wellbeing while being respectful of the overarching concern with threats to use force against a state mounted by state and non-state actors. Overall, acknowledging geopolitical pressures to engage in preemptive responses based on the *rhetoric* of the post-9/11 Bush approach to national security, while being sensitive to the wider allegations of unilateralism that have been directed at American foreign policy, especially in the wake of the Iraq War. The panel also walks a third tightrope that is responsive to the importance of the human rights movement that is a high priority for global civil society while being overtly deferential to the traditional prerogatives of sovereign states, expressed both by the norm of non-intervention and by a recognition that international action is only legitimate if the state that is the site of such behavior fails to address an ongoing humanitarian catastrophe. Each of these moves seems entirely consistent with the Westphalian concept of world order based on the interplay of sovereign states, as modified by the development of international law, and as adapted to a changing global setting. And yet this agenda is subject to contradictory lines of criticism: the Panel's proposals go too far given the geopolitical climate; the proposals are far too modest given the claimed intention of the reformers to live up to Charter expectations as to collective security or to safeguard the world against the menace of unilateralism.

Why too far? The United States, in particular, has made it abundantly clear that it will determine on its own (it will not await what President Bush derisively termed 'permission slips' from the UN) when deciding whether to rely on force to pursue its international security concerns. It will decide without regard to Charter constraints given its insistence that threats to its security and vital interests must be dealt with by preventive and pre-emptive modes of warfare. As long as the veto is available to the five permanent members of the Security Council, any effort to impose *international* restraints on their behavior depends on their *voluntary* compliance. And further, it remains the case that the responsibility to protect is an empty norm without either endowing the UN with independent capabilities or generating a political will on the part of leading states to provide needed levels of support either in advance or in response to humanitarian emergencies. There is no evidence that such conditions will be met. The feeble response to the massive genocidal developments in Darfur for several years in the face of the complicity of the Sudanese government is ample evidence that the political will is absent to support the norm associated with a responsibility to protect even in such an extreme situation. The reformist road advocated by the Panel seems blocked for the foreseeable future by geopolitical resistance and ambivalence that should have been entirely predictable.

Why not far enough? The Panel's proposals purport to change policy without altering the constitutional status of the Security Council's permanent members within the United Nations, and without providing capabilities and institutional procedures to make their recommendations assume a meaningful *political* character. To be more specific, the only way that the Security Council could be meaningfully empowered to implement the suggested supervision over extended claims of self-defense is to deny the availability of the veto to permanent members, but the issue is so delicate that it is not even mentioned, much less creatively addressed. Similarly, the only way that an interventionary mission to discharge the responsibility to protect could become credible would be through the establishment of a UN Emergency Peace Force that was specially trained in advance and independently financed and recruited. Again, such an implementing procedure is not even discussed as a remote possibility. Finally, to make the enlargement of the security agenda to encompass 'human security' more than loose words requires some sort of institutional recognition that these new issues are deserving of inclusion on the agenda of the Security Council to the same degree as war/peace concerns. Because such a recognition would highlight the disparity of economic conditions in the world economy, creating pressures for a more equitable distribution of the benefits of economic globalization than that arising from neoliberal policies, there is no present prospect that the call for a comprehensive approach to security will yield behavioral results, except of a kind that would have been produced in any event, for instance, intergovernmental cooperation to control transnational organized crime.

For these reasons, the only responsible conclusion is that the report of the High-level Panel failed from both a realist perspective of politics as the art of the possible as well as an idealist perspective of politics as the quest for the necessary and desirable. Its most important proposals, although carefully formulated and sensitive to the global setting, only reinforced the mood of despair surrounding issues of global reform. In this sense, perhaps imprudently, the Panel accepted an assignment that seems a 'mission impossible'. Returning to the fork in the road: there is no fork, only the old geopolitical pathway dominated by geopolitics and statism, and not conducive to reform. Kofi Annan's use of this metaphor is an expression of false consciousness, especially as related to its animating subject-matter, which was the combination of American unilateralism with respect to war making and a general atmosphere of inaction in response to humanitarian crises. Prior to the metaphorical call to make the right choice at this supposed fork in the road, the then secretary-general called attention to the dangerous precedent posed by 'this argument' that 'States are not obliged to wait until there is agreement in the Security Council. Instead, they reserve the right to act unilaterally, or in ad hoc coalitions'. He added that '[t]his logic represents a fundamental challenge to the principles on which, however, imperfectly, world peace and stability have rested for the last fifty-eight years'.

Annan admitted that 'it is not enough to denounce unilateralism, unless we also face up squarely to the concerns that make some States feel uniquely vulnerable, since it is those concerns that drive them to take unilateral action'.[8] It is here that there is a failure of comprehension, and an insight into how such a mission impossible is launched. Of course, the whole discourse is beset by the taboo associated with mentioning particulars, that is, which state resorted to war for what apparent purpose. It is obvious from the setting that Annan was talking about the American invasion of Iraq, but to suggest that this invasion was a response to an American post-9/11 sense of 'vulnerability' is to ignore the evidence that the Iraq War was initiated for reasons of grand strategy, and the anti-terrorist claims of an imminent threat were trumped up and irrelevant to the decision to wage war against Iraq. The point here is that if the true pressures on the UN framework are not properly analyzed there is no way to fashion a relevant response. The High-level Panel was completely responsive to the secretary-general's mandate, providing momentary cosmetic relief, but also deflecting a more accurate understanding of the true challenge being mounted by prevailing patterns of geopolitical behavior against the constraints on war making contained in the United Nations Charter.

Decades before the Iraq War, the issue of Charter obsolescence due to geopolitical disregard had been widely discussed and debated.[9] Many international law specialists have pointed to the practice of leading states that cannot be reconciled with Charter constraints on recourse to aggressive war as an instrument of policy, and have concluded that a strict reading of the prohibition on force is no longer *legally* justified.[10] Along the same lines is the argument that the failure of the Security Council to implement the mechanisms intended in Chapter VII to underpin collective security removes an essential element from the Charter approach of simultaneously prohibiting force and promising the victims of aggression the prospect of collective action in a protective response. Michael Glennon has been tireless in the last several years in his critique of what he regards as 'legalism', even Platonism, contending that it interferes with a realization that the UN Charter system for restraining states was never truly implemented as a collective security mechanism, has not been respected by important states, and lacks constraining weight and authority.[11] Glennon goes further, extending a provisional vote of confidence to what he calls 'ad hoc coalitions of the willing' that 'provide an effective substitute' 'on specific occasions' for the Security Council, referring specifically to the Kosovo War launched in 1999 under NATO auspices as his justifying example. He argues that it was correct to disregard the absence of Security Council authorization for a non-defensive use of force, and that the NATO authorization, although not based on international law, was sufficient.[12] The Kosovo example is misleading as the coalition of the willing was responding to a credible humanitarian emergency of limited scope, and not embarking on a geopolitical adventure that rested neither on moral nor political imperatives. To move in Glennon's direction is to endorse the geopolitical management of world politics at a historical moment in which the dominant claimant to that role enjoys diminishing legitimacy as a hegemonic actor and confronts deepening resentment arising from its policies.[13] In this regard, to shore up the advocacy of global policy as carried out by coalitions of the willing, through a historical reference to the relative success of the Concert of Europe in keeping the peace in Europe during the nineteenth century, is profoundly misleading and unresponsive to contemporary realities.

At the same time, the prohibition in the Charter on aggressive war is a key foundation for challenging the legality and legitimacy of state action by either moderate states or the forces of global civil society. To the extent that a post-Westphalian form of democratic and humane global governance is struggling to become a political project, it depends for clarification of its undertaking on the norms associated with the UN Charter and the Nuremberg tradition of imposing criminal accountability on leaders of states.[14]

To summarize, the metaphor as used by the secretary-general to encourage a process of UN reform was influential in guiding those entrusted with shaping an agenda of proposals and recommendations within the Organization, as a bureaucratic order of battle. But it was deeply misleading as a public statement or as a political project because it conveyed the impression that there existed an alternative to geopolitics that could be effectively developed by intergovernmental consensus. By far more appropriate as a metaphorical gesture of credible substance would have been the resignation of the secretary-general precisely because there was no discernible fork in *that* road! 'Without a fork in the road I cannot continue to serve this worthy Organization in good faith!' And elaborating by saying that 'due to the recent circumstances highlighted by the Iraq War, the prevailing path has become untenable, a betrayal of the core principles of the Charter of the United Nations prohibiting aggressive war'. If Kofi Annan, surely a decent person and dedicated international civil servant, had so used the metaphorical moment, two positive results could have been anticipated: first, a wider appreciation that *needed* UN reforms of even *minimal* scope were presently unattainable; and second, a pointed recognition that the United Nations could not function as intended due to the obstructionist tactics of the main geopolitical actor, the United States. Such a posture would have given Annan a voice of his own as well as a huge receptive audience in civil society that might well have regarded the occasion of this resignation as an opportune moment to launch a struggle for the soul of the United Nations.

Whether the path presently being cleared by the more progressive forces in global civil society is more than a utopian gesture will not be known for decades, but it is the only path that makes the abolition of aggressive war, at least potentially, 'a mission possible'. Lending support to this struggle is the only emancipatory option available to those seeking a humane form of global governance.[15] The metaphor 'a fork in the road' can thus be inverted so as to clarify the historical circumstance, acknowledging both the absence of sufficient choice, from within a Westphalian framing of UN reform, and the possibility of choice achieved by way of a rupture with standardized organizational expectations. It is evident that delivering the case for UN reform by relying on a rhetoric of urgency that is immediately contradicted by routinized patterns of performance that are subject to the dual disciplines of bureaucratic inertia and geopolitical grand strategy, is deeply discouraging to those dissatisfied with present arrangements for peace and security. That the outcome of this dynamic, as evident in the two reports, whose recommendations were further diluted in the secretary-general's own later report, *In Larger Freedom*, has been pathetic from a reformist perspective should not come as a surprise to anyone attuned to the refusal of the UN membership to accommodate the pressures of adaptation arising from the multiple dimensions of globalization.[16] Nor should anyone be fooled by the bureaucratic cover that consisted of a hollow celebration that pretended to view the meager and marginal steps taken at the World Summit in 2005 as responding adequately, even impressively, to the original urgent call.[17] What becomes manifest in the course of this cycle of delusion, is a circular and mutually complicit demonstration of the exact opposite from what is officially explicated: namely, the *impossibility* of UN reform. Acknowledging this impossibility is the only way to overcome it. To the extent that Kofi Annan, knowingly or unknowingly, simultaneously articulates the urgency of reform and provides the disguise for its failure, he is playing the villain's role in this geopolitical theater of the absurd. We are left with Glennon's overt dismissal of the UN, and avowal of the primacy of geopolitcs, as a more trustworthy rendering of the global setting in the early twenty-first century than is the false advertising and misleading charade associated with official UN efforts.[18] In the end, better a cynical counsel of despair than an over-dosage of anti-depressants. Better only because it prompts citizen resistance that is rooted in a clear recognition of the depressing realities that exist rather than perpetuating a pattern of escapist delusion while the bodies pile up.

Horizons of aspiration and metaphors of hope

From its inception the United Nations needed to cope with an unacknowledged tension between an idealist search for peace through law and the realist quest for stability through power. On the idealist side, is the unconditional prohibition of force except in instances of self-defense strictly defined to require a prior armed attack, reinforced by collective security mechanisms that were intended to protect states that were victims of aggression.

On the realist side, is the grant of veto power to the five permanent members of the Security Council, further accentuated by the short-term dependence of the Organization on financial contributions from member states, especially the leading ones, and by an overall relationship to the Charter that is premised on voluntary adherence, respectful of sovereign rights. Such normative incoherence is bound to generate disappointment over time, with idealists expecting too much and realists not expecting anything at all beyond discussion along with their fatalist submission to prevailing hegemonic patterns of world politics. The operative impact of this Faustian bargain has been recently evident in relation to the Iraq War, with idealists congratulating themselves because the Security Council refused to authorize the invasion in 2003, while most realists went ahead with their war plans while bemoaning the irrelevance of the Organization. Subsequent to the invasion, despite its flagrant violation of the most basic principle of the Charter and the devastation of a member state, the UN acquiesced in the outcome, lent its support to normalizing the illegal occupation of the country, and refrained from criticizing the invasion and the many excesses of the occupation.

Through the years, mainly off camera, the UN achieved many positive results, often beyond most reasonable expectations, and far beyond what its predecessor, the League of Nations accomplished, especially in such areas as human rights, environmental consciousness, health, care of children, education, and even in relation to peace and security whenever geopolitical actors happened to agree on what to do. A testimony to this net contribution to human wellbeing is that no state, however disturbed by the politics of the UN, has withdrawn from membership in the United Nations over the entire course of its history.[19] This maintenance of universal membership is a great achievement that should not be undervalued, establishing on a voluntary basis the first ever truly global organization entrusted with the safeguarding of the planet.

Given this understanding, it is not surprising that the UN reform process is so clogged. There are three sources of resistance to substantial reform, each quite formidable:

- the amendment process is constitutionally difficult, and is subject to the veto;
- the entrenched advantages of some states, and the diverse priorities of and within different regions, makes it difficult to achieve a consensus on specific steps (unless innocuous);
- the leading states, especially the United States, are unwilling to cede control over vital dimensions of global policy or to allow initiatives within the Organization that express criticism of its global role or specific policies.

With these considerations in mind, it is hardly surprising that the UN has not been able to solve the most pressing demands for the kind of reform that would provide it with enhanced twenty-first-century legitimacy:[20]

- changing the membership of the Security Council to take account of shifts in influence since 1945;

- adapting the concept of self-defense to the current realities of international conflict without giving states the authority to wage discretionary wars;
- acknowledging the impact of the global human rights movement to the extent of creating capabilities and willingness to intervene in internal affairs in reaction to the threat or actuality of genocide or crimes against humanity;
- taking advantage of the end of the Cold War to embark upon a path of negotiated nuclear disarmament, to establish an emergency peace force to deal with humanitarian emergencies and natural disasters, to impose a global tax that provides an independent revenue base, and to create a global parliament in recognition of the rise of civil society.

It is with this understanding of an agenda for UN reform that makes it suggestive to rely on the metaphor of 'horizons' as clarifying, acknowledging formidable difficulties of an authentic reform process without being demoralizing.[21] A basic distinction needs to be drawn between horizons of feasibility and horizons of desire. Horizons of feasibility refer to those adaptations needed to make the Organization effective and legitimate within its *existing* framework, that is, with an acceptance of the normative incoherence associated with the tension between the Charter as law and geopolitics as practice. In contrast, horizons of desire are based on overcoming this incoherence by minimizing the impact of geopolitics. This presupposes solving the challenge of global governance by *transforming* the United Nations in a manner that achieves primacy for the Charter's goals and principles. Such a possibility, currently an impossibility, would depend on a much more widely shared perception as to the dysfunctionability of war as an instrument useful for resolving conflict and creating security. A transformed UN in these directions would provide an institutional foundation for moral globalization, that is, for the realization of human rights comprehensively conceived to include economic, social, and cultural rights, as reinforced by a regime of global law that treated equals equally and was not beset by claims of exception and double standards in the application of general norms, as well as being receptive to an ethos of nonviolence.

As suggested in the discussion of 'the fork in the road', it would be futile to consider such a transformative horizoning as relevant to the present or likely discourse on UN reform within the conventional arenas of statecraft, including the United Nations itself. Even the horizons of feasibility, other than moves to achieve managerial efficiencies and marginal adaptations, seem unpromising, although it is possible to imagine shifts in the political climate that could lead to adjustments in the composition of the UN Security Council to make it more representative, or a successful initiative to establish some kind of emergency force that would give the UN more credibility with respect to interventions for humanitarian purposes. If we take account of the recent past, the most successful reform developments have resulted from 'coalitions of the dedicated' (compare the geopolitical inversion – coalitions of the willing, as in Kosovo, Iraq) that have been composed of like-minded governments and a movement of civil society actors. Both the anti-personnel landmines treaty and the International Criminal Court (ICC) came about despite geopolitical resistance led by the United States, and illustrated the potential reformist capacity of a 'new internationalism' that is neither a project of statist design nor of global civil society, but a collaboration that draws strength from this hybrid agency. Of course, it would be a mistake to attribute transformative potential to this new internationalism, as it is unclear whether it can move beyond *formal* successes. The anti-personnel landmines treaty, while symbolically important, addressed a question of only trivial relevance to the priorities of geopolitical actors, and the ICC has yet to demonstrate that it can make a robust contribution to the effort to make individuals who act on behalf of states other than in Africa or hostile to the West criminally accountable.

The argument being made is based on an acknowledgement of the need for UN reform, while trying to rid the quest of false expectations and empty rhetoric. The metaphor of horizons establishes goals without regard to political obstacles, and then distinguishes between those goals that might be achieved by existing mechanisms of influence, horizons of feasibility, and those goals whose implementation is necessary (and desirable) but for which there cannot be currently envisioned a successful scenario.

These latter goals of a transformative depth are thus situated over the visible horizon. Their pursuit can be understood either as a new political imaginary for world order in the manner depicted by Charles Taylor in *Modern Social Imaginaries*, or as a waiting game for the inevitable breakdown of the Westphalian world order that might under the circumstances convert a transformation of the United Nations into a political project.[22] In this regard, it might be recalled that the League of Nations became a plausible, if flawed, project only after the devastation of World War I, and the United Nations was only conceivable in the wake of World War II. Each project was intended to 'fix' fundamental deficiencies of world order by altering the horizons of world order politics, and each effort moved beyond what seemed previously attainable, yet each fell far short of horizons of desire and longer-term necessities.

A concluding note

Returning once more to the metaphorical motif, this essay contends that there is no fork in either road, and that the metaphor of choice as applied to UN reform is profoundly misleading and distorting. Within the United Nations system, as now constituted, there is no reform choice, and no alternative to the persistence of a geopolitically dominated reality. Outside the UN, the commitment to UN reform by civil society actors is the only worthwhile path, although the realization of its vision cannot even be imagined at this point, but again, there is no choice to be made. Choosing the geopolitical road to the future is to close one's eyes to the near certainty of disaster. The only road that promises a sustainable and benevolent future for humanity now appears utopian, but given the possibility of presently unforeseeable developments, such prospects could become politically viable in the future.

Given this assessment, it follows that the fork in the road metaphor should be rejected except to express the absence of choice despite the necessity of change. If so used, the metaphorical expression should be formulated as 'there is *no* fork in the road'. A reliance on the counter-metaphor of horizons could be helpfully substituted in a dual mode: horizons of feasibility for reforms within existing structures, and horizons of desire for transformations that require radically modified structures. It is the further claim being made here that both horizons are part of an encompassing social imaginary that can be identified as horizons of necessity.

The perspective is guided by a slight variation on the Gandhian ethos of principled engagement: 'at the start, they mock or ignore; later on, they began to listen, then they oppose, and a bit later, they support and even cheer'. At this point, given both our sense of imminent menace and our vision of a humane future, we need to summon the composure to rely on metaphors expressive of a utopian realism, and the stamina to withstand ironic dismissals for years to come; but better to endure irony than to sulk in silence, or worse, resign ourselves to complicity.

Notes

1 The Secretary General's Address to the General Assembly, September 23, 2003, 1–5, 3.
2 See the Cardoso Report on UN–civil society relations, *We the Peoples: Civil Society, the United Nations and Global Governance*, A/58/817, New York: United Nations, 2004; for commentary and general skeptical overview, see R. A. Falk, 'Reforming the United Nations: Global Civil Society Perspectives and Inititatives', in M. Glasius, M. Kaldor, and H. Anheir, eds, *Global Civil Society Yearbook 2005/6*, London: Sage, 2006, 150–86.
3 Cardoso Report, *We the Peoples*, op. cit.
4 Ibid., xi.
5 Ibid., 21–55.
6 Ibid., 3.
7 Ibid., 66.
8 The Secretary General's Address to the General Assembly, September 23, 2003, 3.
9 Perhaps most notably by Thomas Franck in 'Who Killed Article 2(4)? Or: Changing Norms Governing the Use of Force by States', *American Journal of International Law* 64, 809–837, 1970.
10 See A. C. Arend and R. J. Beck, *International Law and the Use of Force: Beyond the Charter Paradigm*, London: Routledge, 1993; A. M. Weisbrud, *Use of Force: The Practice of States Since World War II*, Philadelphia: Pennsylvania State University Press, 1997; see also A-M. Slaughter, 'Good Reasons for Going Around the UN', *New York Times*, March 15, 2003.
11 See M. J. Glennon, 'Platonism, Adaptivism, and Illusion in UN Reform', *Chicago Journal of International Law* 6, no. 2, 613–40, 2006.
12 Ibid., 639; see Independent International Commission on Kosovo, *The Kosovo Report: Conflict, International Response, Lessons Learned*, Oxford: Oxford University Press, 2000, 163–98 for a different approach to legitimate intervention in the absence of UN authorization.
13 See R. W. Tucker and D. C. Henrickson, 'The Sources of American Legitimacy', *Foreign Affairs* 83, no. 2, 18–32, 2004; also R. A. Falk, 'Legality and Legitimacy: The Quest for Principled Flexibility and Restraint', in D. Armstrong, T. Farrell, and B. Maiguashca, eds, *Force and Legitimacy in World Politics*, Cambridge: Cambridge University Press, 2005, 31–50.
14 For fuller exposition, see R. A. Falk, *The Declining World Order: America's Neo-Imperial Foreign Policy*, New York: Routledge, 2004; also R. A. Falk, I. Gendzier, and R. J. Lifton, eds, *Crimes of War: Iraq*, New York: Nation Books, 2006.

15 See A. Badiou, *Meta-Politics*, London: Verso, 2005.
16 *In Larger Freedom: Towards Development, Security and Human Rights for All*, Report of the Secretary-General, New York: United Nations, 2005.
17 *Implementation of Decisions from the 2005 World Summit Outcome for Action by the Secretary-General*, Report of the Secretary-General, October 25, 2005, A/60/430.
18 Glennon, 'Platonism, Adaptivism, and Illusion in UN Reform'.
19 There is one partial exception. Indonesia withdrew for a year in 1965 to form a counter-organization of 'new states', but returned after discovering an absence of receptivity to its efforts, and the importance of membership in the UN even if the climate was hostile to national policies.
20 Many realists were critical of the Iraq War for realist cost–benefit reasons.
21 See R. A. Falk, 'International Law and the Future', *Third World Quarterly* 27, no. 5, 727–38, 2006.
22 C. Taylor, *Modern Social Imaginaries*, Durham, NC: Duke University Press, 2004.

PART III
Beyond politics

10

ANARCHISM WITHOUT 'ANARCHISM'

Searching for progressive politics

Language matters

Recent explorations of the anarchist heritage are to be welcomed, bringing to a contemporary intellectual audience the politically and morally inspiring thought of such major thinkers as Bakunin, Kropotkin, Proudhon, and more recently, Harold Laski and Paul Goodman.[1] This rich tradition reminds us strongly of the relevance of anti-state traditions of reflection and advocacy, as well as the indispensable role of cooperation, nonviolence, community, small-scale social organization, and local solutions for human material needs if the aspiration for a just and sustainable global society is ever to be rescued from its utopian greenhouse. There is every reason to celebrate this anarchist perspective for its own sake, although in a critical and discriminating manner. *Nonviolent* philosophical anarchism has a surprising resonance in relation to the ongoing difficult search for a coherent and mobilizing progressive politics in the aftermath of the virtual demise of Marxist/Gramscian theorizing traditions, along with socialist thought and practice.[2]

At the same time, it should be acknowledged that this anarchist tradition has accumulated a heavy public burden of discrediting baggage, which adds to the difficulty of relying upon it to engender a new progressive mobilization within the current global setting. An immediate barrier to the wider acceptance of philosophical anarchism as a tradition of thought is its strong identification with exclusively Western societal experience, despite the existence of some affinities with strains of late Maoist praxis, especially the distrust of bureaucracies and political parties. In contrast, Gandhi's inspiration and influence is often explicitly or implicitly evident in some recent attempts to espouse nonviolent anarchist perspectives as, for instance, in the Green Revolution that has been ongoing in Iran since its contested presidential elections of June 2009. Even within the Western framework of political thought and action there are two formidable obstacles to reliance on anarchism as political posture resulting from widespread public confusion and media manipulation.

First, is the widely endorsed stereotype of the anarchist as a sociopathic bomb thrower, an understanding given credible cultural currency by way of Dostoyevski's great anti-terrorist novel, *The Devils*. In our post-9/11 world it is unrealistic for public opinion to separate this dominant image of the anarchist from its pre-occupation with terrorists and terrorism.[3] To refer to someone as an anarchist invokes a discrediting term that is generally accepted as such without any qualifications. At best, 'anarchists' are popularly depicted as those seeking to turn peaceful demonstrations into violent carnivals of anti-state behavior, radical activists with no serious policy agenda. The mainstream media blamed anarchist elements for the small-scale violent disruptions that took place during the infamous 'Battle of Seattle' at the end of 1999, which was the first massive populist expression of radical resistance to neoliberal globalization. In certain respects, by playing the anarchist card, the media and pro-globalizing forces were able to divert attention from the expanding resistance to non-accountable, non-transparent, anti-democratic, and hegemonic institutional actors (the World Bank, IMF, and WTO). Most of those participating in Seattle neither regarded themselves as anarchists nor wanted to be portrayed as marching in step behind the black banners of anarchist militancy. The self-proclaimed anarchists at Seattle were also sharply criticized as ignorant about and indifferent toward the substantive anti-globalization concerns that motivated most of the demonstrators.

Second, our ideas about international relations are often associated with Hobbes to the effect that relations among states are characterized by the absence of government, and in realist thinking that emanates from this source, the irrelevance of law and ethics to the pursuit of order and security on a global level. This Hobbesian orientation has been refined in various ways, but most relevantly for my purposes, by the still influential thinking of Hedley Bull and several followers loosely grouped in what is known as the English School.[4] Bull brilliantly chose the title *The Anarchical Society* for his most important publication, providing a useful variant of realist thinking by keeping the link to Hobbes with the adjective 'anarchical' while taking account of the actual 'societal' contributions of international law, the relevance of human values, cooperation among states for mutual benefit, and the managerial role of major states in moderating conflicts and disciplining outlier states.[5]

Bull's basic classical realist understanding of world politics was made explicit in his strong criticism of those that followed what he called 'the Grotian tradition' supporting efforts to transcend the sovereignty of states by an increasing and, in his view, unwarranted reliance on international law and institutions. Bull was harshly critical of such undertakings as the Nuremberg initiative holding leaders of defeated Germany criminally accountable for their wartime policies, and of the naive belief that the United Nations could in the future be empowered to act autonomously as the keeper of world peace.[6] In other words, for Bull the pursuit of peace, justice, and security is best managed by the pluralist dynamics of a system of sovereign states, without a higher law or decision maker. He was, in this respect, as suspicious of and opposed to world empire as he was to world government. This anarchical presumption of sovereign states as the ultimate and preferred arbiters of world order ignores the more recent ecological and energy pressures of the anthropocene age, which do not seem to be manageable by states acting singly or cooperatively due to the long time horizons, uneven adverse impacts, and the magnitude of required adjustments.[7] Of course, such pressures were not apparent at the time that Bull formulated his argument, although a somewhat similar issue was presented by the existence of nuclear weaponry, and the risk of catastrophic nuclear war.[8]

Within the domain of academic approaches to international relations, this work of Bull and the English School is somewhat more congenial to efforts to achieve humane global governance than is the case for its main cognitive rivals in the United States, yet it is also far too wedded to the permanence of the states system as the optimal form of attainable global governance.[9] Structural realists assessing international relations on the basis of anarchic structure shaping a self-help system of rational action try to find regularities of state behavior in the spirit of scientific inquiry, ignoring normative concerns as well as the benefits of cooperative arrangements.[10] Along analogous lines, the work of game theorists and rational choice analysts in the manner of Thomas Schelling and Buena de Mesquita seeks to combine assumptions about the degree to which policies of foreign states, especially bearing on the use of force and war/peace issues, are guided by self-interested calculations of instrumental rationality, as epistemologically confirmed by empirical assessments.[11] Influenced by the model-building approaches of economists, these more formal approaches to the study of international relations, which exert growing influence in the United States, have virtually no connection with the outlook of philosophical anarchism or even with the approach of classical realists in the Bull vein that includes contributors such as John Vincent, Nicholas Wheeler and Timothy Dunne.

Bull's kinship with anarchism is based on viewing the relations among states as a field of human studies in which the potential for behavior in accord with legal and ethical norms is posited as desirable and where opportunities for cooperative action and the promotion of the global public good is affirmed. What sets Bull on a different path from that taken by philosophical anarchism is his overriding concern with pluralist *order* among sovereign states and his acceptance of the war system as a central feature of world politics. In contrast, the philosophical anarchist views *freedom* and *nonviolence* as core values. For Bull, order is established among unequal states exhibiting more or less prudence, wisdom and capabilities in calculating their interests, and benefitting accordingly from the study of history and philosophy.[12] In essence, Bull, as well as other members of the English School, believes that the best hope for moderate international relations is for a careful assessment of the deep lessons of diplomatic history as further informed by philosophical reflection on the nature of leadership, war, and justice, as well as scrupulous review of past concrete instances of statecraft to learn from failures and successes.[13] Bull takes for granted that it will be sovereign states that operate as the dominant political actors for the foreseeable future, and it is not helpful to wipe them off the global map by normative fiat. Anarchists have never devoted systematic attention to how their anti-institutional, anti-war, and nonviolent attitudes would play out globally if ever put into practice. Anarchists are uniformly disposed to deconstruct the state and to repudiate war as the path to human security. It is a genuine challenge for a revived tradition of anarchism without anarchism to develop a global vision that allows its overriding concern with freedom of the individual, autonomy of the group, and harmony among groups to be responsive to the planetary imperatives of a sustainable social life in the early twenty-first century. The most sustained effort to propose a somewhat anarchist-oriented vision of planetary civilization was written without reference to anarchist ideas. Despite this, critics of large-scale polities as regressive presences, perhaps most coherently articulated in Leopold Kohr's *The Breakdown of Nations*, can be read as an anarchist approach to world politics.[14] It is not surprising that Kohr's work has made no impact on subsequent international relations writing, and to the extent it is remembered at all it is by such writers as E. F. Schumacher and Kirkpatrick Sale, who were preoccupied with the downsizing of scale in all forms of political and economic activity. Such thinkers believe that drastic reductions of scale and size are the indispensable basis of humane and ecologically robust societies and patterns of living.[15]

Another aspect of Bull's work antithetical to anarchism is the managerial role assigned to what he calls the 'Great Powers'.[16] He attributes this role to the significance of inequality as a defining feature in the existing world of states, and limits the notion of Great Power to those states that correlate size and resources with preponderant military power.[17] Such an elevated status resting on military capabilities directly challenges the philosophical anarchist predisposition toward nonviolence as a necessary precondition for a just and humane society. As Bull puts it, 'Great powers contribute to international order in two main ways: by managing their relations with one another; and by managing their relations with one another so as to impart a degree of central direction to the affairs of international society as a whole'.[18] In this sense, the anarchical international society as conceptualized by Bull and other classical realists is totally at odds with the philosophical anarchist postulates of desirable modes of societal and political existence.

The argument being made is that there is much to be learned from both societal and internationalist forms of anarchist thinking, but that neither is sufficiently responsive to the historical circumstances nor normative priorities of the early twenty-first century. It would be possible to follow Derrida and speak of 'an anarchism to come', that is drawing selectively on the positive heritage but making it attuned to the contemporary situation, and this could produce arresting intellectual results. Even if this happens, the strong cultural and populist prejudices against the anarchist and anarchism could not be overcome. Any avowal of anarchism as a political orientation would appear to have only a narrow sectarian appeal, and even this restricted to Western audiences. Furthermore, thinking about the anarchical society, even if ambitiously extended far beyond the boundaries of the achievable as set by Bull and his followers, is not helpful with respect to the altered global setting that is inherently reliant on statist approaches that are ill-adapted to meet current global-scale challenges such as climate change. Indeed, the dysfunctionality of a decentralized world order is most likely to give rise to some kind of imperial extension of statism and despotic patterns of rule, which would be regressive with respect to a wide range of emancipatory goals.[19] The kind of agency and political action that is most promising from an emancipatory perspective now features non-state actors, transnational social movements, the rise of a human rights culture, and turns toward ecumenical religious and spiritual outlooks.

Conceptually, such an agenda could be quite easily incorporated into a twenty-first-century re-description of philosophical anarchism (although not the anarchical society of states),[20] but unfortunately the language and cultural associations of the anarchist legacy are so misleading and diversionary as to make an embrace of anarchism a disempowering intellectual and political option in any public discourse. For this combination of reasons, the position taken here with respect to policy and program is the advocacy of 'anarchism without "anarchism"'.[21] In effect, a covert borrowing and affirmation of principal anarchist positions and values found in the serious nineteenth- and early twentieth-century treatments of anarchist thought, but without overt reliance. This posture can be characterized as 'stealth anarchism'.[22]

I would also draw a distinction between anarchism as political practice and public discourse where the perceptions are so warped as to make the use of the terminology confusingly unacceptable, and more academic discourses where reliance on philosophical anarchism might be useful and enriching, especially by linking contemporary efforts at extending this discourse quite explicitly with its intellectual forebears. This proposed dichotomy of treatment seems justified because of the peculiarly contradictory history of the anarchist idea, which signifies recourse to violence in the public mind and a principled commitment to nonviolence as ethos and praxis among serious students of philosophical anarchism.

Searching for a new progressive politics

The normative political priorities of the early twenty-first century, which include issues left unresolved from the past, can be set forth as follows:

- opting for radical denuclearization (as opposed to ongoing reliance on a two-tier approach based on selective and discriminatory non-proliferation);
- protecting the global commons (applying the precautionary principle; extending 'polluter pays' to all forms of harm as a form of strict liability, as in affixing BP responsibility for the Deep Horizon oil spill in Gulf of Mexico; and prohibiting geo-engineering and high risk technologies);
- addressing global warming (reducing greenhouse gas emissions to manageable levels on an emergency basis to ensure that global warming does not exceed 2 degrees Celsius; extending assistance to harmed and threatened vulnerable societies currently experiencing harmful effects of rising earth temperatures, e.g. sub-Saharan Africa, the Pacific islands, Asian coastal regions);

- acknowledging issues associated with water scarcity, and planning for equitable distribution of safe water, acknowledged as a human right;
- eliminating poverty and drastically reducing economic inequalities (moving beyond the ethos of neoliberal globalization);
- enhancing global democracy (accountability, transparency, democratizing participation; reducing economic, and other forms of, inequality);
- diminishing hard power (militarism) and strengthening reliance on soft power (diplomacy, peaceful settlement, nonviolent coercion – 'legitimacy wars');
- achieving self-determination above and below the level of the state (communities of choice and autonomy displacing imposed communities of artifice and domination);
- encouraging de-globalization and local self-reliance (building cooperative, sustainable, voluntary communities at various levels of social order);[23]
- sensitivity to claims of indigenous peoples to maintain traditional ways of life, and to self-determination and sovereignty goals.

Such an ambitious catalogue of normative priorities exhibits the contours of a possible progressive politics to come. There is a deliberate mixture of elements that can be described as urgent and immediate, and others that are less pressing, but no less relevant. The most pervasive critique of current thinking and practice is to contend that the modernist reliance on the sovereign territorial state, understood in Weberian terms as possessing a monopoly of legitimate violence (except for valid private claims of self-defense), is increasingly anachronistic and dysfunctional when it comes to global policy and problem-solving. The primacy of the state as the foundation of human community and the state system that continues to constitute the operative framework for world order needs to be superseded, or modified, ideologically and behaviorally, as rapidly as possible. It is no longer capable of providing minimal security for even the strongest states, much less serve the public good of the state system when considered as a totality.[24] The American situation, especially since the 9/11 attacks, is emblematic of this anarchistic and militarist mode of response structure, exhibiting the futility of hard power dominance, often articulated as 'preeminence' (a military machine that costs as much as the aggregate expenditures of all other political actors in the world!), the neglect of soft power solutions (bullying Iran about its nuclear program rather than seeking a region, and then a world, without nuclear weapons), and a resulting acute sense of fear and vulnerability ('homeland security' without realizing security within or without).

Given this global setting, it is not surprising that neoliberal globalization aggravates these underlying conditions of insecurity and vulnerability.[25] The global economic crisis that started in the United States in 2008 has increasingly been blamed on the greedy opportunism of those seeking to maximize their profits and incomes, especially in the financial sector, while simultaneously disguising the resulting burdens on the general citizenry by offering unsustainable credit arrangements and facilitating cruel forms of indebtedness. In effect, the most exploitative form of social contract ever negotiated in a capitalist setting came into being after the end of the Cold War. It was encouraged and enabled by the prevailing neo-liberal creed of virtually suspending governmental oversight and responsibility in relation to the private sector, rationalized by a horde of economists beneath the idiot banner, 'the market knows best'. This extreme form of social insecurity became prevalent (the 'Washington consensus') in the period following the collapse of a socialist alternative, which allowed a triumphalist capitalist consensus to no longer feel challenged in the slightest by socialist values and programs, or even by Keynesian and social democratic versions of capitalism. Capitalism no longer had strong incentives to offer society the semblance of 'a human face'.

It is a sad commentary on our times that the most coherent and mobilizing voices declaiming these present realities come from the extreme right. The former left does not even provide a sense of oppositional tension. The public reacts to this unidirectional assault on their political sensibilities by seeming to become more and more receptive to proto-fascist approaches to discontent: hyper-nationalism, intensified militarism, xenophobic immigration policy, and an endless search for enemies within and without state boundaries. These pre-fascist symptoms are expressive of a populist urge to end the insecurities of the age by a combination of geopolitical thuggery, political authoritarianism, and ecological denial in relation to global warming, energy policy, and water scarcity. The absence of a left presence is partly a reflection of demoralization resulting from the Sino-Soviet experiences and partly a result of the ideological exhaustion of state-centrism as a transformative nexus, providing sites for radical reform and revolutionary possibilities. While the traditional right is partly resurgent, partly in denial, the traditional left (including 'the new left') languishes in a prolonged depression, having been largely expelled from public space in most of the West-centric world. A partial exception to this dreary picture is provided by the rise of social democratic and populist left politics in several Latin American countries, undoubtedly reflecting the long struggle to loosen the hemispheric chains associated with American hegemony and intervention.

The claim here is that we need to go beyond the progressive promise of traditional left reformist and revolutionary outlooks by *selectively* reviving the direction and underlying orientation of the tradition of philosophical anarchism.[26] This revival is partial and selective, repudiating that portion of the anarchist orientation that relies on violent tactics in some of the most visible manifestations of anarchism in action, although almost totally absent from the serious anarchist literature. It also enlarges and updates the anarchist orientation by incorporating several compatible, yet non-anarchist, sources of inspiration. These allied modes of thought and practice that seem to enrich the contemporary search for a progressive politics include the worldviews and practices of many indigenous peoples, the theory of and experience with legitimacy wars, the imprint of Gandhi and nonviolent struggle generally, social and digital networking, preferential treatment of small-scale and local communities, and the transnational advocacy of an ecological civilization premised on environmental justice.[27]

The re-framing of anarchist thinking

The essential qualities of that part of the anarchist legacy that is linked to contemporary efforts to give substance and direction to progressive politics are the
following: a primary reliance on non-state actors as the bearers of emancipatory
potential; seeking change on the basis of coercive nonviolence and soft power,
including seeking control of the moral high ground in relation to social and political conflict; and reverence for nature and ancient wisdom. There are several focal
points that receive an emphasis in policy and values oriented assessments, including
resisting predatory globalization, hegemonic geopolitics, and political centralization
(that is, opposition to centralizing programs, policies, and visions of the future
whether imperial or federalist in character).[28]

I Globalization from below

I mention very briefly my own attempt to develop a coherent alternative to the
kind of neoliberal forms of economic globalization that were gripping the political
imagination during the 1990s, creating the impression that there were no alternatives to neoliberalism. In simplifying the originality of this period, I drew a sharp
distinction between 'globalization-from-above' and 'globalization-from-below', the
former being the de facto alliance of governments, banks, and corporations that
were generating a particularly menacing form of 'predatory' capitalism that had an
unprecedented global wing spread, was intensifying inequalities, invalidating
regulatory oversight, and operating without significant ideological opposition.[29] In
opposition, was an emergent collection of local, national, regional, and global social
movements, initiatives, and visions, that is, 'globalization-from-below'. Increasingly,
these developments were establishing empowering connectedness through activist
participation at world UN conferences held during the 1990s, demonstrating
against meetings of international financial institutions and groupings such as the
Group of Seven (G-7, later G-8, later still G-20) and the World Economic Forum.
Also, through reliance on the Internet, mobilizing around local struggles for different forms of justice, and withdrawing legitimacy from the state as the source of
security, protection, and identity. A critique of representative and parliamentary
democracy was an additional element of this response to globalization. Such forms
of democracy were viewed as largely shams or worse, seeking validation not by
contributions to the wellbeing of peoples within a spatially delimited and nationally
identified constituency, but merely by the procedural ritual of elections conferring
consent of the governed to governance by rotating elites that were capital-driven
rather than people-oriented.

What made this critique of globalization-from-above and the perspective of
many of those espousing globalization-from-below a virtual species of anarchism in
outlook, was the turn away from either situating hopes in a reforming state, a
revolutionary seizure of state power, or through the global institutionalization of
authority via the United Nations or the establishment of world government.

Furthermore, the analysis of predatory world capitalism viewed the state as being outmaneuvered as a source of public good in several ways: by the rise of the global private sector, by entrusting security to a highly militarized and globalizing hegemon allied with international corporate and financial interests rather than with the national citizenry, and by situating historical agency in a variety of overlapping arenas of struggle and resistance exhibiting self-reliance and a growing confidence in soft power forms of action. In effect, what exists is an emergent movement for global equity and substantive (as distinguished from parliamentary) democracy.

II The post-modern prince

In a comparable fashion, Stephen Gill, borrowing from Gramsci, who of course borrowed from Machiavelli, insists that the center of political gravity is moving away from 'the prince' who controls from above, as well as away from the transformed vision of social order in Gramsci's affirmation of the defining and hoped for historical agency of the Communist Party.[30] Gill is proposing a 'post-modern' adjustment, re-situating the prince in populist movements of peoples challenging the established order in a variety of ways. He also focuses on the dual priorities of overcoming neoliberal globalization (held responsible for various forms of impoverishment, exploitation, and inequality, as well as for a non-sustainable plundering of the planet) and challenging the military reinforcement of this unacceptable economistic world order and the global gendarmerie role played by the United States. From a progressive standpoint Gill sees the displacement of the state through the entrenchment of 'the world market as the principal form of governance' as marginalizing organized labor, revolutionary political parties, and working in overall harmony with such state capitalist countries as China, Malaysia, and Singapore.[31] Gill dismisses the effort to relegitimize world order by positing the idea of 'sustainable development', and locates his hopes for a humane future in the emergence of political forces 'imagining new possibilities and the making of history' and guided by a societally oriented innovative type of 'organic intellectual'.[32] In depicting these new possibilities Gill draws from a variety of sources to posit a set of conditioning factors: a long-term perspective on change; a broadening of the traditional justice agenda to include gender, race, and nature; reliance on a 'movement of movements' without the requirement of a unifying coherent ideology; diversity of organizational forms, ideological perspectives, and policy goals, with shared use of digital tools to achieve effective results and empathy for all those victimized by the established order; due to non-territorial and local sites of activism not easily containable by normal instruments of state police power; and formulating responsive 'feasible utopias' and 'myths' that posit empowerment, autonomy, dignity, and security, and thus providing reassurances that there are benevolent alternatives to neoliberal globalization.[33] Such a progressive imaginary resembles in many of its aspects the approach and activity of the World Social Forum, and represents an antidote to its repudiated step-father, the World Economic Forum, which served as an incubator of neoliberal tactics, strategy, and hegemony during the 1990s.

The affinities with anarchism, as specified here, are sufficiently prominent as to require only slight explication. The essential affinity is the loss of credible agency by states, imperial projects, and the state system to address successfully the ethical challenges of inequality and exploitation, the economic failures of regulation and stability, and the ecological urgencies associated with global warming and critical resource depletion. Yet this circumstance still generates both hope and an alternative imaginary with respect to the future based on the activation of a multiplicity of social forces the world over and a corresponding dynamic of envisioning a just and desirable future for the planet and its peoples. Building community and sustainable livelihoods while marginalizing the role of the state and global hegemon is the essence of the anarchist imaginary, whether inside or outside the porous boundaries of the sovereign state. Of course, in this century, affirmation of community-based polities, while indispensable, is insufficient. There is an urgent need to redress the imbalances produced by many decades of ecological depravity, and this presupposes both a planetary ethos, as well as cognitive and enforcement procedures, that is, relevant knowledge and the capacity to act as and when necessary.[34] Whether twenty-first-century philosophical anarchism can meet this challenge will determine if the legacy must be disregarded and superseded to produce the kind of progressive politics needed at this stage of history and species evolution. It is along such lines that a continuation of the kind of social and moral orientation of the great anarchist luminaries seems so promising, although probably not framed in anarchist language so as to universalize the appeal of core anarchist values and avoid the sort of backlash that is associated with ideological postures discredited by mainstream conventional wisdom. In this regard, anarchism shares the same fate as 'communism', 'socialism', 'the cultural revolution', 'the left', and 'Maoism'.[35]

III Multitude

The middle volume of the brilliantly provocative trilogy of Michael Hardt and Antonio Negri offers a way forward to achieve a progressive politics that could be deepened by drawing on the work of philosophical anarchism.[36] Despite this there is present in this work a somewhat defensive tone that is expressive of the difficulty of relying on anarchist frames of reference. Hardt and Negri directly confront the criticism, 'You are really just anarchists!' and seek to deflect its force by contending 'that our political alternatives are not limited to a choice between central leadership and anarchy'.[37] The confusion in language arises from anarchy being generally understood as chaos, confusion, as in Yeats' famous line 'mere anarchy is loosed upon the world', which in most respects is the opposite of what it means to espouse philosophic anarchism as thought or practice, a complex imaginary animated by a hopeful vision of human potentiality in opposition to the modernist actualities of exploitation, oppression, inequality, and centralization. It is this dormant anarchist worldview that these authors undertake to explicate and advocate in a suggestive and stimulating manner. At the same time this ambiguous interface between anarchy/anarchism is one more reason to avoid articulating progressive politics in an explicitly anarchist language, however rearticulated to make clear that there is no intention to endorse either bomb-throwers or aimless tumult.

In their sophisticated presentation, Hardt and Negri situate the quest for progressive politics in a kind of transitional phase during which period the peoples of the world, the multitude, are joined in a messy, uncoordinated, and diverse process of discovering and formulating a set of 'common interests'. Such common interests of the multitude should be distinguished from older ideas of a 'general interest' by the stress on the transnational singularities represented and affirmed as constituting what is common and original among the diversities of the multitude ('multiplicity of the multitude').[38] The cohering energy that unifies the quests of the multitude arises from the encounter between the biopolitics of social forces seeking to realize through struggle the conditions for a satisfying life, and the biopower of those dedicated to upholding a variety of neoliberalisms and militarisms.[39] In a moving passage, the animating energy of this advocacy of biopolitics is stated as love: 'Without this love we are nothing.'[40] Such a revolutionary stance with respect to the established order resting on an amoral logic of reified capital accumulation represents the countervailing logic of a humanized commitment to emancipatory politics of a radical character. In this regard, there is a resemblance to the radical restructuring of human existence with respect to the fundamentals of economic, social, political, and cultural order that is the essential shared message of philosophical anarchism.

In a more distinctly anarchist idiom, Hardt and Negri identify the most critical feature of their summons to the multitude to be an all-out assault on sovereignty, that is, a challenging of constituted power of all kinds from above. In their words, '[T]he multitude today needs to abolish sovereignty at a global level. This is what the slogan "Another world is possible" means to us: that sovereignty and authority must be destroyed.'[41] This is not an ahistoric call, but rooted in the need to take account of historical specificities: 'The political project of the multitude, however, must find a way to confront the conditions of our contemporary reality.' To do this adequately requires a 'new science' described as 'a new theoretical paradigm to confront the new situation'.[42] Although taking full account of the problems afflicting the planet, this perspective generates a certain non-utopian optimism based on their observation that 'never before has the restlessness for freedom and democracy been so widespread throughout the world'.[43]

In my view, Hardt and Negri offer us a valuable, if deliberately indirect and probably unintended reinvigoration of anarchism that takes full historical account of a networked world reality (globalization-from-below) that is challenged by global forces that threaten the health, wellbeing, and even survival of humanity (globalization-from-above). The multitude is the differentiated 'whole' that must both create the conditions to enable the 'parts' to flourish in particular time/space domains but also must address the integrated and imperial, mainly unified 'whole' that currently oppresses and endangers the 'parts', especially through the mechanisms of the sovereign state, the imperial enforcer, and the neoliberal conglomerate.

IV Legitimacy wars

There is abundant occasion for collective despair if the vital signs of the planetary condition are assessed and then projected into the future, especially given the variety of conscious and unconscious techniques being deployed to ensure widespread and deep denial of 'the real' by the mass of humanity. The psychological mechanisms of denial operate politically to insulate self-destructive behavior from exposure, criticism, and eventual repudiation. A pattern of denial is evident with respect to the continuing reliance on a neoliberal approach to global economic policy despite the disquieting actualities of climate change, energy policy, poverty, and human suffering. Such an assessment is discouraging about our prospects for constructive behavior in the near future. At the same time, there is one virtually unnoticed counter-trend that is more encouraging: namely, the declining efficacy of hard power approaches to security and conflict by way of war and militarism, and the increasing success of reliance upon soft power approaches as measured by political outcomes. From the anti-colonial wars in which the militarily weaker side consistently prevailed to the anti-apartheid campaign that transformed racist and militarist South Africa, to the ongoing solidarity movement that is fighting for Palestinian self-determination on a symbolic global battlefield relying on the weaponry of coercive nonviolence (including boycott, divestment, and sanctions), there is a pattern of political outcomes that defies realist calculations based on military superiority. These legitimacy wars are being won by the side that commands the high moral ground, and is able to mobilize a variety of symbolic sources of grassroots support. Illustratively, it was not sovereign states or even the United Nations that effectively challenged the unlawful blockade of the civilian population of Gaza, but humanitarian missions of political activists and citizen pilgrims on board the Freedom Flotilla that finally caused sovereign Israel to acknowledge, at least in part, its responsibilities to the 1.5 million Gazan civilians living under siege and terrifying oppression.[44] What is becoming manifest is that in many settings of conflict the weapons of the weak, the biopolitical multitudes, are prevailing over the weapons of the strong, the biopower arenas of sovereign authority. At the same time, caught in their maelstrom of failures, without the political will or imagination to move outside the militarist mentality, the horrifying repetition of wars fought with post-modern weaponry (cyber war, drones) that makes killing as impersonal and one-sided as possible goes forward with larger and larger investments in the futile quest for the ultimate enactments of 'shock and awe', as well as a continuing effort to wage an utterly misguided permanent war in battlefields around the world in response to the 9/11 attacks. Instead of learning from failure and defeat, governmental elites are captives of a militarist, hard power imagination that is incapable of coping with security challenges while causing widespread death, dislocation, and destruction among the innocent.

The realities of soft power legitimacy wars offer a vindication of an anarchist confidence in human potential for nonviolent political resolution of conflict and the pursuit of justice. At the same time, the disastrous failures of hard power state centricism, relying on money and technology to achieve goals through threats and uses of force, illustrates the realist fallacy given the post-colonial setting of the twenty-first century.[45] It is my view that these developments in a globalizing world, with the coordinates of globalization as yet undetermined, provide the basis for an extension of philosophical anarchism to the under-analyzed domain of international relations.[46]

A concluding remark

The argument being put forth is that part of the anarchist impulse based on the search for freedom, community, and autonomy has a surprising relevance to constructing a globally responsive progressive politics. It is both instructive and inspirational. Some expressions of this search seem to confirm this claim of anarchist affinities. Despite this, it seems desirable to avoid any explicit reliance on anarchism because it has been so widely discredited in the marketplace of ideas and does have an alienating Western intellectual provenance. Beyond this, it is too easy to conflate the words 'anarchic' and 'anarchistic', thereby creating profound disquiet. What the anarchistic legacy does provide is greater confidence in the appropriateness of a radical imaginary of emancipation that is strongly biased in favor of dispersal and decentralism, and dismissive of making the big bigger in the name of security and order. Part of the contemporary situation is to move beyond discredited centralizing ideologies and governmental visions of a secure and satisfying human future, while acknowledging that there exist global interconnectedness, complexities, and fragilities that must be given their due in a progressive politics viable for the twenty-first century.

Let me end this essay with two final observations. First of all, the fundamental anarchist impulse can be actualized to varying degrees by living locally and in accord with the mandates of voluntary simplicity. In this sense, it is not utopian, although it may be shielded from the harsher truths of the contemporary world by enjoying the paradoxical benefits of security provided by a reasonably well-governed state. Such a search for sustainable community can draw inspiration from the persistence of indigenous nations as well as from the writings of Gandhi, Tolstoy, Paul Goodman, Murray Bookchin, E. F. Schumacher, and countless others who can be loosely associated with anarchist thought and practice. It is my argument that this perspective should form the nexus of anarchism without anarchism.

There is a second strand of thought that involves the combination of the present circumstances of ecological urgency with the decline of hard power effectiveness, that creates a new set of opportunities for an intellectual renewal and adaptation of the tradition of philosophical anarchism to the present historical moment.[47] Here it may be useful to connect explicitly with the earlier writings of Bakunin, Kropotkin, Proudhon, and others, and write and reflect unselfconsciously in the spirit of anarchism *with* anarchism, or put differently, to create a discourse of philosophical neo-anarchism. Here, since the concern is the way in which the world should operate and be organized for the benefit and security of all, the allegations of utopianism must be taken seriously, but not as the occasions for closure of debate and deliberation. After all, since the future is essentially unknowable, what is perceived at present as 'utopian' may yet come to pass. Surely, the peaceful transformation of apartheid South Africa to an unfolding form of multi-ethnic constitutionalism seemed utopian until it started happening. Besides, by holding a critical mirror before the present, and providing an alternative, the political and moral imagination can be liberated from the current gathering sense of doom and gloom. In the more pristine workshop of academic debate, the popular denigration of anarchism and anarchists is not nearly so relevant, and there may be more to gain from retaining the old language than by abandoning it.

Notes

1 See especially the recent articles by A. Prichard, 'Deepening Anarchism: International Relations and the Anarchist Ideal', *Anarchist Studies* 18, no. 2, 2010, 29–57; Prichard, 'What Can the Absence of Anarchism Tell Us About the History and Purpose of International Relations?', *Review of International Studies* 37, no. 4, 2011, 1647–69; compare Richard Falk, 'Anarchism and World Order', in J. R. Pennock and J. W. Chapman, eds, 'Anarchism and World Order', in *Anarchism*, New York: New York University Press, 1978, 63–87.

2 This demise has at least two dimensions: the collapse of the Soviet state, along with the documentation of its continuous reliance on massive repression; the abandonment of socialist economic policy by China, along with its regressive 'socialist' political order and spectacular market success story. Beyond this, the Marxist-Leninist form of revolutionary thought seems ill-adapted to twenty-first-century imperatives, being premised on the revolutionary violence of workers, material abundance, industrialism, state power, and a world of warring sovereignties. For these reasons Marxism-Leninism has lost its emancipatory potential, even its historical relevance, although socialist values continue to animate most anti-capitalist struggles, as well as resistance to neoliberal globalization.

3 Even such sophisticated observers as J. Habermas and J. Derrida viewed the post-9–11 world as an aspect of 'the age of terror'. See G. Borradori, *Philosophy in a Time of Terror: Dialogues with Jürgen Habermas and Jacques Derrida*, Chicago: University of Chicago Press, 2003.

4 See T. Dunne, *Inventing International Society: A History of the English School*, Basingstoke: Macmillan, 1998.

5 Bull, *The Anarchical Society: A Study of Order in World Politics*, New York: Columbia University Press, 1977.

6 Bull, 'The Grotian Conception of International Society', in H. Butterfield and M. Wight, eds, *Diplomatic Investigations*, Cambridge, MA: Harvard University Press, 1968, 50–73. See also Bull, *The Anarchical Society*, op. cit.

7 On the anthropocene, see S. Dalby, *Security and Environmental Change*, Cambridge: Polity, 2009; S. Dalby, 'Geopolitical Trends in the Near Future: Welcome to the Anthropocene!' paper presented at workshop on 'The World in 2030: Geopolitics and Global Climate Change', UCSB/UNU, Santa Barbara, California June 24–25, 2010; also R. A. Falk, 'A Radical World Order Challenge: Climate Change and the Threat of Nuclear Weapons', *Globalizations* 7, nos. 1–2, 137–55, 2010; also S. Žižek, *Living in the End Times*, London: Verso, 2010.

8 Daniel Deudney mounts a strong conceptual argument for limited world government as essential for the management of nuclear weaponry. See his chapter entitled 'Anticipations of World Nuclear Government', in *Bounding Power: Republican Security Theory from the Polis to the Global Village*, Princeton, NJ: Princeton University Press, 2007, 244–64; see

J. Schell, *The Fate of the Earth*, New York: Knopf, 1982, for deep analysis of the non-sustainability of world order in which state actors possess nuclear weapons; also see E. P. Thompson, 'Notes on Exterminism, the Last Stage of Civilization', in Thompson, *Beyond the Cold War*, New York: Pantheon, 1982, 41–79.

9 For an excellent study of international relations that both explicates the British School and relies upon analogous modes of inquiry, see R. Jackson, *The Global Covenant: Human Conduct in a World of States*, Oxford: Oxford University Press, 2000, 58–76.

10 K. Waltz, *Theory of International Politics*, Reading, MA: Addison-Wesley, 1979: see also Waltz, 'The Spread of Nuclear Weapons: More May Be Better', Adelphi Papers, London: International Institute for Strategic Studies.

11 T. C. Schelling, *The Strategy of Conflict*, Cambridge, MA: Harvard University Press, 1960.

12 This is the central theme of Bull's *The Anarchical Society*, op. cit. Note 5. As he puts it (xii): 'Of course, in common with most men [sic] I do attach value to order. If I did not think of order in international politics as a desirable objective, I should not have thought it worthwhile to attempt this study of it.'

13 For an example of the latter, see the principal work of Bull's talented student, R. John Vincent, *Non-Intervention and International Order*, Princeton, NJ: Princeton University Press, 1974; another excellent work in this vein, sensitive to human values, is N. J. Wheeler, *Saving Strangers: Humanitarian Intervention in International Society*, Oxford: Oxford University Press, 2000.

14 New York: E. P. Dutton, 1978. It is noteworthy that there is not a single reference in the Kohr bibliography to an author that would be considered to fall into the IR tradition. See also Kohr, *The Overdeveloped Nations: The Diseconomies of Scale*, New York: Schocken Books, 1978.

15 Most notably E. F. Schumacher, *Small is Beautiful: A Study of Economics as if People Mattered*, London: Blond and Briggs, 1973; and K. Sale, *Human Scale*, New York: Putnam, 2nd edn, 1982.

16 See Bull, *The Anarchical Society*, op. cit., 200–229.

17 Ibid., 201–2.

18 Bull, *The Anarchical Society*, 207. Michael Mandelbaum, an American writing in a spirit that is akin to the British School except for his enthusiasm for the role of the United States as a virtual world government, is similarly convinced that without such a presence chaos would diminish the wellbeing of all actors. But to favor this kind of centralism in a pluralist framework for human relations contradicts the fundamental anarchist claim and insight. See M. Mandelbaum, *The Case for Goliath: How America Acts as the World's Government in the Twenty-first Century*, New York: Public Affairs, 2005.

19 See important strictures on departing from the 'international' and embracing the 'global' in R. B. J. Walker, *After the Globe, Before the World*, New York: Routledge, 2010.

20 It should be observed that the anarchical society hypothesis was always antithetical to the anarchist vision of a good society. At its core, the former was statist and pluralist, while the latter was anti-statist and decentralist.

21 The attractiveness of the anarchist tradition in the context of the present is well formulated in a stimulating book: see S. Critichley, *Infinitely Demanding: Ethics of Commitment, Politics of Resistance*, London: Verso, 2007, especially 119–28.

22 For useful survey, see G. Woodcock, *Anarchism*, New York: World Publishing Co., 1971; for a lively narrative account of a mixture of popular and academic perceptions of historical anarchism with a somewhat provocative linkage to contemporary concerns about transnational terrorism, see A. Butterworth, *The World that Never Was: A True Story of Dreamers, Schemers, Anarchists and Secret Agents*, New York, Pantheon, 2010.

23 A congenial alternate listing of normative vectors with affinities to the spirit of non-violent anarchism can be found in the preface of Boaventura de Sousa Santos, ed., *Democratizing Democracy: Beyond the Liberal Democratic Canon*, London: Verso, 2005, xxx–xxxiii.

24 Of course, arguments about the adequacy of the state system from an ethical perspective have existed throughout the entire modern period, indeed ever since the original

Westphalian framings of world order in the early seventeenth century by such figures as Grotius and Hobbes. One line of rationalist critique was associated with Kant's view of the moral evolution of international political life, enabling a possible 'perpetual peace', resting on political republicanism and demilitarization. What seems different over the period since 1945 is the apocalyptic shadow being cast over planetary life, initially by the prospects of large-scale nuclear war and more recently by ecological collapse, both caused by human not natural agency. For recent assessments, see Falk, Žižek, op. cit. Note 7. It should be observed that human experience has always been haunted by apocalyptic dangers, but previously due to threats to civilizational survival posed by natural disasters such as disease, drought, or flooding.

25 For three excellent analyses along these lines see J. H. Mittelman, *Hyperconflict: Globalization and Insecurity*, Stanford, CA: Stanford University Press, 2010; J. A. Camilleri and J. Falk, *Worlds in Transition: Evolving Governance Across a Stressed Planet*, Cheltenham: Edward Elgar, 2009; S. Gill, *Power and Resistance in the New World Order*, London: Palgrave, 2nd revised edn, 2008.

26 A notable attempt to set forth a reformist program based on social democratic values was made by D. Held, *Global Covenant: The Social Democratic Alternative to the Washington Consensus*, Cambridge: Polity, 2004. But such an attempt seems too beholden to Westphalian statism to offer insight into the distinctive problems and opportunities of this historical moment. See also A-M. Slaughter, *A New World Order*, Princeton, NJ: Princeton University Press, 2004.

27 Critchley, *Infinitely Demanding*, op. cit. Note 21, proceeds from a similar ethical/political standpoint, reinforced by sophisticated readings of Western philosophy.

28 There are many complexities, and tradeoffs. For instance, arguably regional forms of centralization, as in the European Union, may produce greater autonomy for ethnic and cultural minorities by weakening the internal role of the state in the lives of the citizenry. It may be that regionalism combined with transnational networking and activism is the best available strategic move to weaken the grip of the state on global policymaking and on the lives of peoples caught within the confines of territorial sovereignty. See T. E. Paupp, *The Future of International Relations: Crumbling Walls, Rising Regions*, New York: Palgrave, 2008.

29 R. A. Falk, *Predatory Globalization: A Critique*, Cambridge: Polity, 1999.

30 S. Gill, *Power and Resistance in the New World Order* op. cit. Note 25, especially 237–69.

31 Ibid., 258.

32 Ibid., 261, 265.

33 Ibid., 266–68.

34 For one perspective see R.A. Falk, 'The Second Cycle of Ecological Urgency', in J. Ebbesson and P. Okawa, eds, *Environmental Law and Justice in Context*, Cambridge: Cambridge University Press, 2009.

35 But see A. Badiou's extensive writings; particularly relevant is *The Communist Hypothesis*, London: Verso, 2010.

36 See M. Hardt and A. Negri, *Multitude: War and Democracy in the Age of Empire*, New York: Penguin, 2004.

37 Ibid., 222.

38 Ibid., 356, also see 355–56.

39 Ibid., 206, 348–58.

40 Ibid., 353: ' … love serves as the basis for our political projects in common and the construction of a new society', at 352.

41 Ibid., 353. This idea of destroying sovereignty is specifically focused on the primacy of the state as the locus of sovereign biopower. 'Sovereignty in all its forms inevitably poses power as the rule of the one and undermines the possibility of a full and absolute democracy.' At 353.

42 Ibid.

43 Ibid. Hardt and Negri confront the criticism that their faith in the multitude and biopolitics is utopian, at 226–27.

44 On May 31, 2010 the Freedom Flotilla carrying 10,000 tons of humanitarian assistance to the entrapped civilian population of Gaza was attacked in the middle of the night by Israeli military forces while sailing in international waters. The attack resulted in nine deaths of Turkish nationals in the lead vessel in the flotilla, the *Mavi Marmara*. The lethality and brazen unlawfulness of the attack caused widespread international outrage, and a rupture of diplomatic relations between Turkey and Israel. The resulting pressure also caused the Israelis to announce a termination of the blockade with respect to all items other than arms and ammunition and to break temporarily with their practice of non-cooperation with UN inquiries into their behavior in occupied Palestine by agreeing to participate in an international panel appointed by the UN secretary-general.

45 For an elaboration, see R. A. Falk, 'Nonviolent Geopolitics', Chapter 2 of this volume.

46 A notable, yet preliminary and inconclusive effort to do just this, can be found in T. G. Weiss, 'The Tradition of Philosophical Anarchism and Future Directions in World Policy', *Journal of Peace Research* 12, 1–17, 1975.

47 For useful depictions of the ecological emergency see G. Dyer, *Climate Wars: The Fight for Survival as the World Overheats*, Oxford: One World, 2010; C. Hamilton, *Requiem for a Species: Why We Resist the Truth about Climate Change*, London: Earthscan, 2010.

11

HOW TO LIVE TOGETHER WELL ON PLANET EARTH

Interrogating the Israel–Palestine conflict

Comprehending the Israel–Palestine ordeal

Derrida, in an illuminating essay 'Avowing – The Impossible: "Returns", Repentance, and Reconciliation', directly and indirectly sheds light on the Israel–Palestine conflict in ways that circumvent and transcend a widely endorsed conventional wisdom that has led nowhere but to recurrent cycles of violence and deepening distrust for more than six decades. Yet to take advantage of Derrida's distinctive and suggestive modes of understanding requires distancing and differentiating, as well as appreciating. Derrida's fundamental discourse is metapolitical, although with a variety of political implications that he explicates in valuable and suggestive ways, the assessment offered here is basically political in the sense of seeking to identify and understand conflict-resolving and conflict-sustaining aspects of the Israel–Palestine struggle.

The argument of this essay is anchored in Derrida's thought, although in a dialogic and critical spirit that highlights his approaches, but also takes account of some alternative ways of improving the life circumstances and human security of Israelis and Palestinians.[1] These alternatives are less philosophically probing of the underlying conflict, but seem somewhat more promising as historically realizable political projects for living together well in the context of short- and middle-term future relations within Israel/Palestine. This essay relies on a comparison between Derrida's radical thinking about impossibility (as permanently embedded in human experience and yet morally essential as horizon and to encourage the striving needed to fulfill human potential) and a more unidimensional and mundane view of impossibility (as currently not plausibly realizable, accepting the conventional realist limitation of imagination that can only be overcome by unanticipated and improbable historical developments).

Derrida is aware on several levels of the seemingly endless dance of death that has for so long entrapped the Israeli and the Palestinian peoples. He is also sensitive to the connections of the Israel–Palestine conflict with the intensification of current lethal combat zones, both regional and global. Such concerns are explicit in Derrida's final phase of philosophizing undertaken in the shadow of the 9/11 attacks on the World Trade Center and the Pentagon. In *Philosophy in a Time of Terror* Derrida interprets this global setting as dominated by 'two political theologies, both, strangely enough, issuing out of the same stock or common soil of what I would call an "Abrahamic" revelation'.[2] Derrida makes explicit this linkage between the macrolevel geopolitics of counter-terrorism in the inflamed Middle East and the Israel–Palestine microlevel struggle. He asserts, 'It is highly significant that the epicenter … of all these "wars" is the confrontation between the state of Israel (another "democracy" …) and a virtual Palestinian state (one that … has not yet given up on declaring Islam the official state religion …)'.[3] Derrida also observes here that Israel has 'not cut the umbilical cord with religious, indeed with ethnoreligious authority'.[4] Such a deepening of reflective awareness strengthens the case for casting the net of inquiry far beyond the horizons of conventional wisdom.

Conventional wisdom with respect to Israel/Palestine continues to control public discourse on the conflict despite its unbroken record of futility. It basically reaffirms the concept of partition as applied to historic Palestine, although not as an initiative of the UN between two equal claims on the territory as was controversially attempted in 1947. The idea in recent decades has been to bring about a meeting of minds on the part of representatives of the antagonists seated at an international negotiating table, with the United States sitting at its head both purporting to be neutral and objective in *this* role while acting openly and essentially in an unbreakable partnership (labeled 'special relationship') with whatever Israeli government is in power at the time. The hoped-for end result of achieving 'peace' is generally asserted to be two nominally sovereign states, geographic neighbors coexisting peacefully side by side. (The gross disparities between the two 'neighbors' in their present condition and with regard to any likely negotiated outcome has been treated by mainstream commentators in the West as unmentionable, inevitable, realistic, and intrinsic.) One state, Israel, would remain a regional superpower with a formidable arsenal of nuclear weapons; the other, Palestine, would struggle for oxygen if it is, in fact, allowed to come into existence as a nominal sovereign state accepted as a member of international society. This Palestine would have to be willing to accept total vulnerability as an assured feature of its own demilitarization, disempowered as a state by being denied in advance any discretion or capabilities to uphold its own security in the face of perceived future threats to its existence and interests, however real, and consigned to living under humiliating conditions of constant economic, political, and social subordination to its Israeli neighbor.

Such a 'peace' is so emptied of justice and elemental collective dignity as to be almost certainly challenged from within the wider Palestinian community, which will be likely interpreted in the West not as a consequence of a response to injustice and indignity, but as a vindication of those Israeli voices who proclaimed over and over again the 'impossibility' of any peace with the Palestinians, or more generally, the Arabs. The Israeli argument in the end is that the Palestinians remain intent on destroying the state of Israel, and throwing its Jewish inhabitants into the sea, thus disregarding the repeated assertions by various Palestinian leaders of an acceptance of pre-1967 Israel provided Israel withdraws from the territory occupied in the 1967 war and properly addresses the refugee problems. Even aside from the asymmetry of such a peace between two peoples, now equal only in their shared humanity, there are two intractable problems with this conception. First of all, with an evolving set of circumstances that has continued for more than 60 years, the smaller Palestinian reality contracts further and further, while the Israeli reality expands in such a way that what may have seemed somewhat mutual and equitable decades ago now appears as one-sided and deformed. Israel has established such weighty facts on the ground (e.g. settlements, Judaization of Jerusalem) and heavy non-negotiable demands (e.g. no right of return for Palestinian refugees, no shared or divided control of Jerusalem) so as to repeatedly reshape the bargaining process of realist diplomacy to the disadvantage of the Palestinians. Indeed, in many respects, what is treated as de jure occupation is now more aptly described as a combination of de facto annexations.

In effect, the Palestinians are force-fed an increasingly one-sided arrangement that is given a totally misleading imprimatur of reasonableness by whoever happens to be 'the honest broker' in the White House at the time. For the Palestinians what is called 'peace' is ever more a slap in the face designed not only to legitimize unlawfully achieved disparities but also to depict the Palestinians as rejectionist and determined to eliminate Israel when, in reality, they are only resisting a permanent condition of the subordination of future Palestinian security and development to Israeli will and whim that has become ever more self-aggrandizing in response to the policies of its extremist right-wing leadership.[5] As Derrida affirms, the fears of the Jewish mainstream in Israel for their own future are genuine, associated with the long dark shadow still cast by memories of the Holocaust, and for Derrida himself, in his own personal inerasable memories of life as a Jewish child in the harshly antisemitic atmosphere of colonial Algeria. These are genuine elements of an Israeli–Jewish collective consciousness that *partly* explains Israeli non-negotiable security requirements, which are interwoven in complex ways with territorial ambitions and biblical claims. What such a reality induces at mainly Palestinian expense, however, is a lethal spiral between escalating Israeli demands for security, which to the extent accepted, give rise to intensifying Palestinian insecurity, as well as to various deprivations associated with being encouraged by Washington to swallow unacceptable demands.[6]

Second, the current Israeli leadership that seems completely resistant to striking a fair compromise is probably not prepared to accept even an international arrangement that is slanted so strongly in its favor. Ironically, such stubborn Israeli rejectionism may disclose the hollowness of the conventional wisdom on the conflict as habitually seen from the perspective of the favored Israeli side. Such a disclosure suggests that the peace process could have been all along for Israel nothing more than a diversionary theater presentation whose primary role has been to shift attention in such a manner as to facilitate the accumulation of ever more irreversible facts on the ground until the goal of a genuine Palestinian state no longer seems plausible even to those who were once its most ardent and influential advocates. The separation wall, draconian occupation, ethnic purification policies in East Jerusalem, relentless expansion of settlements and an Israelis-only road network on the West Bank, appropriation of water in occupied Palestine, undisguised refusal to repatriate refugees, and frequent violent incursions – all are creating a growing impression that the peace process, if not always, at least lately, has become a charade masking an annexationist, colonialist, and apartheid reality.

Negotiations probably never have been intended by the Israeli leadership to culminate in an actual peace agreement, but at best were designed to give an acceptable public relations exhibition of an unacknowledged, yet real, Palestinian surrender of self-determination rights coinciding with an Israeli dynamic of creeping annexation ('facts on the ground') relentlessly taking place on the West Bank and in East Jerusalem. If this is so, the peace process from beginning to end was nothing more than a nasty mind game played over and over for the sake of the liberal West and undoubtedly for portions of the Israeli populace and diasporic Jews. Neither the West nor Israeli public opinion exerted significant pressure on Israel to make a fair peace, and the United States, with multiple forms of leverage, was particularly culpable. It was sufficient for Israel to make periodic *rhetorical* avowals, however disingenuous, of its commitment to a consensual process that would bring about a new condition of coexistence. If this happened, it was hoped that it would undercut anti-Western popular sentiments in the Arab world with a variety of geopolitical benefits. Such a perception fused in the political imagination some kind of 'solution' to the conflict with the promotion of Western, especially American, strategic interests in the Middle East, especially related to oil reserves, stemming the Islamic tide, and ensuring that only Israel would possess nuclear weapons. This geopolitical dimension of diplomacy has become particularly pronounced in the twenty-first century given the priority accorded to energy policy and counter-terrorism in Western grand strategy. The still unresolved encounters in Iraq and Afghanistan despite the winding down of the American combat role, and the ongoing tensions with Iran are by-products of this global problematic. All of these geopolitical potholes would be easier to repair, so prevailing political reasoning supposes, if the Israeli–Palestinian conflict could be finally resolved, and the irritant of the conflict removed from the regional and global setting, with little concern devoted to whether the substance of such a removal would be consistent with international law, and even less, with the requirements of justice.

There is also an influential and related argument that, since 'peace' now seems unachievable by the parties to the conflict, and yet is such a high geopolitical priority, it must instead be imposed from outside. In effect, it is contended that the United States as the main producer and consumer of the conventional wisdom on the conflict must lend credibility to its own fable by rescuing the peace process from total disillusionment. Exponents of this reasoning hold that this can be done only by dictating the terms of coexistence between the two peoples in a manner that ratifies most of Israel's essential demands while purporting to be guided by a sense of justice beneficial for both sides.[7] Such an approach turns the historic clock of diplomacy back to the colonial era where it was common practice for European diplomats to draw the boundaries of political communities in the Global South without consulting the populations affected. The results were generally disastrous – natural communities divided in often arbitrary fashion by European ignorance, arrogance, and ambition, postponing for generations efforts to reconstitute more natural political communities based on ethnic, religious, spatial, cultural, and historical affinities. Indeed, much of the bloody turmoil afflicting the peoples of the Middle East can be traced to the dirty work of British and French diplomats who selfishly divided the spoils of the collapsed Ottoman Empire after the end of World War I. The United States, as unconditional ally of Israel and arbiter of the conflicting claims of the two sides, combines this imperial role of past colonial powers with a contemporary normative pretension that supposedly provides parties with the guidelines as to what is fair and just to resolve the conflict in a manner that accords with post-colonial realities. Of course, past colonial empires also always claimed a higher purpose, often expressed crudely as the 'white man's burden' or in a more sophisticated way by claiming for themselves a civilizing role of benefit to non-Western societies. Yet here too such a scenario for solution is wishful thinking as the post-colonial historical circumstances matter when it comes to shaping national destinies. A conflict as fundamental as that between Israel and the Palestinians cannot be solved by a diktat from Washington even if, as is not the case, the United States had the capacity and will to impose a just solution. The process of envisioning a solution has become more and more difficult without breaking the bonds of conventional wisdom altogether by abandoning the presumed basis of peace as some arrangement of permanent partition (the two-state consensus) rather than in a restored unity for Palestine, which until recently has been advocated only by isolated and idealistic voices in the wilderness. No longer surprisingly, in view of the cumulative settlement phenomenon, there have recently surfaced in Israel right-wing versions of a one-state solution in a series of variations on the following template: relinquishing Gaza forever, thereby getting rid of 1.5 million Palestinians; expanding the settlements indefinitely; denying the Palestinian diaspora any right of return; promising eventual second-class Israeli citizenship to the captive Palestinian population, and extending the hegemony of a Jewish state to the West Bank and East Jerusalem.

Different understandings of 'impossibility' inescapably confront any effort at this stage to point the parties toward those forms of peace that might be genuine and sustainable.[8] It will be explained in a later section that this represents a deliberate repudiation of the conventional wisdom that politics is 'the art of the possible'. The claim here is that such a politics of 'the possible' can produce only despair for those seeking justice and peace for the Palestinians, and even for the Israelis. Derrida's thinking, although using impossibility in a less immediately political sense, but rather in a profound series of 'deconstructions' denoting inherently unresolvable dilemmas or aporias of thought and action bearing on living together, is highly relevant in this context by proposing a daring conceptual leap from 'impossibility' to 'responsibility', that is, detaching the burden of decision both from any criteria of guidance and from the vague, and sometimes dangerous, admonition to exercise good faith. Many individual and collective disasters have emanated from the good faith and sincerity of fanatics, perhaps most ominously, the Holocaust. By referencing the Nuremberg trials against surviving Nazi leaders, Derrida convincingly treats the Holocaust as a historically definitive turning away from deference to the unconditional sovereignty of states and unaccountability of their leaders.[9] In effect, sincerity is never enough. Respect for fundamental human rights must be retained as the Archimedean threshold of political acceptability without ever surrendering to an unjust fait accompli.

Derrida's relevance

Against such a discouraging background of assessment, and taking note of the daily torment experienced by the Palestinians, Derrida's guidance to living together well is refreshing and possibly liberating, but only if understood as a series of signposts for thought and not solutions for the policy puzzles. Derrida both encourages detachment from the conventional dead-end wisdom that has long shaped the mainstream discourse of the Palestine–Israel conflict, and avoids the correlative temptation to advocate some type of colonialist intervention disguised as conflict resolution achieved through the exercise of a supposedly benign global leadership.

Derrida is suggestive both at the level of generality and of particularity. He points to 'peace' as 'an enigmatic concept if ever there was one' ('Avowing', 11), and makes clear that it is not to be confused with 'armistice', 'cease-fire', or 'peace process' ('Avowing', 11), nor with the sort of ultimate or utopian peace associated with such words as 'perpetual' or 'messianic' that provide an imaginative horizon for that which is desired and desirable.[10] These visionary signposts point to outcomes that are not within the realm of attainable futures, and hence, appear *politically* irrelevant in the narrow sense of projects that are undertaken with the means envisioned to attain the end. So what could be a relevant horizon of (just) peace for these two peoples locked so rigidly in conflict?

Of course, Derrida gives no easy answers or clear paths, only hints and calls for responsible decisions in the presence of radical and irreducible uncertainty, decisions that are hence inseparable from accepting high risks and dangerous uncertainties. Among the hints is the clear differentiation between the absence of war under conditions of cease-fire and armistice, and even worse, occupation (gradations of *living together badly*), and an avowal of peace that involves a search for *how* within a given set of conditions the process of living together can be transformed into *living together well*, or at least, much better. Derrida insists that this quest for peace requires sensitivity to the demands of law but is far from synonymous with the implementation of legality. In Derrida's words: 'I do not wish to grant too great a privilege to the juridical sphere, to international law and to international institutions, even if I believe more than ever in their importance.'[11] To succeed with law and beyond law, a peace process must engender such movements of the heart as trust, good faith, sympathy, and compassion, taking the fears and perceptions of 'the other' into account ('Avowing', 15). More specifically, 'Palestinians and Israelis will truly live together only on the day when … peace comes into bodies and souls' ('Avowing', 11). By putting the threshold of peace so high for these peoples so long mired in distrust, bad faith, and hostility, Derrida is perhaps here unwittingly encouraging, or at least creating a respectable space for, a politics of despair, with which I disagree for reasons made clear below.

It needs to be appreciated that diplomacy as practiced by governments is dramatically more modest about its idea of peace, and even more humble in its accomplishments. In general, the diplomat proclaims success, and may even receive a Nobel Peace Prize, if antagonistic parties can only be made to agree, even if the agreement reflects the unfair outcome of coercion or bribery rather than genuine consent and fulfillment of respective rights, or deliberately puts to one side certain intractable issues so as to have the appearance of an agreement. President Jimmy Carter's Camp David Accords in 1978 were appropriately appreciated as bringing an end to a condition of war between Israel and Egypt, including Israeli withdrawal from the Sinai peninsula, but this step toward peace was achieved only by an American commitment to pay the parties significant continuing annual subsidies for the indefinite future and by leaving the Palestinians adrift. From such diplomacy the best that Palestinians and Israelis can ever expect is a less violent form of unjust living together, that of a durable cease-fire and armistice, a long-term truce, reduced tensions and violence, and above all, an end to occupation, achieved at the high costs of inscribing illegality, injustice, and hierarchy on the lives of both peoples, but with grossly unequal effects as between oppressor and oppressed.

At the same time, despite these difficulties, it would be irresponsible in the special sense imparted by Derrida to abandon the search. There are other valuable hints in Derrida's text. I find especially crucial the stress on the additional ethical burdens placed on the strong, thereby taking a more humanistic account of disparities of power than is customary for realists. It is the worldly 'realist' stance that reduces collective human interaction to working out the implications of existing disparities of power, what 'experts' refer to as facts on the ground in the Palestine/Israel setting. The ultimate expression of this realist feature of international relations is to consider as legal beyond questioning or revision 'peace treaties' that ratify the fruits of aggressive war, and disavow the international norm that sovereign territory cannot be validly acquired by force. Derrida reserves this kind of calculus, insightfully and realistically, for his more compelling sense of the real as always incorporating a sense of the impossible as enhancing the potential of what exists. He suggests that an initiative for peace must proceed 'in a manner that is first of all wisely unilateral' ('Avowing', 11), a willingness by the stronger side to act without seeking an exchange or a reciprocal action, a genuine search for reconciliation. One suspects that such an Israeli posture, if genuine and of sufficient magnitude, would have a contagious effect, leading quickly to Palestinian countermoves that could create a benign circle of respect and engagement, and might enable the start of a true peace process.

It should be carefully observed that Derrida puts the enigmatic qualifier 'wisely' before the word 'unilateral', suggesting limits perhaps intended to be associated with avoiding a provocative vulnerability in the form of a repudiation from within (as enraging one's own constituency by giving away too much without receiving anything in return) or without (creating a temptation for adversary extremists by what might be interpreted as exhibition of weakness rather than a show of strength). Suggestive of the issue in the Israeli/Palestinian context was the assassination in 1995 of the Israeli prime minister, Yitzhak Rabin, by a right-wing Israeli extremist, Yigal Amir, who seems to have acted in good faith, apparently at the behest of others in a right-wing sect, intending to save the country from the peace that Israeli extremists believed would follow from the recently signed Oslo Accord, and either doom the Jewish state and Zionist project over time or at least foreclose its maximalist vision of reconstituting biblical Israel. As subsequent events have shown, Amir need not have thrown his life away, nor taken the life of Rabin, as it is highly unlikely that had Rabin lived, a viable Palestinian state would have emerged from the ensuing negotiations in any event.

Similarly, the assassination in 1981 of Anwar Sadat, president of Egypt, was attributed to Egyptian extremists who were deeply opposed to Sadat's normalization of relations with Israel, especially his signing of the Sinai Peace Treaty in 1978, widely viewed as an unforgivable betrayal of Arab unity and the Palestinian struggle. Sadat's gestures were interpreted differently depending on national and ideological perspective. For the Israeli mainstream and liberal Americans, Sadat was perceived at the time to be an angel of peace, but for most Palestinians, and the Arab 'street', Sadat was a cowardly and opportunistic figure ready and willing to turn his back on Palestinian claims and rights, while subscribing to the word 'peace' without concern for its substance.[12]

There is a parallel path of respect for rights leading toward genuine peace that Derrida does not consider, although he is acutely sensitive to the role and limits of law, and more generally, to the importance and yet insufficiency of a juridical framing of living together, either well or badly. Such a framing is particularly problematic in the Israel/Palestine context because it is insufficiently sensitive to the circumstance of *these* two peoples living together better in the early twenty-first century. As Derrida perceptively notes, both positive and negative potentialities can be realized along a spectrum of endlessly varied permutations. A positive law-based initiative would entail a belated Israeli acknowledgment that reconciliation depends on a mutual acknowledgment of respective *rights*, but coupled with an attitude of reconciliation and compassion, perhaps institutionalized in the form of a truth and reconciliation commission. Such an acknowledgment would come as an utter surprise, amounting to a rupture with the consistent and effective Israeli insistence on shifting the diplomatic conversation away from respective rights toward the need to work out adjustments that are responsive to existing facts, that is, in effect, ratifying prolonged Israeli unlawfulness in their administration of the occupation.

If we contemplate this rupture, however unlikely it seems, there is a further benefit: the Palestinians would then have something to give in exchange as well as to receive. Despite their anguish over the *nakba*, they themselves could also, if so inclined, help construct an atmosphere of trust by recognizing the anguish of the Holocaust, thereby framing the interaction of the two peoples as based on a shared compassionate appreciation of the historical suffering of 'the other'.[13] With the help of such a manifested and mutual awareness, a turn away from facts on the ground and toward law/rights could *begin* to overcome the deepening imbalances and open wounds arising from long-sustained and acute disparities in power and decades of failure to protect Palestinian rights. It is not that the discourse of law is inherently generative of justice, but it can be, as here, a partial corrective for embedded injustice, that is, where rights have been systematically occluded by force and facts. This has long been the disillusioning experience and ordeal of the Palestinians, who point to the consistent failure over many years to implement dozens of UN resolutions affirming their rights. As a result many Palestinians held the view until recently that only violence would yield any results, pointing to Hezbollah's success in prompting Israeli withdrawal from Lebanon in 2000 and armed resistance as inducing the Israeli 'disengagement' from Gaza in 2005.[14] Yet there has been in the last several years an encouraging development – this Palestinian sense of dependence on violent resistance is giving way to an increasing reliance on soft power strategy, epitomized by the worldwide boycott, divestment, and sanctions (BDS) campaign, or more broadly, by engagement in a global legitimacy war of the sort that toppled the apartheid regime in South Africa in the early 1990s.

Against this background, the willingness of Israel to acknowledge the relevance of Palestinian rights under international law, as conditioning the politics of reconciliation, would exhibit Israeli sincerity and seriousness to an extent never previously displayed. Yet from another vantage point, as significant as such a turn would seem, it would still only amount to a belated recognition of entitlements on the Palestinian side that were long suppressed by Israeli diplomatic muscle and force of arms. Derrida constructively points out that a reconciling process is unlikely to move very far ahead without some real and perceived *sacrifice* being made on all sides, but to qualify as a 'sacrifice' an action must voluntarily come from within each of the antagonists rather than be imposed from without by a powerful geopolitical actor. Derrida's presentation also makes it clear that an act of sacrifice should never be confused with a *concession* made as a result of negotiations or even as a calculated step to achieve an eventual advantage (for instance, dismantling some or all of the West Bank settlements in the expectation of permanent unified control of Jerusalem or of Palestinian abandonment of demands associated with the right of return of refugees).

Such a rights-based approach to peace, from the perspective of the sort of rational calculations that dominate realist diplomacy, would seem to suggest major substantive benefits for the Palestinians and major drawbacks for the Israelis. It would from this worldly viewpoint seem impractical in the extreme, and even irrational. On every major contested issue in the conflict (refugees, Jerusalem, settlements, borders, water) international law is clearly (at least as clear as law can ever be) on the side of Palestinian claims to a degree that would make legal counter-arguments seem puerile and unpersuasive. That is, there are several Israeli legal counter-arguments that could certainly be advanced, but they are so much against the grain of prevailing and neutral legal (and ethical) understanding as to possess little political weight if objectively assessed. If a rights-based approach to peace negotiation were to be adopted, it would almost certainly resolve issues in contention in favor of Palestinian claims. Put differently, the post-1967 grievances, and equally the pre-1967 grievances of the Palestinians seem overwhelmingly legitimated by international law.[15]

And significantly, since the PLO National Council declaration in 1988, the most substantial pre-1967 Palestinian grievances (with the exception of the refugee issue) have been effectively renounced and foreclosed, including the earlier insistence that the establishment of a Jewish state within the British-mandated territory of Palestine was unlawful from its moment of origin, as well as the subsequent, more limited contention that Israel, as a territorial entity, should be confined to the borders of the 1948 armistice. These borders had already greatly enlarged Israeli territory beyond the UN partition boundaries established by the international community as a fair apportionment of historic Palestine (minus Jordan) as between the two entities.[16] In effect, without demanding or receiving reciprocity, the Palestinians have already made major, largely unacknowledged concessions to the Zionist project of establishing a Jewish state on Arab lands, moves that Derrida might have termed a wise unilateral initiative given the overall circumstances. This Palestinian self-limiting posture definitively *sacrificed* significant law/justice claims arising from the establishment of a Jewish state within the Palestinian Mandate as a colonialist scenario.[17] What makes this gesture toward reconciliation particularly impressive is that Palestine was (and remains) the obviously weaker party, and despite its vulnerability made such a pronounced effort more than 20 years ago to transform a frozen conflict into a negotiable disagreement with the manifest intention of establishing a new reality of living together, hopefully well, or at least tolerably.

The Palestinian side was almost certainly inhibited from describing its behavior in the language of sacrifice owing to an entirely understandable anxiety about generating fury among the Palestinian people for giving away basic rights that were inalienable, and hence could and should not have been given, and certainly without receiving anything in exchange. In retrospect, it can be seriously asked in Derrida's suggestive language whether this was a *wise* instance of Palestinian unilateralism, which has now been inscribed in the political consciousness of all parties as the baseline from which any serious negotiations should start. Even Hamas demands only withdrawal to the 1967 boundaries along with the end of the Gaza blockade as its preconditions for long-term arrangement of peaceful co-existence. In effect, since the Palestinian initiative of 1988 gained little or nothing from the Israelis, it may not seem to have been a wise sacrificial initiative, at least as viewed retrospectively. Perhaps at the time it seemed like a bold and sensible wager on breaking the deadlock given the limited options at the disposal of the Palestinians.

Later, after the societal mobilization of the Intifada (1987), followed by the Gulf War (1991), there seemed to be a serious American-led effort to find a solution for the conflict through providing an international framework that would create pathways to accommodation. Edward Said strongly argued that the main result of this effort, the Oslo Declaration (1993) was to give effect to an unwise and subservient unilateralism on the Palestinian side that amounted to a surrender. Subsequent developments have largely upheld his otherwise cynical assessments of the so-called peace process.[18] Can Israel ever be expected to shift the fulcrum of its negotiations from 'facts' (that is, power and status quo) to 'rights' (that is, sacrifice and withdrawal) for the sake of reconciliation and peace, achieved in the spirit of compassion and historic compromise? And if not, can the Palestinians ever be expected to give their consent to a set of circumstances that is disastrously disadvantageous from the perspective of their rights, hopes, aspirations? If these questions are answered negatively, as would seem to be the case from a political perspective, but not from *certain* religious perspectives, then deep or real peace is necessarily part of that messianic horizon that Derrida identifies, and not a worldly possibility. This is a depressing realization, and hopefully not the whole story. What we should by now realize is that the political processes, as so far known to us, can only be expected to achieve either a victors' peace or a nominal peace (essentially dictated by Tel Aviv, ratified by Washington, and swallowed in Ramallah). Such a peace, at best another armistice or truce hidden behind a more grandiose description of what was achieved, would need to be harshly enforced at every stage to be at all stable, unless ethnic cleansing or a consummated genocide would eliminate the Palestinian presence altogether. Short of an outright Palestinian surrender, continuing resistance by the Palestinians would almost certainly be the inevitable by-product of such a peace, and given regional trends, could lead to an expanded war zone and reliance by both sides on more destructive weaponry and tactics. Any such outcome would certainly be trumpeted as a genuine peace by the Western media and negotiating governments, and might mislead public opinion in the West. At the same time it is almost certain to be greeted with great suspicion by those who have in the past and present acted in solidarity with the Palestinian struggle, or feel that too much has been sacrificed to accept such an unequal arrangement.

In some respects, an illuminating analogy is the deceptive acquiescence of many surviving indigenous communities in their dismal fate. Of course, this acquiescence takes a variety of forms, ranging from hidden opposition at the margins of various modern societal arrangements to different degrees of co-optation and opportunism, but it should never be confused with authentic acts of acceptance or confused with a satisfactory rendering of justice.[19] One expression of the tension wrought by such forms of peace is the behavior of Puerto Ricans who vote for US statehood in the afternoon and then go to a local bar to sing independence songs. In effect, the calculative advantages of tax breaks and food stamps for an impoverished island people induces a pragmatic vote for a subordinated affiliation associated with statehood within the federal structure of the United States, while the impractical dream of most Puerto Ricans remains for their country to become a fully independent and sovereign state standing on its own with its own presence on the global stage.

In the face of the discouraging prospect of genuine peace being achieved by intergovernmental diplomacy, a shift to religious orientations by both Palestinians and Israelis has been observed. When religion is put forward as an alternative to politics, this shift must be clarified. For one face of religion is the accentuation of the worst tendency of politics to extinguish compassion and to interpret conflict in a completely narcissistic, absolutist, friend/enemy or faithful/infidel dualistic, and belligerent manner. The extremist wings on both Israeli and Palestinian sides have grown in influence while the conflict has persisted through the decades, exhibiting this abandonment of politics in favor of religion. Reliance on fundamentalist religious identities gives rise to non-negotiable demands that are completely indifferent to the consequences for the feared and hated 'other', whose otherness is demonized so as to be treated as not deserving of respect.

But there is more to religion than such extremist versions. Religion should not be treated as the essential foundation for peace, but neither should it be demonized. Demonization of the Islamic other became an acceptable component of public discourse, especially in the United States, after the 9/11 attacks and in response to the rise of the so-called 'religious right' and evangelical Christianity.[20] It should be remembered that the inclusive potentialities of religion provide the strongest and most widely adhered-to basis for a compassionate and ecumenical approach to conflict and reconciliation, as well as offering a serious engagement with the imperatives of universal principles of justice.[21] Both Judaism and Islam have strong inclusive traditions that have recently been hidden or marginalized by the politically motivated prominence given to the minority views of exclusivist extremists. This misleading and exaggerated presentation of religion exerts a baneful historical influence, accentuated if allied with lifeworld expansionist and xenophobic undertakings.[22] If there is to be societal support for actualizing the mainly hidden compassionate and inclusive potentiality of religion as an indispensable basis of reconciliation for Israel and Palestine, it will depend on a reconfiguring of religion along these more universalistic lines.

In an elemental sense, a peace process that is truly about peace is necessarily and inevitably, albeit partly, a religious undertaking that cannot be adequately grasped by reliance on the bargaining language of the bazaar or even of the diplomatic language of international negotiations. And maybe for that reason the existential outcome for the parties locked in conflict will likely not be genuine peace because their respective imaginations are set too securely within a *politically* grounded mindset, or worse, rendered unconditional, that is, *apolitical*, by exclusivist religious affirmations.[23] Tragically, this suggests that what we have been calling a 'peace process' is almost certain to give rise to one of several non-peaceful outcomes: generating new cycles of violence, leading to the eventual annihilation or surrender by the weaker side, or, at best, producing a permanent cease-fire and an end to occupation, whether negotiated or imposed, and whether or not denominated as 'peace'.

By moving outside of politics in the direction of religion, the main civilizational custodian of both compassionate and narcissistic ethics, we observe more clearly the unfolding of frustrating narratives, afflicting in different ways and in distinct registers, of the suffering of the adversaries known as Israel and Palestine, abstractions that hide the fears, hopes, and daily struggles of people in their life situations. In effect, peace is not attainable by political means, at least as practiced by governments and bureaucratic entities, a depressing conclusion to be sure. It should be depressing for both sides, because it means that even the dominant party can never relax, can never trust, and must constantly act to instill fear and loathing on the part of the dominated other. Such a pattern of neither peace nor war has been increasingly evident in Israeli security policy: building an unlawful separation wall on the Palestinian side of the green line resulting in further encroachment on occupied Palestinian territory, attacking a defenseless Gaza with ultramodern and cruel weaponry, and even threatening aggression against Iran, rationalized in advance as a necessary 'preventive war'.

There are at least three other ways of conceiving the political in relation to the Palestine–Israel conflict that pave the way to more hopeful scenarios, which will be discussed in descending order of plausibility. Each is improbable, and for that reason, promising as a vector for constructive thought (since the 'probable' is irrelevant from the perspectives of peace and justice that guide this inquiry). As argued above, the probable is stuck in a matrix that seems definitely incapable of yielding a genuine, or even a sustainable, peace for the two peoples. None of these ways being proposed here is directly considered in Derrida's essay, but each could be incorporated in his presentation without disturbing his overall framing of the inquiry.

A first alternative would involve exploring analogous conflict patterns to discover the conditions under which progress toward peace was made. For instance, the Irish experience of recent years qualifies as one where an apparently irreconcilable conflict was resolved to a significant, although partial, and as yet still uncertain degree. The context suggests that many factors led to this generally favorable set of developments, but the most crucial seemed a change of heart on the part of the main external actors, the United Kingdom and the United States, in their approach taken toward the Irish Republican Army (IRA). What changed was the willingness to see the IRA as a political other, with grievances and legitimate claims, rather than as a terrorist spoiler of the status quo that must be eliminated and could not be treated as an actual, or even, a hypothetical negotiating partner. Such a shift, never publicly acknowledged, appeared to make a crucial difference, inducing a spirit of reconciliation, compromise, and mutuality culminating in the Good Friday Agreement. Despite some bloody setbacks, a momentum for reconciliation produced a set of conditions that comes close to achieving a sustainable peace (although doubts and grievances remain and regressive incidents occur), which while falling far short of realizing the full meaning of peace in Derrida's sense, of course an impossibility, did achieve an outcome that had seemed 'impossible' in the lesser sense used here, and was desirable as compared to what had previously existed.[24]

Could not some similar process emerge in Israel, or on the part of the United States or the European Union as external actors, treating the Palestinian other, including Hamas, as a human subject and political actor with rights, status, and feelings, as well as seeking enough common ground to be able to redeploy the language of peace and peace process in a credible manner *for the first time*?[25] Derrida has some interesting and pertinent comments on his hopes that Europe might become a different kind of political actor, more swayed by law and justice, but admits that he discerns no present evidence supportive of such a hope.[26]

What makes this approach unlikely to be embraced is the width and depth of disparity in material conditions, intensified by a prolonged occupation that deliberately sought to give this constructed reality an appearance of permanence and irreversibility. The extent of common ground seems too minuscule to enable any dramatic movement from the *here* of occupation (really annexation) to the *there* of Palestinian self-determination in the form of a distinct truly sovereign state. That is why humane skeptics on the Palestinian side, from Edward Said to Saree Makdisi, have increasingly opted for a single democratic secular state (one polity for two peoples) that entails the abandonment of a Jewish state, and thus of the main Zionist rationale.[27] In other words, both sides would have to renounce their separate super-nationalistic goals in exchange for the benefits of a sustainable peace by adopting a merger (or partial submergence) of their respective nationalisms, signaled by a new name for this sovereign entity that would be more or less coterminous with the British Mandate of Palestine. In effect, then, the one-state solution would be an Israel/Palestine version of the Irish breakthrough toward accommodation, but taking into account the drastically different circumstances, and hoping for the best under the most difficult of circumstances; although not without concern that this hope for the best could end up as an embodiment of the worst, which would be a single state dominated by Zionist ideology and Israeli secular control.

When describing the formation of states, and specifically Israel, Derrida observes that their birth is always accompanied by what he calls 'originary violence', a violent imposition on whatever form of societal community previously existed at that place and a set of exclusions bearing on the future that arises as soon as defensible borders are drawn, from which 'no state can escape' ('Avowing', 22).[28] On the Israeli side especially, and particularly on the part of dedicated Zionists, we might expect a renewal of originary violence if a wider Israeli swing toward a one-state outcome were ever to occur, but that should not necessarily doom the project. As Derrida also points out, the imposing of law requires reliance on force to achieve compliance even if its goal is the elimination, or at least the mitigation, of violence. The political preconditions for the formation of a single state to embrace the two peoples are difficult to set forth in advance. These would likely reflect a political form that expressed the popular will of both communities as discerned by legitimate representation at the leadership level and consent and consensus at the popular level, which does not currently exist, nor is it easily imagined. An additional difficulty of implementation, even if some degree of political resistance could be somehow brushed aside or rendered minimal, is that the disparities that presently exist would undoubtedly be preserved and reproduced in new forms in a unified state. Eliminating or at least mitigating these disparities would depend on a religious revisioning of the conflict through an outpouring of empathy on both sides that seems unimaginable, a stretching of plausible projections to an unreasonable extreme. The South African compromise miraculously achieved by Nelson Mandela nevertheless allowed the white elite to retain their privileged material and social positions. Such an outcome, itself an illustration of the impossible happening to an extent, suggests the problems contained in what remains an inspiring instance of a largely nonviolent transformation despite the extremely violent circumstances of acute abuse and exploitation during the last stages of apartheid. Even if we embrace the ambiguous utopianism of a secular one-state 'solution' to the Palestine–Israel conflict as a practical political project, there are these further concerns about the persistence of originary violence and the degree to which law and force are made available to protect regimes of unequal rights and opportunities so as to maintain pre-existing economic, social, and cultural hierarchies.

A second alternative approach takes seriously the eventual possibilities of bottom-up politics associated here with the mobilization of global civil society in the shape of a Palestinian global solidarity movement.[29] Social change has throughout history been dependent on such struggles, and some argue that most successful challenges to oppression have resulted from them.[30] The American civil rights movement was one impressive example, but undoubtedly the most relevant example for this essay is the anti-apartheid movement that exerted such pressure on the South African racist regime as to bring about an entirely unexpected change of heart and mind, featuring Nelson Mandela's release from jail and the subsequent, equally unexpected, consensual establishment of a multiracial constitutional democracy. This came about not because of a sudden moral awakening on the part of the Afrikaaner leadership in South Africa, but because of the multiple pressures exerted from difficulties of governability within the country and as a consequence of a worldwide movement, fully supported by the UN, leading to the isolation and delegitimation of the apartheid government as resting its authority on the bare claim of territorial sovereignty, subverted by a set of racist arrangements that had been officially declared a crime against humanity by the collectivity of governments represented at the United Nations. Derrida persuasively stresses this development of criminalizing the behavior of sovereign states and their leaders as a decisive moment in the moral evolution of humanity. He traces the emergence of this sovereignty-transcending criterion of 'crime against humanity' directly to the Holocaust, which allowed international law to move morally and legally forward via the Nuremberg Judgment.

In important respects, the Palestinian Solidarity Movement is correctly perceived as the successor to the anti-apartheid movement. Particularly since the Gaza attacks of 2008–9, a mobilization of support for Palestinian justice and self-determination has taken hold in all parts of the world, but to a far lesser extent at a governmental or intergovernmental level. There is under way a robust BDS movement (that is, boycott, divestment, and sanctions) modeled on the anti-apartheid movement, and achieving some symbolically important results, including an escalating spiral of economic, sports, and cultural boycotts in recent months.[31] It is difficult to evaluate the effectiveness of this mobilization because it will be denied as having any impact by the established centers of power and opinion unless and until the target government decides on making a radical and entirely unexpected, and likely abrupt, move in the direction of accommodation. This was the case with regard to South Africa, and it is likely to be so for Israel, assuming that a moment of transformation does eventually arise. At this time, such an eventuality seems totally implausible, but so it did in the case of South Africa just months before it began happening. Visiting there in the apartheid era, I was struck over and over again by how the white consensus was articulated in survival terms – it's either us or them – while the African consensus was equally captive to the hard power mythology of conflict and violence – we will prevail, but it will take a long time and be bloody. The idea of reconciliation and transformation was not acknowledged on either side, even in private conversation, until it began to happen!

Of course, Israel/Palestine is not South Africa. The Palestinians are not blessed with a Mandela, although there are important nonviolent leaders and tactics that slip below the radar of the global media.[32] The Israelis are burdened by a history of persecution that makes its leadership risk-averse and overly reliant on force to achieve security. Beyond this, Mandela made it easier for the white establishment by his refusal to challenge economic and societal apartheid, limiting his demands to the dismantling of political apartheid. For this reason, it may be that a fierce struggle lies ahead in the likely event that the remnants of apartheid come under increasing pressure from an impoverished and still exploited African majority. What is relevant, however, is to take note of how often political struggles are not settled by force of arms, but rather on the symbolic battlefields of legitimacy wars. Whether we consider the American defeat in Vietnam, the collapse of communism in Eastern Europe and the Soviet Union, or the removal from power of despotic leaders in Iran (1979) or the Philippines (1985), the importance of victory in legitimacy wars is repeatedly demonstrated. But winning a legitimacy war is a far cry from ensuring a corresponding political result. The plight of the Tibetans or Chechens or any number of entrapped ethnicities in hostile political frameworks demonstrates the sad historical truth that legitimacy matters *decisively* only under certain conditions. The Palestinians waging their struggle at the present time have yet to show that they have the capacity to make the outcome of this legitimacy war matter enough to the Israeli leadership to make the option of reconciliation an attractive alternative to persisting conflict.

A third mode of hopeful conceiving is to take serious account of the unanticipatable as an element of the wider reality of the Palestine–Israel conflict. At present, given the circumstances described above, and the outlook of the relevant political actors, the rational and realistic political mind cannot conceive of genuine peace as an outcome, that is, a peace based on living together *well*. The most that can be rationally imagined is a somewhat better cease-fire, agreed upon and reinforced by a partial Israeli withdrawal and sweetened by international economic assistance, but built on unacceptable and unlawfully constructed disparities and by a persisting lack of respect for Palestinian rights, especially in relation to refugees, exiles, and Jerusalem. In contrast, what Derrida seeks and demands by way of peace is an entirely different modality of living together than as occupier and occupied or as Jew and Arab, drastic differentiations of identity inevitably tinged with bitterness, fears, false narratives, and anxieties, and the reinstitutionalizing of ethnic hierarchy. Perhaps the optimal form of a mutual agreement was developed a few years ago by the concerted and courageous efforts of civil society peace representatives of both Palestinian and Israeli peace camps, with the Israeli participants being fringe political players, while the Palestinian participants were closely associated with the core leadership at the time of Yasser Arafat. Reflecting this disparity in representation, what could be agreed was inscribed in arrangements proclaimed to the world as 'peace' but retaining the core inequities that the Palestinians had been accumulating over the years, indeed for so long as to make even Palestinians accept their existence. These Geneva proposals certainly diminished the one-sidedness of intergovernmental horizons but still came nowhere close to prescribing a just peace, sensitive to the fundamental and equal rights of both peoples, and may even have fallen short of achieving a sustainable peace, the form of impossibility insisted on here. There is no doubt that good faith and a search for reconciliation animated this effort, as well as a disavowal of the sterile Oslo peace process. Still, the participants in this alternative search were pragmatists influenced by considerations of realism and conflict fatigue, making the outcome of their efforts to find a more balanced conception of peace still far too deferential to the demands of Israel as the more powerful party to produce a sustainable peace, much less a genuine peace.[33] Such an outcome reinforces the impression that a sustainable peace is presently unattainable despite maximizing rational efforts, and thus fails the litmus test of lifeworld politics as the art of the possible. It also confirms Derrida's admonition that peace for Israel/Palestine will not and cannot be achieved through bargaining or calculating relative advantages via governments. An altered will in society and among elites is also indispensable.

But suppose instead, in a situation where peace with justice is not attainable by normal politics, that there is recourse to what might be called 'extraordinary politics', politics as the art of the impossible or the politics of impossibility. The viability of such considerations rests on our confirmed inability to anticipate the future, and our experience of being consistently surprised by the unanticipated.[34] Many historical struggles for social and political justice succeeded despite the seeming impossibility of such an outcome. This was true of the anti-slavery movement, of many anti-colonial struggles, more recently of the anti-apartheid movement, and throughout history of the many movements of resistance that defied the logic of superior military and material power. In relation to the Palestinian struggle it appears concretely to mean at present investing hopes for the future in the conduct of the legitimacy war without calculating or depicting in advance how to achieve a just outcome or what its contours would be. As suggested earlier, the structures and practices of a prolonged coercive occupation amount to a continuing crime against humanity in the Nuremberg sense, and this adds clarity and consensus to solidarity with the Palestinian quest for rights and justice as the foundation of peace. Because of such moral/legal pressure, an alternative to an oppressive stalemate or an unsustainable long-term cease-fire is gradually implanting itself on the global collective consciousness, as well as among Palestinians and Israelis, and might over time encourage outside actors to play a constructive peacemaking role.

In such a 'hopeful' understanding of the Palestinian plight, it has been necessary to break the bondage of reasonable expectations or feasible proposals. Only the unreasonable and unfeasible appear presently useful. And what was discussed above needs to be considered in combination, not as a matter of alternatives. Of course, there are no assurances of success, far from it, and that is part of the point. The search for any assurance in advance as the prudential basis for concerted action contradicts the foundational engagement of a politics of impossibility in a mysterious, yet strange, kind of hope that arises out of the depths of hopelessness, and cannot be validated by an appeal to evidence. Implicit in this exploration of impossibility has been a skepticism about any further reliance by either side on violence as the basis of emancipation or security, while acknowledging the importance of Derrida's analysis of originary violence as accompanying the formation of every sovereign state. If the Palestinians are to enjoy the benefits of a sustainable peace, it must be accompanied by some realization of justice. Moving from here closer to there will almost certainly be largely, although neither exclusively nor necessarily, the result of a globalized nonviolent movement that undermines the stability of existing structures at the level of mind and heart. This is the major teaching of late twentieth- and twenty-first-century conflict, and the most enduring lesson of the South African transformation.

Notes

1 An important ambiguity, not commented on by Derrida, should be taken into account throughout this chapter. References to 'Israelis' and to 'Israel' tend to suggest a monolithic reality that obscures a spectrum of Jewish attitudes (including toward a variety of Zionisms), and more important the reality that 20 percent of the population of pre-1967 Israel is Palestinian, and has been living as a second-class, discriminated, and mainly alienated minority in a self-proclaimed Jewish state. Such conditions are themselves incompatible with Articles 26 and 27 of the International Covenant of Civil and Political Rights. It should also be emphasized that the conditions that exist at present should not be treated as symmetrical in assessing the burdens of the conflict on Israelis and Palestinians living under occupation. In every material, political, and psychological sense conditions are grossly unequal to the disadvantage of the Palestinians, which is particularly true given the unlawful character of an occupation that has gone on since 1967, entailing severe encroachment on fundamental human rights that increases with the passage of time, especially due to settlement expansion.

2 G. Borradori, *Philosophy in a Time of Terror: Dialogues with Jürgen Habermas and Jacques Derrida*, Chicago: University of Chicago Press, 2003, 117.

3 Ibid., 117–18 note 1; I would personally question whether Israel, given its increasingly harsh approach to internal dissent and to its Palestinian minority, deserves the

characterization of 'another democracy', although the inverted quotes in the Derrida text suggests an intention to question whether the Israeli claim to be the only democracy in the Middle East is to be accepted at face value.

4 Ibid., 118.

5 There is ongoing discussion as to whether the rightward drift of Israeli internal politics has much bearing on Palestinian prospects for the exercise of their inalienable right of self-determination. On one side, are those who insist that more moderate Israeli political outlooks, in the manner of Rabin and Peres, were prepared to strike a real compromise with the Palestinian people. On the other side are those who argue that even moderate Israeli leaders coveted the West Bank and Jerusalem and were not willing to end the settlement process or agree to a Palestinian right of return as endorsed by the UN General Assembly in resolution 194.

6 A variation on 'the security dilemma' is depicted by R. Jervis in *Perception and Misperception in International Politics*, Princeton, NJ: Princeton University Press, 1976, 58–116.

7 Best articulated by H. Siegman, 'Imposing Middle East Peace', *Nation*, January 25, 2010, 18–20; but see M. Benvenisti, 'The Case for Shared Sovereignty', *Nation*, 18 June 2007, 11–16.

8 It is not a word game to insist that the impossible is necessary. It is a way of criticizing conventional endorsements of a two-state solution as an outcome that would not bring peace, and at this stage, given Israeli policies associated with the settler movement enacted for more than 40 years and a cumulative effort at ethnic cleansing in East Jerusalem, the preconditions for a viable Palestinian sovereign state are missing, even if the Israeli political will existed, which is not the case. Impossible is meant here not in the Derridean positive sense, but in a negative sense of pretending that there exists a correspondence between the phrases 'two-state solution' and 'an end of the conflict'.

9 It was the Holocaust, as perceived at the end of World War II, which generated the sovereignty-transcending idea of 'Crimes against Humanity', which represents a large move to curb the absolutist pretensions of Westphalian modernity. For Derrida's comment on this development, see *Philosophy in a Time of Terror*, 132–33; for Habermas' comment see ibid., 38.

10 The provenance of the reference to perpetual peace is, of course, to Kant's famous essay bearing that name, but also conveyed with a subtle irony of Kant's given his association of the name with an innkeeper's sign, which promises a different form of 'perpetual peace'.

11 Borradori, *Philosophy in a Time of Terror*, 119.

12 For a subtle and sophisticated inquiry into the ethics and politics of assassination in the context of Gandhi, see A. Nandy, 'Final Encounter: The Politics of the Assassination of Gandhi', in *At the Edge of Psychology: Essays in Politics and Culture*, Bombay, India: Oxford University Press, 1990, 70–98.

13 The *nakba* is usually translated as 'catastrophe', and is the Palestinian term used to identify the mass expulsion of Palestinians from pre-1967 Israel in the course of the 1947–48 war.

14 'Disengagement' should not be confused with 'withdrawal'. Israel in the eyes of most legal commentary remains the occupying power, subject to international humanitarian law, especially as set forth in the 4th Geneva Convention of 1949.

15 I have argued frequently to this effect. See R. A. Falk, 'International Law and the Peace Process', *Hastings International and Comparative Law Review* 28, no. 3, 2005, 331–48.

16 As has been often noted, the Palestinians, along with the Arab countries bordering Israel, rejected the UN partition plan contained in GA resolution 181, contending that the imposition on Palestine of a Jewish homeland was unacceptable and colonialist, that is, in flagrant disregard of Palestinian rights of self-determination.

17 For an excellent study of the evolution of the conflict, which confirms the impression that the Palestinian side was victimized in terms of rights and reasonable expectations at every stage, see V. Kattan, *From Coexistence to Conquest: International Law and the Origins of the Arab–Israeli Conflict, 1891–1949*, London: Pluto, 2009.

18 For Edward Said's still influential views, which have a certain prophetic character, having been largely vindicated by subsequent events, see *The End of the Peace Process*, New York: Pantheon, 2000.

19 F. Fanon, *The Wretched of the Earth*, Harmondsworth: Penguin, 1967; H. K. Trask, *From a Native Daughter: Colonialism and Sovereignty in Hawaii*, Monroe, ME: Common Courage Press, 1993.

20 Widely read authors such as S. Harris, *The End of Faith: Religion, Terror, and the Future*, New York: Norton, 2004; and C. Hitchens, *God Is Not Great: How Religion Poisons Everything*, New York: Twelve, 2007, have reinforced the tendency to demonize religion and to treat religion as reducible to its extremist embodiments.

21 For my attempt to portray this dual face of religion see R. A. Falk, *Religion and Humane Global Governance*, New York: Palgrave, 2001; for an impressive grappling with these issues see N. Hashemi, *Islam, Secularism, and Liberal Democracy*, Oxford: Oxford University Press, 2009.

22 For representative critical reflections from Jewish and Muslim perspectives, see M. H. Ellis, *Israel and Palestine out of the Ashes: The Search for Jewish Identity in the Twenty-first Century*, London: Pluto, 2002; C. Muzaffar, ed., *Religion and Global Governance*, Kuala Lumpur, Malaysia: Arah Publications, 2008.

23 Politics is being conceived here as the art of the possible, a rationalistic calculation resting on some sort of agreed bargain that is not receptive to nor particularly concerned about considerations based on empathy or equity.

24 I did witness in 2005 a revealing acknowledgment by an important actor, the former British prime minister John Major, who at a private breakfast in London contended that significant progress in conflict resolution occurred only after he and others treated the IRA as a political actor rather than a terrorist organization; he contrasted such an approach with the demonization of al Qaeda by George W. Bush in the aftermath of the 9/11 attacks.

25 Such a posture has been made easier to adopt by Hamas' 2006 electoral victory in Gaza combined with its continual proposals for a long-term cease-fire with an implied acceptance of a sovereign Israel with 1967 borders.

26 Borradori, *Philosophy in a Time of Terror*, 116–17.

27 See S. Makdisi, *Palestine Inside Out: An Everyday Occupation*, New York: Norton, 2008, esp. 263–98; V. Tilley, *The One-State Solution: A Breakthrough for Peace in the Israeli–Palestinian Deadlock*, Ann Arbor: University of Michigan Press, 2005; A. Abinimah, *One Country: A Bold Proposal to End the Israeli–Palestinian Impasse*, New York: Metropolitan, 2006.

28 Here, Derrida follows and extends the thinking of Walter Benjamin in his 'Critique of Violence', in *Selected Writings, vol. 1: 1913–1926*, trans. E. Jephcott, Cambridge, MA: Belknap Press of Harvard University Press, 1996.

29 For general insight into this political perspective see M. Kaldor, *Global Civil Society: An Answer to War*, Cambridge: Polity, 2001; see also R. A. Falk on globalization-from-below in *Predatory Globalization: A Critique*, Cambridge: Polity, 1999.

30 H. Zinn, *A People's History of the United States: 1492–Present*, New York: HarperCollins, 2003; E. Wolf, *Europe and the People Without History*, Berkeley: University of California Press, 1982.

31 Although initiated in 2005, BDS (that is, the boycott, divestment, and sanctions) movements become a serious challenge to Israel after the Gaza attacks at the end of 2009. See www.bdsmovement.net for information. See R. Wiles, ed., *Generation Palestine: Voices from the Boycott, Divestment, and Sanctions Movement*, London: Pluto Press, 2013.

32 In this regard, I would call attention to a series of remarkable hunger strikes, by Palestinians being held in Israeli prisons without trials or even formal charges, as well as the political party Al Mubadara founded and headed by Dr Mustafa Barghouti, committed to non-violent resistance, democratic principles, and a peace process shaped by international law.

33 The Geneva Accord or Geneva Initiative was a comprehensive unofficial text of a peace agreement prepared by prominent Israelis and Palestinians, released in 2003. The Israeli

participants were viewed as much further removed from government policy than were the Palestinians who took part; see D. Ross, *The Missing Peace: The Inside Story of the Fight for Middle East Peace*, New York: Farrar, Straus and Giroux, 2004.

34 See N. N. Talib, *The Black Swan: The Impact of the Highly Improbable*, 2nd edn, New York: Random House, 2010.

12

SHALL WE REVIVE THE WORLD ORDER MODELS PROJECT (WOMP)?

Exploring horizons of desire in the early twenty-first century

The initial endeavor of the World Order Models Project (WOMP) in the mid-1960s was to invite representative scholars from around the world to contribute coherent ideas in book length studies of 'feasible utopias' to be realized by the 1990s.[1] The only constraint was to accept a common framework of world order values. Many collaborative meetings were held over the next two decades in different parts of the world and a series of books was published. The proposals were intended to become political projects with transitional scenarios from 'here' to 'there'. In retrospect, the proposals uniformly exhibited the impatience and optimism of their authors, as little in the world of world of states evolved in the directions being proposed. Several of the studies could be read today as if projecting preferred futures for the 2030s, 40 years later. The essay that follows considers whether it would be worthwhile to try again, assembling a new generation of scholars to set forth their proposals for creating a preferred future within an agreed framework of world order values (peace; social, political, and environmental justice; developmental and ecological sustainability; global citizenship and transnational identities) and a group of diverse participants representative of the main civilizational and principal progressive ideological traditions in the world.

A second phase of the original WOMP undertaking attempted to produce an aggregated set of proposals that would meet with assent from the range of scholars who represented the diverse perspectives already reflected in the earlier efforts to project preferred worlds for the 1990s. Despite earnest efforts over a period of several years, the undertaking was abandoned as futile; there was insufficient common ground even among such a likeminded group, itself grounds for reflection! In this respect, the optimism of the earlier proposals was refuted by the pessimistic inference to be drawn from this experience where even scholars who had affirmed the shared values were unable to produce a collaborative document that depicted in general outline a feasible utopia.

The question raised in this essay is whether after an interval of almost 20 years it might be of value to start over. Surely, there is a growing realization that the most serious problems facing humanity in the early twenty-first century seem insoluble by the institutional and diplomatic mechanisms available to a world of sovereign states, even as augmented by a vast array of NGOs and a thickening series of transnational networks engaging the participation of non-state actors. Even such basic Westphalian concerns as territorial sovereignty, conflict management, security and the use of force for humanitarian ends are not easily accommodated within the structural and ideological frames and political procedures that have shaped world order thinking and practices for the past four centuries. It has become increasingly obvious to thoughtful persons throughout the planet that these unresolved global challenges are ticking time bombs of the greatest magnitude. These threats seem so severe from the vantage point of the present that without the emergence of innovative and effective means to safeguard and promote the *human* interest, civilizational collapse seems almost inevitable in coming decades.[2]

Against such a background, it seems irresponsible not to exert our imaginative powers to the utmost! This is what prompts my sense that it is a matter of urgency to use our imaginative resources to the fullest to devise more appropriate ways to govern the world.[3] In this spirit, I would encourage the revival of WOMP, and other similar scholarly endeavors tasked with developing comprehensive proposals for the sustainable and equitable governance of planet Earth. It might be an appropriate challenge for the Alliance of Civilizations initiative of the United Nations.

Points of departure

A decade after the start of the twenty-first century there exists a storm cloud of despair that casts a dark shadow across the future of humanity, giving rise to anguished cries of quest: 'another world is possible' or 'imagine a better world'. These cries are anguished because they combine a realization that what exists and is emerging is unacceptable, and what seems necessary and desirable is at this time politically unattainable, although it just might be at least imaginable. In starkest terms, this is the gauntlet thrown down on the path cleared in past years by the WOMP process and similar endeavors throughout the world: is it useful to depict in broad contours solutions to vexing global challenges even if they appear to be politically unattainable? We know how to comment on what is currently attainable, and we can make certain assessments as to what is necessary, as well as depict the gap between the attainable and the necessary. The primary challenge of WOMP is to extend the imaginative reach to the horizons of the desirable, that is, to explore as best we can the exotic terrain often derided as 'utopia' from divergent civilizational and ideological perspectives.

For those of progressive outlook, the anguish itself seems to center on two clusters of issues: the absence of any serious challenge to the persistence of predatory globalization as the ideological foundation of world order; and the lack of political will on the part of state-centric world order to cope with global warming, nuclear weaponry, embedded militarism, and mass impoverishment in effective and equitable ways. These unmet challenges in the setting of the ongoing 'war on terror' (what the Pentagon has dubbed as 'the long war', and does move toward the Orwellian image of a total state dedicated to permanent war in the name of 'homeland security' but for the sake of a domestic imperium) in which every citizen is simultaneously treated as a potential terrorist suspect who is continuously vulnerable to being criminalized by malice or accident as each person is encouraged to report on whoever acts suspiciously. Such a societal circumstance creates a rarely articulated realization that constitutional democracy and human rights are withering on the vine, to be replaced by 'creeping authoritarianism', or more alarmingly, by a drift toward fascism, whether or not so named. These concerns are aggravated by the lack of ideological plausibility associated with Marxist, socialist, and even social democratic modes of thought. As a result, we are living in the midst of a crisis of confidence in the ranks of the historic left that shows no signs of being overcome, despite periodic ripples of hope, such as followed the uprisings known throughout the world as the Arab Spring, and its less consequential sequel in the form of the Occupy Movement.

Somewhat further in the background, although menacing in its potentiality, is the unwillingness of the geopolitical magnates of world order to seek in good faith the elimination of nuclear weaponry from the military arsenals of sovereign states, preferring reliance on a two-tier structure of nuclear have and have-not states. This dualistic structure epitomizes geopolitical reliance on double standards as the core reality of world order, also exhibited by the persistence of the veto in the operations of the United Nations. These double standards seriously compromise the legitimacy of the United Nations and seriously erode the authority of international law. The proliferation preoccupation is also a geopolitical mind game, convincing the political leadership of the world, and much of the public, that the main danger of the weaponry arises from the behavior of the political actors that do *not* have the weapons rather than from those that possess, develop, and might threaten to use them in the future, and have in the past actually threatened use. In the beginning the non-proliferation commitment was supposed to be balanced against the disarmament commitment of the nuclear weapons states, but with the passage of time two revealing developments can be discerned: a hardening of the non-proliferation ethos, making its implementation a pretext for aggressive war; and the de facto suspension of the disarmament commitment (as somewhat disguised by the silent substitution of arms control).

For those with a more mainstream or conservative outlook the sources of pessimism are elsewhere: in acute vulnerability to Islamic extremism; in the related clash of civilizations giving rise to a new cold war; in the absence of sufficient fiscal discipline threatening economic implosion; in the burdening of market forces with an array of social goals; in the decline of traditional values and the embrace of decadence; in the rise of China and other non-Western centers of economic and political power; in the erosion of ethnic identity via immigration, legal and illegal;

and in an American political gridlock resulting from the disappearance of bipartisan centricism (what Arthur Schlesinger, Jr, dubbed years ago as 'the vital center'.)

There is also a deepening uncertainty about the reshaping and management of world order in the near future. There is a growing consensus about the relative decline of the United States, but less agreement on whether this will morph into a process of absolute decline or produce a militarist last ditch effort to restore American global preeminence. There is also the prospect of the regionalization of world order with countries such as the United States, China, Brazil, India, and the EU playing roles as regional hegemons. Such a prospect has been analogized to the character of world order in the twelfth century when regional empires prevailed in the main regions of the world.[4]

At present, the state-centric world controls the dynamics of *global* problem-solving in one of several ways: a continuing hegemonic role for the United States; a shared duopoly or oligopoly of managerial authority in which the United States is joined by China, or by the BRIC countries; a statist pluralism in which norms of behavior are set by 'consensus', interpreted as unanimity as at the Copenhagen climate change conference or as super-majority as at its Cancun sequel in 2010.

It is against this background that the question of a rebirth of WOMP takes shape, at least in my mind. Is there an intellectual landscape on a global level that would be receptive to systematic, transnational, and comparative explorations based on a shared value set prepared to set forth proposals as to the contours and character of those political changes in the near future that could restore hope and inspire citizen engagement throughout the world? Assuming that such a substantive resonance exists, is there the will and capability to provide the financial and organizational basis for a project of this global scope to become more than the figment of a vacationing imagination? It is important to underscore that WOMP 1 was not content with critique and diagnosis, but did produce visions of preferred worlds and transition scenarios for the passage from here to there. The fact that none of these visions were realized within the allotted time span is not fatal to the enterprise, but the disappointing real world changes dramatize the need for taking stock of the past effort. And it raises an important issue: should a hypothetical WOMP 2 put more stress on what is attainable, or should it accept its role as cartographer of the highly unlikely, yet desirable and necessary, in the domain of 'future worlds'? If we are unable to provide answers to these questions and concerns, we should be prepared to agree that 'the second coming of WOMP' is unable to do more than provide a congenial venue for nostalgia. Arguing somewhat against myself as to our capacities for self-appraisal, I am reminded of W. H. Auden's plea: 'We who are about to die demand a miracle.'

Undoubtedly, this way of posing the problem of reviving WOMP is too stark. Perhaps, instead, we need to envisage something far less ambitious than the initial project with its working groups throughout the world and its periodic meetings of research directors in various national settings. Possibly, all that is practical would be to produce something as modest as a single edited volume that invites contributions from a likeminded group, as augmented by added invited contributions, conceptualized and heavily edited by post-WOMP 1 public intellectuals and scholars; without the infusion of 'new blood' the second coming would likely be an embarrassing rendering of 'WOMP resurrected'! Perhaps, this initial gathering will not be able to find a path to the future, even a modest one, and if this is so, we should have the integrity to acknowledge that we also are victims of this deactivating mood of despair.

What WOMP missed

Perhaps it is covering up failure, but the magnitude of what WOMP missed in terms of developments and new challenges does in a perverse way provide a source of hope. By realizing the limited capabilities of projecting the future, it suggests that certain 'impossibilities' are realizable, and that normative commitments should not be put aside merely on the ground of infeasibility. To put this assertion methodologically, and epistemologically, the 'impossible' happens for better and worse. For better, the end of the Cold War, the liberation of Eastern Europe and minority peoples within the Soviet Union, the peaceful transition of South Africa to a multiracial constitutional democracy whose first president was Nelson Mandela, the election of an African American as president of the United States: each of these outcomes seemed to be an impossible goal except in retrospect.

For worse, the resilience of a state-centric world order (despite its post-Westphalian features)[5] and of the neoliberal capitalist ideology and practice (despite its 1998 'crash' and normative failings) are dispiriting realizations as of the present. Beyond this, the unanticipated emergence of the multidimensional climate change challenge to the future of human wellbeing combined with the exceedingly weak institutional and psychopolitical capabilities for collective problem solving whenever major private sector economic interests are at stake and mobilize in opposition.[6] Most dispiriting of all was the interaction between the mega-terrorism of the 9/11 attacks and the hyper-militarism of the American-led response, spreading warfare without resting security primarily on soft power instruments (law, intelligence, addressing legitimate grievances).[7] Of course, the American neoconservative leadership in 2001 used the attacks to launch a pre-9/11 grand strategy designed to satisfy the global and Middle Eastern ambitions of the United States that accompanied the collapse of the Soviet Union.[8]

Disappointment followed from the earlier world order achievements as measured by several instances of benevolent problem-solving: public order of the oceans; regulating ozone depletion; suspended sovereignty and mining claims relating to Antarctica; responding to ozone depletion. These success stories resulted from fairly enlightened hegemonic leadership by the United States, relatively small economic interests at stake (except in relation to the law of the seas), creative bargaining of competing interests and varying national priorities (for instance, freedom of navigation for naval vessels versus enlarged coastal claims to living and non-living resources). Significantly, these agreements were achieved despite the then prevailing Cold War atmosphere of acute geopolitical tensions, and the absence of comparable world order achievements in the subsequent era of globalization seems both surprising and a decline in the sort of benign hegemonic leadership earlier exercised by the United States.

Why? The collapse of American global leadership due to the internal rise of ultra-nationalist forces, especially after the 9/11 attacks, moves to the political right, combined with foreign policy failures and a major economic recession that has given rise to an anti-internationalist public mood.[9] Beyond this, the unevenness of circumstances among states, and their differing views on the fair distribution of responsibilities, make reaching lawmaking agreements much more difficult than in the past, especially if the scale of economic obligations is large, as is the case in the climate change negotiations. The reaction of global civil society, favoring building global democracy from below, does not presently seem responsive to the gravity of the dangers posed and harms being caused by global warming. It lacks the staying power and dedication that was so evident during the anti-war movement that flourished in the last stages of the Vietnam War or the anti-apartheid movement that spread globally in the 1980s.

Comments on the two phases of WOMP 1

The guiding idea of WOMP 1 was to encourage principal authors, representing most principal civilizational and ideological traditions (but not necessarily typical and certainly not exhaustive of variations within these traditions), to set forth in a detailed manner their preferred worlds for the 1990s, together with according attention to the transition problem. An impressive scholarly output resulted in the late 1970s.[10] The overall impression was one of diversity, reflecting distinct civilizational and ideological identities and differing relationships with the hegemonic order, an overall lack of consensus as to the nature of a preferred world except for a negative consensus exhibiting hostility to world government or world federalism, and a positive consensus as to the normative framework of inquiry established by the agreed values, whose degree of abstraction allowed an almost limitless range of appropriate interpretations. The negative consensus created an abiding tension in WOMP 1, as it was a disavowal of the views of the principal organizer and convener of the project, who remained committed to institutional centralization of a governmental character as the necessary and attainable basis of an acceptable world order. The positive consensus created an atmosphere of commonality sufficient to engender a high degree of mutual respect for the differing responses to the underlying challenge to depict a preferred world for the 1990s.

A later attempt was made in WOMP 1 to have the original participants plus several prominent newcomers cooperate on producing a consensus model of a preferred world for 2010, or thereabouts. In this second phase of WOMP the undertaking was named 'The Global Civilization: Challenges for Democracy, Sovereignty and Security'. This phase did not yield any genuine agreed product, although there were several workshops and some publications, but of a character that exhibited mainly the views of the author.[11]

The continuing work of WOMP was best reflected in the pages of its magazine, *Alternatives*, which tended to express the disunity of opinion among public intellectuals about how to promote a just world order, as measured by priorities and horizons of opportunity. There did remain a semblance of coherence due to an implicit sharing of values: minimizing violence, enhancing economic wellbeing, human rights, ecological sustainability, and political identity. And with the notable exception of Mendlovitz, shared skepticism about world government as neither necessary nor desirable, and certainly not attainable except possibly in an imperial or despotic form. Despite this, it was Mendlovitz's entrepreneurial energies, managerial enthusiasm, and leadership talents that kept the project alive so long.

What now?

My own view is that this could be a *kairos* moment for a new version of WOMP. There is a far greater recognition than in the 1980s that the range of world order challenges is overwhelming the problem-solving capabilities of the current hybrid world order that combines Westphalian and post-Westphalian features with bewildering complexity. This sense of frustration reflects several developments since the 1990s: the lost opportunities for nuclear disarmament and a stronger UN after the collapse of the Soviet Union; the rise and militancy of non-state actors; trends toward economic, informational, and normative globalization; the lack of policy response to the scientific consensus on climate change; UN gridlock regarding reform or responding to humanitarian catastrophes (e.g. Gaza); interest in and support for democratizing world order, including transparency and accountability for state actors and greater participatory rights for non-state representation (e.g. a global peoples' parliament); and the persistence of dysfunctional militarism as exhibited both by non-defensive uses of force on the part of states and by the size and character of military expenditures, a pattern epitomized by the American response to the 9/11 attacks.

What could be expected to emerge from a newly constituted WOMP endeavor? And for whom? The originality of WOMP is to propose visions of international relations, globalization, development, justice, sustainability, and governance that are rooted in a normative conception of a better world for people(s), insist on a scale of change that is transformative in character (rather than reformist or managerial), and sets forth the vision as a political project (not a utopia) capable of realization if certain formidable preconditions can be satisfied. By and large this WOMP perspective has been skeptical of the transformative potential of state or existing international institutions, and relies for its principal historical agency on the emergent capabilities of popular movements of a progressive nature and global civil society activism as selectively reinforced to varying degrees by some governmental and intergovernmental actors, by some parts of the United Nations system, and by some regional actors.[12] What I have called 'the new internationalism', involving the collaboration of civil society coalitions and sympathetic governments, as occurred in both the movement to ban anti-personnel landmines and even more strikingly in the global effort to establish the International Criminal Court. The prior work of WOMP is both suggestive of what a revived WOMP might undertake, but also of the need to reinvent WOMP for the twenty-first century.

One further clarifying note: Although WOMP may have initially harbored grandiose expectations of directly influencing policymakers, its real audience was among intellectuals and activists throughout the world. Perhaps, there was some ambiguity on the part of WOMP authors as to whether or not to win over elites worried about global developments and interested in avoiding future catastrophes such as a new world war fought with nuclear weapons, the recurrence of a global depression of the sort that afflicted much of the world during the 1930s, and mass famine and chaos generated by demographic growth that exceeded the carrying capacity of the planet. The appeal to elites, especially in the West, tends toward world federalist types of visions, and this turned out to be unacceptable to WOMP authors, and would probably remain so in a WOMP revival. Non-western elites, to the extent that they are dedicated to development and social justice, should certainly be invited to participate and conceived of as a potential audience.

A final reflection: the Alliance for Civilizations project, launched within the UN system, essentially as a constructive alternative to the 'clash of civilizations' hypothesis associated with conservative thinkers such as Bernard Lewis and Samuel Huntington, presents an interesting contrast to WOMP. It was conceived and implemented at a governmental level, with the Spanish and Turkish governments acting as co-chairs, having the intention of promoting inter-civilizational respect and understanding beyond tolerance, but without any transformative mandate so far as the structure and operating principles of world order are concerned. A revived WOMP might start from a similar point of departure as the Alliance of Civilizations, but with its main target audience being public intellectuals, and its promise being a credible cluster of transformative visions reflective of inter-civilizational diversity of outlook and circumstance and sensitive to the distinctive challenges and opportunities of the early twenty-first century.

Yet putting forth these conceptual and normative arguments in favor of the revival and continuation of WOMP is far from presupposing that the human commitment and imaginative and material resources are sufficiently present to attempt such a Promethean task that many might prefer to regard as better described as 'Sisyphean'. I have personal doubts about the viability of such an undertaking, given the immensity of both the entrepreneurial, organizational, and imaginative challenges if a revived WOMP is conceived to reproduce the earlier experience on a comparable scale. I would be more hopeful about more modest conceptions of a new project, less universalist in reach and more content to rely on voluntary participation and Internet potentialities, and that is not subsidized by any entity with an agenda of its own. In any event, I would welcome being surprised by credible expressions of enthusiasm, engagement, and capability of whatever scope.

To some extent, WOMP reflected an Enlightenment and humanist faith in reason as the foundation of human progress, which was, of course, a crucial component of the Western hegemonic projection of power, interest, and value. Whether this Enlightenment orientation is too tainted by its Western past, too limited as well as by its secularist confidence in science and technology and its disdain for religion and tradition, to serve us well in the present is a foundational question. It leads naturally to a related issue as to whether WOMP, if it were to continue, should do its best to disavow this legacy, or at least to incorporate non-Western perspectives into the very sinews of the undertaking.[13]

Notes

1 For overview, see S. H. Mendlovitz, ed., *On the Creation of a Just World Order: Preferred Worlds for the 1990's*, New York: Free Press, 1975; for other books in the series see R. Kothari, *Footsteps to the Future: Diagnosis of the Present World and a Design for an Alternative*, New York: Free Press, 1974; A. A. Mazrui, *A World Federation of Cultures: An African Perspective*, New York: Free Press, 1976; R. A. Falk, *A Study of Future Worlds*, New York: Free Press, 1975; J. Galtung, *The True Worlds: A Transnational Perspective*, New York: Free Press, 1980; G. Lagos and H. Godoy, *Revolution in Being: A Latin American View of the Future*, New York: Free Press, 1977.

2 An important WOMP participant, Robert Johansen, wrote a pioneering book appealing for the incorporation of the human interest in the defining of national interests while shaping American foreign policy. R. Johansen, *The National Interest and the Human Interest: An Analysis of United States Foreign Policy*, Princeton, NJ: Princeton University Press, 1980.

3 Taking a far more ecumenical and cosmopolitan approach to the themes explored in a recent elegant study: M. Mazower, *Governing the World: The History of an Idea*, New York: Penguin Press, 2013.

4 Charles Kupchan mounts such an argument recently. C. Kupchan, *No One's World: The West, the Rising Rest, and the Coming Global Turn*, Oxford and New York: Oxford University Press, 2012.

5 See W. Brown, *Walled States, Waning Sovereignties*, New York: Zone Books, 2010; also R. B. J. Walker, *After the Globe, Before the World*, New York: Routledge, 2010.

6 G. Dyer, *Climate Wars: The Fight for Survival as the World Heats*, Oxford: One World, 2010; and C. Hamilton, *Requiem for a Species: Why We Resist the Truth About Climate Change*, London: Earthscan, 2010.

7 My own early attempt to interpret this interaction is to be found in R. A. Falk, *The Great Terror War*, Northampton, MA: Olive Branch Press, 2003; for a somewhat later reassessment, see Falk, *The Costs of War: The UN, International Law, and World Order After Iraq*, New York: Routledge, 2007.

8 This geopolitical sleight of hand, combined with the large gaps in the official version, has fueled suspicions that 9/11 was either allowed to happen or an inside job. For the most persuasive assessments along these lines, see D. R. Griffin, *The New Pearl Harbor*, Northampton, MA: Olive Branch Press, updated edn, 2008; see also his alarming critique of the efforts to discredit a prominent Obama appointee's proposal to infiltrate and discredit the criticism of the 9/11 official story: Griffin, *Cognitive Infiltration: An Obama Appointee's Plan to Undermine the 9/11 Conspiracy Theory*, Northampton, MA: Olive Branch Press, 2011.

9 For different interpretations, see S. Wolin, *Democracy Inc.: Managed Democracy and the Spector of Inverted Totalitarianism*, Princeton, NJ: Princeton University Press, 2008; and P. Beinert, *The Icarus Syndrome: The History of American Hubris*, New York: Harpers, 2010.

10 See books cited in Note 1 above.

11 The most direct claim of a collective effort was made in relation to my book (R. A. Falk, *On Humane Governance: Toward a New Global Politics*, Cambridge: Polity, 1995), which is

described on the title page as 'The World Order Models Project Report of the Global Civilization Initiative'; other publications are described in Saul Mendlovitz's preface, vii–ix.

12 I have tried to depict this potential for transformative politics in a recent article. R. A. Falk, 'Anarchism without Anarchism: The Search for Progressive Politics in the Early Twenty-first Century,' *Millenium Journal of International Studies* 39, no. 2, 381–98, December 2010.

13 In this regard, see T. Weiming, *Significance of Concrete Humanity: Essays on the Confucian Discourse in Cultural China*, New Delhi: Centre for Studies in Civilizations, 2010.

INDEX

Note: *n* attached to a page number denotes an endnote, with appropriate number.